D0251580

To Play Again

To Play Again

A Memoir of Musical Survival

Carol Rosenberger

[swp]

SHE WRITES PRESS

Copyright © 2018 by Carol Rosenberger

All rights reserved. No part of this publication may be reproduced, distributed, or transmitted in any form or by any means, including photocopying, recording, digital scanning, or other electronic or mechanical methods, without the prior written permission of the publisher, except in the case of brief quotations embodied in critical reviews and certain other noncommercial uses permitted by copyright law. For permission requests, please address She Writes Press.

Published 2018
Printed in the United States of America
Print ISBN: 978-1-63152-326-7
E-ISBN: 978-1-63152-327-4
Library of Congress Control Number: 2017950295

For information, address:
She Writes Press
1563 Solano Ave #546
Berkeley, CA 94707

Cover design © Julie Metz, Ltd./metzdesign.com
Interior design by Tabitha Lahr

She Writes Press is a division of SparkPoint Studio, LLC..

Dedicated to the memory of the heroic **Amelia DaCosta Stone Haygood** (1919–2007). Amelia believed that the impossible could become possible and helped to make it so for many. Her remarkable life was devoted to enabling and encouraging others in significant ways. Amelia's unique insight and generous participation transformed the arc of my own life, and I am honored to recount, within this memoir, a few of the many stories that could be told about my dear friend.

Contents

Chapter One

⤸

Chopin Interrupted

"That's something no one can take away from you!" said the tall man, whose large hazel eyes were glistening with tears. He bent over slightly and gripped my hand so firmly that I couldn't help wincing. "Oh, sorry, I mustn't hurt those valuable hands!" he added and relaxed his grip, looking down at my hand as if he expected it to have extra fingers or other strange properties.

There was still a long line of people who had come backstage to greet me after my performance, but he lingered for a moment longer. It was intermission, and the musicians of Michigan's Pontiac Oakland Symphony—the men in tails and the women in black gowns—were milling around, playing their warm-up scales and snatches of music for the second half of the program. I could hear somebody humming a melody from the Beethoven Third Piano Concerto, which we'd just played. The year was 1955. I was twenty-one, and felt on top of the world.

There's nothing quite like the afterglow of performance. You work yourself up to a nervous pitch beforehand; you walk on stage with exaggerated calm; you bow and smile to the audience, trying to keep your hands from shaking as you begin. You hear the sound as if it's coming from somewhere else, as if it's not really connected with your hands on the keyboard.

But gradually the music takes over, and the nervousness is transformed into excitement. It heightens everything you want to express about the music embedded so deep within your being; and suddenly you feel that you're one with the music and the audience. There's nothing else in the world but that current from the source to the sound and back, a pulsing current that seems to stretch toward eternity. That's what your entire life is about. You've always known that, but you know it more clearly at such moments.

The man with the hazel eyes was right, I had thought, as he walked away. Usually backstage comments don't register. I'm too high after the performance. I remember faces and expressions and handclasps and embraces, but words usually get lost in the music I've just played. I remembered that comment, though. It was a little like a reassurance of immortality; my piano playing would always be there, no matter what.

I'd been playing the piano for as long as I could remember. My earliest memory is of the keyboard high above my head as I stood in front of it, holding onto it for support. I still remember the excitement of reaching up to the smooth white keys and pressing one of them. The sound drew me into it; I floated with that sound, as it seemed to fill me and the space around me. Even then, I couldn't get enough of that sound and the thrill of producing it.

After nineteen years of bonding with the instrument and many performances over the latter half of those years, I still felt that way about playing the piano. But now it was more than my greatest joy. It was *me*. It was my very identity. If anyone had asked me that key psychological question, "Who are you?" my immediate response would have been, "I'm a pianist." Then I might have thought to add, "I'm Carol Rosenberger."

I was "on my way," as one says of a concert career. Literally, I was on my way to Europe, where I planned to enter some of the big competitions, which have served as important springboards for young talent. I also wanted to play for two of my particular heroes among twentieth-century musicians: Nadia Boulanger and Walter Gieseking.

I wonder if there is a time for every young person when the dream seems perfect—when one has experienced enough to know what is possible and has not yet discovered what is impossible.

It's incredible, as I look back on the day when the most shattering event of my life occurred, that I had no premonition of disaster, no vague unease. Instead, I felt almost euphoric that warm August morning as I climbed the elegant curve of the steps outside the Palace of Fontainebleau in the beautiful little French town of the same name.

The legendary Nadia Boulanger, revered teacher of many greats among twentieth-century classical composers (Aaron Copland, David Diamond, Walter Piston, Roy Harris, Elliott Carter, to name only a few), was the director of the music conservatory housed in one wing of the palace. I was thrilled to have history all around me. It was here, on these very steps, that Napoleon had said adieu to Josephine. As a young person from a young culture, I wanted this older culture to reveal some of its secrets. Surely Europe, with its direct line to the past, must hold all sorts of clues to the mysteries of Art and Life. I didn't want to miss anything.

I was thinking that morning about my first session with the formidable Boulanger, known to everyone as "Mademoiselle," which had taken place just a few days before. She didn't have much time for private sessions during the summer, but she had listened carefully as I played the Chopin B-flat Minor Sonata for her. Her gray-white hair was drawn back into an ascetic bun, and her eyes burned with the intensity of her own devotion to music. Mademoiselle had asked me many questions in her French-accented English. She wanted to know all about my repertoire, what I thought my strengths were, and what needed to be filled in. She had said that she found my playing "sensitive and intelligent" and pointed out some musical connections that I might have missed. Best of all, she made an appointment to hear me play again. As I was about to leave she added, "You will go far."

And now I was on my way to the practice room where I spent eight hours a day of concentrated but exhilarating work. When one says "practice room," any musician or onetime student of music automatically thinks of a tiny cubicle, bare of furniture, with piano and bench literally on their last legs, where sound ricochets mercilessly to and fro, and ear fatigue is chronic. But this practice room was a large, airy, high-ceilinged room with a fine Erard grand piano in one corner. The room looked out on one of the palace gardens; and I could sometimes hear, mingled with scraps of sound from pianos, voices, and violins in other practice rooms, one of the brilliant peacocks screaming from below.

I don't think it's the coloring of sentimental memory that makes me remember this as one of the best days I'd ever had at the piano. I was working on the Chopin sonata that I had played for Mademoiselle and with which I was planning to enter a competition in three weeks' time. Though it's perfectly logical that I would have been playing the Chopin that day, it does seem a strange coincidence. That piece, with its life-death juxtaposition in the powerful Funeral March, formed an eerily apt musical setting for the sharp turn my life was about to take.

I remember how satisfying it was to dig my hands into the rich figuration of the first movement. It was going particularly well. This sonata had been one of my biggest successes in public performance, but I felt that now it was flowing better than ever. A heightened vision of the piece was forming in my mind, and I felt just on the brink of realizing it.

Suddenly a sharp pain shot through my left hand.

It was a kind of pain I'd never felt before. I don't know *how* I knew, but I knew it wasn't a muscle ache. I'd had those on occasion when I'd plunged into practicing after a few days away from the piano, or when I had practiced too many octaves at one sitting. But this was different. Something about it made me think of the Novocain needle in a dentist's office.

I knew I should stop practicing for the day. Protecting my hands was an automatic reflex. I avoided sharp knives, kept a safe distance from a closing car door, and had developed a similar list of automatic responses that any serious pianist would recognize. You just don't take chances with the investment of a lifetime.

I got up from the piano and walked around the room, shaking my hand and swinging my arm. Even though I knew it wasn't a muscle ache, I couldn't think what else to do. But the pain didn't stop.

Chapter Two

⤨

The Attack

That evening over dinner I discussed the strange pain with my closest friend, Martha Ritchey. Martha and I had met at Carnegie Mellon's music school in Pittsburgh and arranged to come to Europe together. She was a slim, sharp-featured girl with short, sleek hair turned in a sweeping curl over each ear. Her blue eyes softened her face, and a little perpetual frown was a clue to her extremely active mind. Martha was a singer, and even in ordinary conversation had the singer's precise diction and careful delivery. Her speaking voice had a tone that sounded disdainful to those who weren't used to it, but I knew it hid an excess of idealism. Martha expected too much of the world, and was always being disappointed. I saw myself as more realistic, and therefore less vulnerable.

Martha's first reaction was exactly what I thought it would be. "*Anybody* could expect some sort of pain after practicing eight hours!" she enunciated, as if I were slightly stupid not to have thought of that. I had to smile. Martha joked about it sometimes, but I knew she looked upon my singleness of purpose with more than a little awe. Then her frown deepened. "Maybe you're not entirely over the flu yet."

It had never occurred to me that this strange pain could have anything to do with the flu epidemic that had hit Fontainebleau a couple of weeks before, and had spread rapidly and widely. Everybody had been sick for a few days with a slight fever and a variety of familiar viral symptoms. I had been a little wobbly after about three days in bed, but was feeling fine now. I couldn't imagine that there was any connection. I took another sip of wine, enjoying the feeling of warmth it gave me. I didn't often drink wine, because it interfered with my reflexes, but tonight I thought it might relax me, might dull the pain, which had begun to spread up my arm.

"Why don't you take a day off practicing tomorrow?" Martha suggested, her tone of voice telling me she was anticipating resistance to that idea.

"But I missed three days already with that stupid flu!" I protested, shaking my head. "And the contest is only three weeks away."

This was a competition sponsored by the conservatory. The prize was $600 and a couple of appearances in Paris. I had been telling myself that all competitions were totally unpredictable and that one couldn't take any of them too seriously; but at the same time I was thinking how helpful the $600 would be and planning what I might play in Paris.

"Well, a lot of people are saying that you'll probably win," Martha assured me, "so why don't you relax a little tomorrow?"

"I'll see how it is in the morning," I compromised. It was sure to be better by then.

But the pain woke me up the next morning. It was more intense and had continued spreading up my arm to my left shoulder and into my neck and upper back. I had a severe headache, too, which seemed to be connected. It was bewildering. I couldn't imagine what I could have done to hurt myself to this extent. I felt abnormally tired—and dizzy, too, when I tried to get out of bed. I sat on the edge of the bed and stared out the window. The morning was bright and clear, but I felt enveloped in a haze. The only thing that was really in focus was the pain.

On the little table beside my bed sat my silent practice keyboard, a reminder of what I should be doing today. It was silent in that it produced no music; its plastic keys made a thump as they went down and a clack as they came back up. But it was useful for exercises and for reinforcing patterns with my fingers when I couldn't get to a piano. I shook my head at it wistfully. I wasn't going to be able to practice today.

I looked over at the desk, where I wrote long letters home to my family on onionskin airmail paper. But today I didn't feel like writing a letter; besides, the last thing I wanted was to worry my family.

What could I do about the pain? Heat was good for stiff or sore muscles; maybe heat would be good for this pain, whatever it was. Perhaps the pharmacy down the street would have a hot-water bottle? I got shakily out of bed and made my way over to the armoire—the most charming thing about this little room on the top floor of the old Hôtel d'Albe. It was ornate and appropriately antique, and a logical substitute for a clothes closet. Today, it seemed unreasonably far away from my bed. I opened the armoire and held onto the door, wondering what I should put on. As I reached for a shoe my hand seemed to drift shakily past it. Nothing was working as it should this morning.

Just putting on my clothes was tiring, and they felt scratchy, as if my skin were unusually sensitive. Usually I ran down the creaky wooden stairs, but this morning I went slowly, hanging onto the banister. The familiar musty smell of the d'Albe had always seemed to give it an exciting air of antiquity, and I had loved the idea of living in a hotel that had history in its favor. But now the combined odors of must and coffee made me feel slightly queasy.

As I made my way out into the bright sunshine, I wondered how I could feel chills on such a warm day. My body felt heavy;

my head felt light. The dizziness was coming in regular waves; with each crest I would almost black out. I knew I should stay close to a wall, a railing, or a gate—something I could hang onto when the waves came. There was a rhythmic pounding in my head, as if iron hands were grabbing my temples, letting go, then grabbing them again.

I held onto the counter and tried to describe to the pharmacist what I wanted. His voice seemed to come from far away, and I had to sort out syllables before I answered. My high school French teacher would not be proud of me, I thought.

I tried to walk steadily as I left the shop, clutching the precious hot-water bottle, but was glad when I got outside and could lean against the wall until the dizziness let up enough to allow another few steps. It occurred to me that I could have asked someone to get the hot-water bottle for me. Why hadn't I thought of that?

Back at the hotel again, suddenly the steps looked very steep. I had loved having a room on the top floor, but now it didn't seem so appealing. Just take one step at a time, I told myself, then rest, then one more step—and *hang on*. My room seemed a haven when I finally reached it, and it was a relief to put on my pajamas again. I had never been so grateful for the washstand in my room; I could fill the hot-water bottle immediately.

I lay face down on my bed and pushed the comforting warm bottle onto my upper back, where the pain was most severe. "Please, Hottie," I said to it, "do your stuff." When I was a small child in Michigan, my mother used to bring me a hot-water bottle on the cold winter nights. She would slide it into my bed and put it at my feet. As soon as she had kissed me goodnight and left the room, I would pull the hot-water bottle up and put it beside me on the pillow, its head and neck out of the covers and the body of the bottle tucked in. I would pat it comfortingly. "Now, Hottie, you can breathe, too."

I was hoping that Hottie would now return the favor and relieve the pain. But I soon noticed something else. There was a regular, rhythmic twitching or jerking sensation along with the pain. It felt as if I were bouncing up and down on the bed. I don't know how long I had been lying there when Martha knocked and came in. She took in the hot-water bottle and my prone position.

"Are you worse today?" she asked, and when I nodded, she felt my forehead. "Well, no wonder, you've obviously got a fever. I wish one of us had a thermometer!"

"Don't worry about that," I told her, a little impatiently. "The problem is the pain."

"Would it help if I massaged your back?" she asked. I was sure that it would. But she stopped almost as soon as she had started.

"Carol, there's something very strange!" she said, sounding worried. "Your muscles are jumping and jerking!" So she could feel it, too.

Martha gently replaced the hot-water bottle and said she would be back in a few minutes. She returned with a thermometer and two other friends, Marge Marçallino and Carol Stein. I lay there with the thermometer in my mouth and listened to my three friends talking in low tones. It was good having them all there; they could talk with each other and I didn't have to reply.

Marge, a tiny, olive-skinned girl with huge dark eyes, was spending the year in France on a scholarship from the Rotary Club in her native Hilo, Hawaii. She had a delightful combination of practicality and Hawaiian ease in enjoying life, and had rapidly become a good friend. Carol, one of the twin daughters of violist Lillian Fuchs, was a gifted violinist. Everything about her was intense: her eyes, her voice, her way of playing. She and her sister Barbara, a cellist, and I were planning to enter the Fontainebleau Chamber Music Competition as a trio.

Carol swung her long, brown hair and put her hand on my shoulder. "My mother gave me the name of a doctor in Paris to call in case of emergency," she told me, her voice rising in pitch with eagerness and concern. "I'm going to call him now."

I started to protest, but didn't. Whatever had taken hold of me so violently had crowded out all normal thought processes, so I might as well let someone else think for me.

Things were beginning to blur. Someone was notifying Mademoiselle, and someone else brought me some food, which I didn't even want to look at. Carol returned from her telephone call to a Dr. Lipsitch in Paris.

"He told me you should be brought to the hospital right away!" she told me, impressed with the order. The hospital! That seemed a long way. I thought vaguely that I really didn't want to leave this bed. But I was in someone else's hands now.

"Larry is going to drive you," Carol went on. Larry Isaacs, a tall, lanky Southerner, was one of our few friends who had a car. It looked as if I had no choice.

Marge and Martha helped me into two sweaters and a pair of slacks over my pajamas. I wanted another pair of socks, too, as well as my coat. It seemed inconceivable to me that everyone else could be comfortable in their light summer clothing.

I noticed as I got up that I seemed to have lost control of my body. The pain and the muscle jumping had taken over, shaking me continuously and playing their cacophonous tutti inside me.

Four people were trying to help me down the steps—practically carrying me. Everyone seemed to have forgotten how to smile; they all looked grim. Oh God, I thought, they're scaring themselves. They're overdramatizing the whole scene. I wondered why I couldn't stop them, until I realized that I was leaning heavily on them.

I was bundled into the front seat of Larry's little Fiat. Carol and Martha got in back; they looked cramped, I thought, leaning forward as if they could somehow be of more help from that position. Larry tried valiantly to amuse us with his imitation of a broad American accent in French, using his drawl to perfection. Ordinarily we all loved this act, and I tried to smile, but Carol and Martha stared grimly ahead.

They took me to a small private room in the American Hospital in Neuilly-sur-Seine on the outskirts of Paris. The room looked out on a garden surrounded by trees, and there were neat borders of yellow flowers under the trees. It was sunny and green and too bright. I felt drab and even more miserable in contrast. Inside the room, everything was crisp and white, and I was suddenly aware that I hadn't combed my hair or had a bath for what seemed like a very long time. I didn't belong in this pristine atmosphere. Why had I let them bring me here?

A nurse who looked scrubbed and energetic and spoke with a British accent came in to welcome me. "What are your symptoms?" she asked. My mind was working too slowly.

"My symptoms? Well, uh . . . I seem to be twitching . . ."

"Twitching?" She laughed and I could almost feel myself squirm. I must have used the wrong word. Maybe she thought I shouldn't be here, if all I was doing was twitching. But she was already helping me out of my slacks.

"May I leave my sweaters on?" I asked. "I've got chills." That was probably a symptom, too, I thought, after I'd said it.

"Oh, yes," I remembered, "and pain . . ." but she was nodding, as if she already knew that.

The bed was smooth and white and cool, while I was nothing but pain and muscles jumping, sweat and chills. My rumpled bed at the Hôtel d'Albe had felt more appropriate.

I faded in and out of my feverish fog. At one point a young intern came in with a chart and a pen in his hand. "Take this off, please," he smiled pleasantly, pointing with his pen to my outer sweater. I struggled to remove it.

But that wasn't enough. Now I was to remove the other sweater, the socks, the pajamas, everything. My hands were trembling so much that the smiling young man had to put his pen and paper down on the chair and help me. With every layer we removed, he seemed to find it more amusing. I must look ridiculous with all this, I thought. He probably can't believe how cold I feel. It occurred to me that I had put the thicker socks on over the thinner ones, just as I used to do when I went ice-skating. He handed me a hospital gown—only a hospital gown, to replace all of this?

"I've been having chills," I explained again.

"Oh, you'll be warm here," he assured me, still laughing. I thought to myself that he wouldn't find it so funny if he felt this cold.

He started to ask me a long list of questions. After the effort of getting my clothes off, my mind was wandering wearily, and his questions filtered unevenly through my fog.

Then a short, stocky nurse came in and told me I would have to be weighed. As she was helping me out of bed, my left leg seemed to give way and I lurched to the left. I probably would have fallen if she hadn't grabbed me, her strong grip digging into my right arm. As I looked over at her to apologize, I noticed that her expression was severe and her eyes frightened—the same look my friends had had when they were helping me out of the d'Albe. She steadied me, helped me over to the chair, and said she would be right back with a wheelchair.

"No!" I tried to shout at her. "I can walk! I'm just a little weak!" But she was resolute, and into the wheelchair I went. Evidently I had failed in the one chance she was going to give me to hold myself up on my own two feet. As she wheeled me down the hall, I hunched down in the chair and hoped no one would see me. Surely this was all some kind of fearful comedy.

I had not really recovered from the humiliation of being wheeled to the scales when Dr. Lester Lipsitch swept cheerfully into my room. He had a pleasant face and a resonant voice that made him sound very confident. I could tell from his speech that he was a New Yorker. He had his own list of questions, but it seemed to me that the intern had asked many of the same things. I wondered vaguely why they couldn't have gotten together over this. But now he wanted more than answers to questions. He wanted me to move my foot.

"Push up," he said, and resisted my foot so that it was almost impossible. "Hold. Good. Push away from me . . . hold . . . good. Push toward me . . . hold . . . good." I pushed and pulled in every direction and position, with legs, arms, head, and torso. My legs trembled; my arms trembled more; but he didn't seem to notice.

"Pull your abdominal muscles in," he ordered, his hands on my belly. I pulled. The muscles shook. "Pull them in," he repeated. I pulled again. He glanced at me and his look wasn't cheerful. Did he think I wasn't cooperating? Something was wrong. But then he smiled quickly. "Good," he said.

How could it be "good" so suddenly when his expression had told me clearly that it had *not* been good the instant before? But my private fog rolled in again, and I let his smile take over. He had obviously been giving me muscle tests, and the "good" must mean that I had passed them.

"We are going to keep you here for a few days," Dr. Lipsitch said cheerfully. "We don't know what you have, but we'll get you well as soon as we can."

A few days? "I'm entering a piano competition in three weeks," I told him anxiously. "Do you think I'll be all right by then?"

He was still cheerful. "We can't be sure of that right now. I just want you to rest. I don't want you to get out of bed at all for the next few days."

"Not *at all?* I can at least get up to go to the bathroom, can't I?" I pleaded, pointing to the toilet and washbowl in the corner of my room. They couldn't have been more than three steps from the bed.

"No," he said easily. "I want you to stay right in bed until we figure out what you have." He said it so casually that I wondered if this was standard procedure in France, or his usual way of treating a patient. He must not have an aversion to bedpans. Or maybe he thought I had something besides the flu. Why else would he tell me I couldn't get out of bed at all?

Soon the pain and haziness took over again. At one point a nurse brought dinner, but it seemed too much effort to eat. She also brought a sleeping pill. Maybe that would shut out the pain for a while. Maybe I would feel better in the morning.

But when the nurse woke me up at dawn to take my temperature, the pain and muscle jumping were still there. I thought irritably that if she had only let me sleep a little longer, maybe some of the pain would have gone away. Then another nurse came in with a basin and towel. She handed me a warm cloth. I started to wipe my face but my hands were trembling, and it seemed hard to get the cloth in the right place. The nurse took the cloth out of my hands and finished giving me my "bath." How I hated having someone else bathe me. I began to suspect that I might be even weaker than I was yesterday.

Dr. Lipsitch came in surrounded by a group of interns, repeated his "push-pull-good" tests, and declared: "You're doing very well!" Since I felt that I was weaker than yesterday, and the pain and jerking were no better, I wondered in what way I was doing well. But I felt I shouldn't ask him; he seemed to have his own rhythm for the visit and was already on his way out the door. Besides, my mind was working slowly, and the whole group of interns would hear anything I said. Maybe they would find me as funny as the first intern had yesterday.

Nurses came and went. Around noon my door opened to another figure in white. I glanced up and then looked again in amazement. It was Martha, gowned in a long white hospital coat. She laughed at my surprise and said she had come in on the train. I knew it was a long ride, and was so grateful to her for coming that I was close to tears.

"Where did you get that?" I asked, indicating the hospital coat.

"It was hanging outside your door. The nurse wouldn't let

me come in without it. There's also a bowl of disinfectant sitting there. I'm supposed to rinse my hands in it when I leave."

"French hospital procedure?" I wondered aloud. She shrugged. "Quaint, isn't it?"

A nurse came in with my lunch tray. "Help yourself before I contaminate it," I suggested, as soon as the nurse had left. "I haven't been hungry."

But Martha shook her head. "No, I think the hospital staff should be aware of your lack of appetite."

"Oh," I had to laugh, "I doubt if anyone here has heard of my legendary appetite." In my only other hospital experience, a tonsillectomy at age two, I had supposedly amazed the nurses by eating a full breakfast the morning after surgery. I could remember very few occasions in my life when I hadn't felt like eating.

I looked down at my lunch tray and grasped the fork. I tried to lift a bite of salad as far as my mouth, but it was too much effort. I put the fork down to rest my arm for a minute. It was odd how *heavy* the fork seemed. The food looked less inviting.

"I just don't seem to be hungry," I told Martha.

"You seem to be having trouble lifting the fork," she observed, with her serious look. "Why don't I try feeding you?"

That was a startling idea. Yesterday I would probably have refused, but today it seemed logical to let someone else lift that heavy fork. Strangely enough, with Martha doing the work, I was able to eat the entire lunch.

When Dr. Lipsitch came back that afternoon, Martha confronted him. Her penetrating gaze and clear diction could be a commanding combination.

"Carol *is* able to eat if someone feeds her!" she declared.

Dr. Lipsitch looked surprised. "But I *want* her to be fed, of *course!*" he answered, as if stunned that no one was doing so.

"Well, the nurses don't seem to be aware of that," Martha shot back. He said he would take care of it immediately.

It was strange how good it felt to have someone speak

for me. How often I had found myself speaking for someone: defending my younger brother, Gary, if other little boys ganged up on him; being spokesperson for a group at school if they wanted to approach the faculty about a problem. It was a role in which I had always felt comfortable. But now, with the pain and weakness and fogginess, I wasn't in a strong position anymore. I was glad to let Martha take over.

From then on the nurses fed me every meal. Those next days blur in my memory. I remember Martha and Marge coming in from time to time, bringing books from friends at Fontainebleau. I wasn't able to hold a book up to read, but didn't mind because even when Marge or Martha read to me, I couldn't concentrate very well. One day Martha brought me a special gift from Mademoiselle: wild strawberries from the Forest of Fontainebleau. She said that Mademoiselle, who was a devout Catholic, was having prayers said for me. That struck me as sweet and a little melodramatic.

Dr. Lipsitch continued to wear his cheery smile when he came in every day to give me the muscle tests, but I was more and more puzzled at his "good" that punctuated every test. Even I could tell that I was getting weaker all the time. It was increasingly hard to make any movement, and I even needed nurses to help me turn over.

One evening when the night nurse was changing my damp hospital gown, she relaxed her grip on my shoulders for a moment. I tried to maintain my sitting position but seemed to have no control. I fell backwards on the bed. She looked startled.

"I seem to be . . . paralyzed . . . or something . . ." I said, by way of apology. I was also expressing for the first time a fear that had been pushing its way through the brain fog. It seemed as if my condition was expanding beyond the category of mere weakness. I wanted to discuss it with her, but her angry glare stopped any further conversation.

Suddenly I realized that for the first time in my conscious

life I was as dependent on someone else as a small child would be. She and the other nurses, all of them strangers, had the power to enable me to sit up, turn over, take nourishment; without them I couldn't move. And yet from childhood on, I had always been referred to as "so independent." I had always felt that I could handle difficult situations. "Here! Let me! I can do it!" had been my most characteristic response. How bewildering that now all I could do was cry.

I seemed to have lost control, not only of my muscles, but also of my emotions. I cried if the nurse was abrupt with me. I cried if I tried to turn over and couldn't; I cried because I couldn't lift a teacup. It was as if my emotions had been scraped raw; there was no longer that protective insulation that one never notices until it has vanished. What should have been a minor irritant felt like a major emotional upset. It was further upsetting that I couldn't discuss my fears with anyone. I didn't want to worry Martha or Marge; the doctor insisted I was doing well; and the night nurse was angry with me for using the word "paralyzed." I felt more lonely and isolated than ever.

One evening I decided to call Martha at Fontainebleau. There was a phone by my bed, and by using both hands I could get the receiver to my ear, but the switchboard refused to put the call through. Though I really didn't want another encounter with the night nurse, I rang for her to straighten this out.

"I need . . . to call . . ." I began, when she came into the room. But she interrupted me.

"No calls after 9:00 p.m.," she said, looking less angry than the other night, but still severe. Then her voice softened a shade. "I'm sorry but it's the rule."

I cried a long time that night from sheer panic and rage. I had never felt so alone. I was alone in a foreign hospital, alone in a foreign country. I felt out of touch with everyone close to me. And now they wouldn't even let me touch base with a phone call.

When Dr. Lipsitch came in the next morning I tried to tell him in my increasingly shaky voice about the phone call incident. The weakness in my abdominal muscles was making it hard for me to get out more than a word or two in one breath. I had noticed that my breathing was becoming shallow. Stranger still, my voice was sounding increasingly high-pitched and thin. I knew enough about singing to be aware that I was instinctively placing my voice higher in the facial "mask" in order to be heard at all. But it made me sound somewhat childish.

"Am I . . . in some kind . . . of prison?" I heard myself say in this strange child's voice and, to my horror, started crying again. I couldn't seem to stop.

Dr. Lipsitch turned to the nurse. "She may call outside anytime she wants," he ordered. I was so grateful to him for that kindness that I kept on crying. I didn't know how to explain to him that any emotion at all seemed to end up in the same place.

It was worrying me that Dr. Lipsitch hadn't come up with a diagnosis of this strange illness. As I faded in and out of consciousness, I tried to figure out what could have happened to make my muscles so weak. One morning I ventured to express to him an idea that had come during my hours of feverish fantasies.

"Could it be . . . some strange . . . kind of . . . cold . . . in my muscles . . . that makes it . . . seem like paralysis?" I had uttered a dangerous word, but didn't know how else to put it.

Surely no one could get angry with me for saying that it just *seemed* like paralysis. The doctor's brown eyes looked gentle behind the glasses that magnified them. He smiled as if I had said something charming. But I hadn't been trying to charm him; I had been trying to get at what was wrong with me. Couldn't he at least consider the possibility?

"No," he answered, "I don't think that's it. Just rest and don't worry." He sounded his usual cheerful self, as if he weren't a bit worried at not having arrived at a diagnosis. His manner seemed to tell me that he was doing his job, and I should stick to mine.

I couldn't believe it. He was actually expecting me not to worry about a strange disease that left me helpless? If no one knew what it was, then how could it be treated? I barely managed to hold back the tears until he left the room.

A day or two later Dr. Lipsitch swept into my room with a broad smile. He seemed pleased about something, and came over to my bed and took hold of my hand. This was certainly not his usual procedure. Wasn't he going to give me the muscle tests today, I wondered?

"Your fever has dropped this morning," he said, smiling warmly down at me. The tone of his voice, and the thought that perhaps this strange illness was at last relaxing its grip, made a surge of emotion shoot through me and tears spring to my eyes.

"From now on," he continued, "you'll stop getting weaker and start getting stronger." He seemed so sure of what he was saying! The relief of it made me unable to say anything. Then he gave my hand a reassuring squeeze.

"We didn't want to tell you until your fever had gone down. What you've had is an attack of polio."

Chapter Three

⚜

The Unthinkable

The sun was streaming into my room. The rooftops of Neuilly were sharp against the sky beyond the garden. But my mind reeled instantly from the assault of the word Dr. Lipsitch had just uttered.

Polio . . . the terrifying disease that struck every summer back home in Michigan . . . danger lurking in swimming pools and movie theaters . . . paralysis . . . wheelchair . . . braces . . . iron lung . . .

Polio . . . a grade school friend rushed to the hospital . . . then confined to a wheelchair . . . even months later, thin, tired, trembling. Wasn't I trembling all the time, too?

Polio . . . a playmate of my little brother's . . . suddenly in an iron lung, then out again. But when he'd come back from the hospital he was weak, and cried at the slightest thing. Wasn't that a description of me?

Polio . . . trying to get the newly approved vaccine just before I left for Europe, but being told to come back later, as there were only enough supplies for children . . .

Dr. Lipsitch was still giving me his incongruous smile as these appalling thoughts reverberated through my brain.

"People are afraid of the word *polio*," he said. "That's why we didn't want to tell you until your fever had gone down."

"When did . . . you know . . . ?" I managed to say.

"I was fairly sure when Carol Stein called me from Fontainebleau. That's why I had you brought to the polio wing."

The *polio wing!* He had known right from the beginning? And he hadn't told me? Cheerfully, smilingly, he had chosen the moment of revelation?

None of this could be real, could it? He was standing here telling me I'd had polio, but the sun was still bright and he was still smiling and I was still *me*, somewhere underneath the weakness and the trembling and the weepiness. My polio must be different from anyone else's polio.

In the midst of this unreality, one all-consuming question was pushing its way into my consciousness. I was afraid to ask and yet was compelled to do so. I couldn't conceive of a negative answer.

"I'll be . . . able to . . ." I hesitated. I had been going to say "play the piano," but Dr. Lipsitch jumped in with his own interpretation.

"You'll be able to walk out of the hospital when you leave."

Walk? It had never occurred to me that I might not walk again. That shocking thought crowded out everything else for the moment.

The doctor went on. "You'll be weak for a while, but from now on you'll start getting stronger again. You'll be able to live a normal life."

He gave my hand another reassuring squeeze. That must be the answer to my question. A normal life was piano playing and a concert career. So this "weakness" must be temporary?

As I look back on that morning, I wonder what was in the doctor's mind. Was he trying to reassure a weak and still very ill patient that life would go on? Preparing me for a gradual letdown rather than giving me a sudden shock? Or had he not taken in the fact that I was a concert pianist?

Did Dr. Lipsitch see me as lucky that I would be able to walk with only slightly paralyzed legs? And did he view the more severe paralysis of my back, abdominals, shoulders, arms, and hands as less important? I had told him I was a concert pianist. Didn't it occur to him that my entire piano-playing apparatus had been destroyed?

All I know is, from that moment on, a giant misconception began to form in my mind. I was only too eager to believe that it would be just a matter of time before this "weakness," as he insisted on calling it, would go away and allow me to continue.

I believed, or was encouraged to believe, that the continuity of my life would not be broken—that *my* polio was somehow different from anyone else's and that I would be able to resume life as usual.

As Dr. Lipsitch went on to give me the muscle tests that morning, it suddenly occurred to me that the "good" punctuating every test was merely a formula to reassure the patient. How had I failed to recognize it?

I had even suspected that he might be giving me the tests for polio. And yet the "good" had reassured me, just as he had intended. I had thought I was passing his tests with flying colors. He had almost given himself away with his surprise that first day when he tested my abdominals. His sharp glance at me belied the "good," and yet I had dismissed it.

How ironic that even as I lay there, concentrating on the tests and feeling stupid that I hadn't guessed, I was accepting a much larger deception: that soon the muscles would be truly "good" once again.

Martha came in that day while the nurse was feeding me and offered to take over. We didn't like to talk in front of the nurses. She had been told the news already, but had not been all that surprised.

"There's been a respirator sitting outside your door almost

from the beginning," she confided. "Doctor Lipsitch asked me not to mention it to you. I shuddered every time I looked at it."

I marveled at all this secrecy. "I wonder . . . if I'd have . . . guessed . . . if I'd known . . . about the . . . respirator."

"I don't know. They certainly tried to throw you off the track."

"Especially . . . the night nurse . . . when she . . . got so angry . . . when I said . . . *paralyzed.*"

"I don't think she was angry, Carol. I think she was frightened. After all, she had her orders not to let you know, and there you were, talking about paralysis."

"This may . . . sound strange . . . but you know . . . it's a relief."

"To be able to talk about it?"

"Well, and . . . to know . . . that *they* know . . . what it is. I was afraid . . . I'd just . . . keep getting . . . worse and worse . . . and they'd . . . never find out. . . ." That thought, and the relief, made me start crying again.

"My God, Carol, were you that worried?"

I jerked my head down and then back up. I couldn't really nod anymore. The motion just wouldn't go smoothly.

"Why didn't you tell me?" she said.

"I didn't want . . . to worry . . . *you.*"

Martha was so surprised that I'd been thinking of her in the midst of all this that her little frown almost disappeared for a moment. I had a sudden urge to laugh through the tears. I tried not to, because it never came out as a laugh anymore. My abdominals were so weak that they wouldn't separate a laughing sound into a "ha-ha," and the result was something like a strange, inhuman cry: "Haaaaaaaaaaaaaaaaa," a semi-wail.

Almost worse than having no laugh, though, was having no cough. I had never realized that you needed core muscles to cough. Without them you feel that you are about to strangle, and all you can do about it is a weak little "aaaaaaa."

"You know . . . I've got to . . . tell my family . . . somehow."

"Don't worry. Mademoiselle has already sent them a cable."

"A cable? But that'll ... frighten them!"

"She said she would word it so that it wouldn't be frightening."

I wasn't to know for some time about the cables that whizzed back and forth while I lay in the hospital. Mademoiselle tried to be reassuring, but my parents were spending many a sleepless night trying to decide if they should come to Europe or have me flown home. In spite of this, the letters from my mother were calm and cheerful.

Now that the fever had dropped, I was allowed out of bed when the nurses changed my sheets. They would help me up and put me on a chair with armrests, where I had a different view of the garden. I shivered with pleasure to be sitting up again, even for a few minutes.

One day I was wheeled to the scales to be weighed. A nurse propped me up just long enough to get a reading. I had lost sixteen kilos, she said. Let's see, sixteen kilos would be about . . . thirty-five pounds! That couldn't be right! I had been in the hospital only ten days. And after that first day, with the help of the nurses, I had eaten everything that had been brought to me. It didn't make sense.

But on the way into my room we passed a mirror that I couldn't see from my bed. One glance was shocking. The face that looked back wasn't mine; it bore no resemblance to the one in the mirror at the Hôtel d'Albe. It was thin and drawn, and its white emaciation was covered by an angry red rash.

Once back in bed, I thought about the strange face in the mirror. Could all that muscle jerking and twitching have melted off thirty-five pounds?

I didn't yet know about muscle atrophy: the shriveling and wasting away of muscle tissue whose motor neurons have been permanently destroyed by polio. I didn't know that the weight loss was a telling measure of the atrophy my muscles had undergone. My understanding of any of this was far in the future.

Now that the fever had dropped and the danger of contagion

had passed, I had more frequent visitors. No one commented on my appearance, and my fog made me forget about it most of the time.

One day Marge wrote a letter to my parents, partially dictated by me. We presented the story of my illness as if I would soon be up and pursuing my normal activities. I wasn't really kidding *them*. I was kidding *myself*.

Martha and I were already talking as if I would be playing again in no time. I asked her to bring in my copy of the Mozart sonatas. She helped me prop up the sheet music so that I could see the first two pages. This was better than reading! It took so much effort to reach out and turn each page that I soon tired of reading and lost concentration. But I could just lie there with the sheet music in front of me and learn the music one phrase at a time. That way I wouldn't need to turn pages very often.

The nurses noticed this unusual activity and must have reported it to Dr. Lipsitch.

"Well, I hear you've been practicing Mozart!" he said, the next time he came in.

"I thought I . . . might as well . . . be learning some . . . new repertoire."

He smiled, but his next words were a surprise. "I think we'd better wait a while for that," he said easily.

That seemed strange, but perhaps it was simply a little early for me to begin "doing" anything. I did have one question, though.

"How soon . . . will it be . . . until I can . . . start playing . . . again?"

"Oh," he said casually, "it won't be too long."

A warm feeling flooded through me. When I had asked earlier how soon I could leave the hospital if I had someone to take care of me, he had said "not too long." When I had pressed him for an estimate of time, he had said he would release me to the right convalescent situation in a week or so. Perhaps, therefore, "not too long," when it referred to my playing the piano again, was also only a matter of weeks.

When I search now for clues to the source of that extremely unrealistic attitude, I think not only of the doctor's evasiveness, but also of my life experience at the time. I thought I knew about illness. I had had chickenpox, scarlet fever, flu, and had been sick for as long as six weeks. But at the end of the acute stage of any of those illnesses, I soon functioned normally.

I knew, of course, that polio was far more serious. I was frightened and shocked at the very word, but also puzzled. I didn't know what had happened to me. And the doctor's false reassurance—his attempt to portray my condition as something temporary—kept me from knowing what I probably didn't want to know, anyway.

I still slept fitfully because of the pain throughout my upper body. Gradually I began to recognize that the pain and trembling were related to muscle weakness. I didn't dwell on the fact that the pain was there no matter what I did or didn't do. I had to try to put things into a frame of reference I could understand.

Lifting a very heavy weight, I reasoned, made normal muscles shake a little. The next day those normal muscles would be sore. Now my muscles, in their severe state of weakness, were straining in a similar way to do the simplest things: to maintain a sitting position for a few minutes, even when I leaned back against something; to try to turn my head even slightly when someone came into the room.

A good example was my effort to lift a fork. When the nurse would bring a tray and raise my bed to a sitting position, I would first anchor my forearm on the tray, then lower my head a little and simultaneously raise my hand a little so that food met mouth. It wasn't easy, since both head and hands were trembling with the effort. It was as if the fork weighed fifty pounds.

Another challenge was the ordeal of getting my digestive tract to function properly, despite the laxatives I was fed at every meal. While I had been confined to bed, I had blamed the problem on the bedpan. But now, I was beginning to recognize that it was due to the lack of abdominal muscle. After the nurse had helped me over to the toilet in the corner of my room, I would strain and tremble with effort, trying to dig my elbows into my belly to push muscles that wouldn't contract. But my arms were too weak to be of any help. And my back was so weak that it was hard to keep my balance.

One morning while I was sitting there, weeping as usual from the effort and the frustration, Dr. Lipsitch and his group of interns swept into the room. He caught sight of me.

"Oh, is our girl busy?" he joked. "We'll come back later."

It was humiliating that they had witnessed my failure to perform such a basic function, and symbolic of my feeling of helplessness.

I was becoming more and more determined to leave the hospital, so Martha and Marge and I began mapping out our strategy. Now that it was merely a question of recuperation, of gradual regaining of strength, we reasoned, why did I have to stay in the hospital?

Why couldn't I lie in bed back at Fontainebleau, where my room was already paid for, and there were friends who could bring meals and help with everything the nurses could do for me? Marge and Martha were traveling to Paris much of the time anyway. Wouldn't it be easier for everyone if I went back to Fontainebleau?

We put together our case, and Martha and I presented it to Dr. Lipsitch one morning.

"We could move Carol into a room on the first floor," she assured him. "There would be a bathroom just outside the door, so she wouldn't have to walk very far. Marge and I would be in the room with her, so there would be someone around all the time. And there are several of us who could easily take turns bringing Carol her meals."

"I know I'll . . . get better . . . faster . . . there," was my contribution.

Dr. Lipsitch looked a little surprised and amused that we had it all worked out and were pleading so strong a case. He laughed and shrugged his shoulders.

"Well, I guess I can let you go if you will promise just to rest in bed until I see you again." He went on to say that I would have to be brought back to Paris every week or so for him to check my progress.

I promised to do nothing but rest. I would have promised *anything* to get out of the hospital.

The day I was to leave, Martha brought me a skirt and blouse to put on. As she helped me into them, we were surprised at how much too big they were. Strangest of all were the shoes. When she put them on for me, I was reminded of the feeling I once had as a small child when I had put my feet inside my father's shoes. They had felt amazingly big and also very heavy. Now my own shoes felt as if they had lead weights on the soles, or as if they were glued to the floor.

When the hospital doors opened and I was wheeled to the waiting car, it felt as if I were being released, not only from the hospital, but also from illness. This must be the end of illness and the beginning of Life as Usual.

The brightness outside was dazzling, and the green everywhere sent shivers up my spine. I don't know if it was an especially brilliant day in Paris, or just my state of mind, but as we drove slowly back to Fontainebleau, everything seemed to spring at me in its clarity.

It reminded me a little of the time I had first put on glasses when I was eleven. My vision had been deteriorating so gradually that I hadn't recognized the blurring until a teacher at school suggested that I should have my eyes tested. The day I walked out into the sunshine wearing my new glasses, the leaves on the trees had startled me with their clear detail, just as they did today.

But today it was not only the leaves on the trees. Everything I saw seemed to have an exaggerated effect on my emotions. Maybe the polio had intensified every experience, pleasurable or otherwise. Perhaps I couldn't take anything in stride. *In stride*, I thought, and tried to keep from laughing my semi-wail. It would be a while before I was striding.

Chapter Four

❧

A View from the Broom Closet

Marge was waiting for us when we arrived, looking as excited as I felt. As we walked slowly into the Hôtel d'Albe, she on one side and Martha on the other, I felt as if I were entering the normal world once again. I was leaning heavily on them both, and was surprised that Marge's slight frame seemed so strong.

They took me to Marge's room on the first floor. No more stair-climbing for me! One of the beds had been moved over by the window so that I could look out onto the street. I hadn't been up more than an hour or so, but already the bed was very inviting. My back and neck were aching from the hour of sitting in the car.

Once I was lying down, I looked around at the other thoughtful touches I was sure that Marge, with her Hawaiian background, had been responsible for: the bowl of fresh fruit she had arranged on the table, the cans of fruit juice sitting on the windowsill, the flowers on another table that had been placed at a considerable distance from my bed.

I smiled to myself. Martha must have told her about my flower allergy. Anyone around me at concert time knew that I asked the ushers to hold the flowers until after the performance.

I had learned to do this when I had played my first solo recital at the age of eight. Someone had placed flowers close to the piano, and I had to turn my head away from the audience at crucial moments, wrinkling my nose and trying not to sneeze.

I was touched by Marge's welcome and by my friends' eagerness to make me comfortable.

"I hope it's not going . . . to be too hard on you . . . to have me here," I said, realizing as I said it that I was a little late to be expressing such thoughts.

"Oh, Carol," they both started to say at once. Marge finished. "Think of all the time we'll save now that we don't have to travel on the train every day!"

"Haaaaaaaaaaaaaaa," I laugh-wailed.

"Besides," Martha added, "you don't know how many volunteers we have to help bring meals to you."

As if on cue, Carol Stein breezed in with my lunch tray. She had also brought me some fruit and patisserie for later. She threw herself into a chair and launched excitedly into the latest Fontainebleau gossip, which I was eager to hear. I was only vaguely aware of Martha tucking the towel around me as Carol described the competition I might have won. All through lunch I listened, fascinated.

The first couple of times I spilled something, Carol jumped to my side. "It's OK," I reassured her, "I do this . . . all the time."

I had a few twinges of distress while she talked about the competition, but after I had finished lunch, while Carol was detailing who would be doing what at the end-of-summer performances at Fontainebleau, I felt the tears welling up.

What was the matter with me? After all, this was what I had looked forward to in my days in the hospital: friends dropping by and keeping me in the mainstream—vicariously, at least. But the contrast between this normal world I had been a part of such a short time before and the world that was now mine—the pain, the weakness, the trembling—was striking me more violently now.

Here I was, back in the place where I had been function-ing at the height of my powers. The other musicians Carol was talking about were going on with their lives, but mine had come to a screeching halt. I didn't think I could stand to hear any more about them.

"I have to make a trip . . . to the bathroom," I interrupted hastily. Carol helped me out of bed and supported me while we walked the few steps to the bathroom door.

"I'll be OK," I said, hearing my voice shake as I turned away from Carol. I didn't want to cry in front of her.

"I'll wait here in the hall for you," she assured me.

I sat down and bunched up what I could of my pajama top around my mouth. The tears and sobs were coming, and I didn't want Carol to hear them. Hearing about other performers was too painful a contrast—while I had been reduced to an improp-erly functioning neural tube, with an alimentary canal that had become a primary concern, and a frequently fogged cerebrum. "I must stop this," I kept telling myself.

I looked around the "private bathroom," at the collection of mops, brooms, and cleaning rags. It was actually the maids' combined bathroom and storage room. The washbowl was a large laundry tub. I sat there looking through my tears at a spider crawling among the array of cleaning implements. Since nothing about me was functioning properly, didn't this catch-all room suit my damaged body better than the sparkling cleanli-ness and smooth whiteness of the hospital? Years later, when I read Kafka's *Die Metamorphose* for the first time, I pictured Gre-gor's room as the broom closet-bathroom at the Hôtel d'Albe.

As Carol helped me back to bed, I felt ashamed for losing control. She must have realized that something was wrong, and tried to keep the conversation light. I responded with a "That's great!" or with a head jerk, my present version of a nod. But I no longer wanted to hear about the world of performance that did not include me. Years later, I was to remember that moment as the beginning of what would be a gradual distancing from other serious musicians.

The next day Mademoiselle came to see me, bringing along her own doctor. She had just received a cable from my parents asking her to prevent, if possible, my release from the hospital. They had read with dismay my enthusiastically dictated letter telling them I was leaving its prisonlike confines. They cabled Mademoiselle that they would feel safer with me in the hospital until one of them could get there.

My parents had communicated all of this to Mademoiselle rather than to me because they hadn't wanted to tell me the reason for their delay in rushing to my side. My maternal grandmother, my beloved Nana, who had lived with our family since before I was born and was my lifelong pal, had suffered a heart attack. Nana was recovering but needed care. My mother, who had been preparing to come to France, was now urgently needed at home, so they decided that my father would come instead.

The news about Nana was a shock. I tried to say that there was no reason for either Mom or Dad to come to France; that they should stay home and take care of Nana. But they were too concerned about me to accept anyone's reassurances, including mine.

Mademoiselle clearly had her own doubts about my returning to Fontainebleau so quickly—another reason she brought her doctor to take a look at me. He was a kindly Frenchman who gave me a cursory version of Dr. Lipsitch's daily muscle tests. Then he asked me to sit up. He watched while I turned laboriously onto one side, pushed with my legs against the bed, braced my trembling arms and half-slid myself into a sitting position. It took me at least a minute to achieve this feat, and I was perspiring when I finished. He turned to Mademoiselle and told her that I must rest, take a holiday—perhaps in southern France—and try to get my strength back gradually.

"I'm surprised he didn't tell you to take a sip of cognac every hour on the hour," Martha said wryly, after he and Mademoiselle had left. It was a joke among the young American musicians at Fontainebleau that the typical French remedy for anything was cognac and/or a holiday.

"He didn't even ask to see you walk," Marge noted.

"I guess there is . . . no way . . . anyone can help," I mused. Two doctors had now said that I simply needed time to recover.

Walking, even leaning on someone, was still a strange sensation. I knew that my legs were now the strongest part of me. But there was nothing to guide my feet. I couldn't really tell where to lean my weight; and the rest of me wasn't able to give any support at all.

Of course! I thought one day, as I headed for the broom closet. There was no support from my back or abdominal muscles. The entire "core" was so weak that I seemed to wobble the way babies do when first learning to walk.

It was a strange reversal of my preconception of polio as something that paralyzed the legs, after which patients learned to support themselves with still-powerful arms and upper bodies. I was in the opposite condition.

A more optimistic part of me wanted to believe that since I could walk I would soon be doing everything else. I noted each tiny improvement. But since I had begun to lose perspective on muscle strength and coordination, I hadn't the remotest idea of how far I still had to go.

Perhaps this is a natural protection within an ill person's psyche. One adapts very fast to a total change in outlook. When you have been unable to feed yourself, lifting a fork is a very big achievement. When you haven't been able to get out of bed at all, walking a few steps to the bathroom is an adventure.

A cable from my father announced that he would arrive the next day. I slept more fitfully than usual that night, knowing that he was flying over the ocean. I had never been concerned about plane flights, but worrying about new things was another characteristic of my post-polio state.

Though I knew when to expect him, I still had the feeling of a deus ex machina when he walked into the room. He smiled his open, wide smile that made people like and trust him instantly.

"Hi, sweetheart," he said, his eyes and voice full of emotion. He looked at me as if he wanted to see into my muscles, see into my insides, to know how I felt. He came over to the bed and hugged me as if I were still the person he and Mom had waved goodbye to a few weeks before. They had driven me from Detroit to New York Harbor so I could sail to Europe on the SS Liberté. I looked up at him, meeting his blue-eyed gaze that always said he feared nothing and no one.

As a child, I had a favorite comic strip in the Sunday paper called "The Spirit." The Spirit was a sort of god in human guise who could be wherever he chose, and who unraveled seemingly impossible tangles in human events. He had something in common with Superman, but didn't have to change costume. The Spirit wore a dark suit and sunglasses shaped very much like my father's, and I thought that he and Dad looked somewhat alike.

I had seen other similarities between Dad and The Spirit. Dad could see into the mysteries of any machine and make it work—or build it himself. He could handle a car as skillfully as a test driver. He moved quickly and was impatient with foot draggers, but he had always found time to reason with me.

As a toddler I had been sure I would not like tomato juice. This was unfortunate in our household, as my mother and grandmother prepared quantities of home-canned, thick, pulpy tomato juice to be stored in our cellar over the winter. Dad persisted in making me admit that I had never tried it. The next step was to lead me inexorably to the conclusion that since I had never tried it, I had no way of knowing whether or not I would like it. I was all the more impressed with his reasoning when I had grudgingly taken a tiny sip of the tomato juice. I loved it!

As I looked up at my dad now, I wished he didn't have to see me in this state. Everyone had always said I was the feminine version of my father—that I looked "like a Rosenberger," that I had the energy, drive, independence. I had come to Europe to *accomplish things,* just as he had gone from the Iowa farm where he had grown up to Detroit to become a highly respected executive engineer at General Motors. He respected my ambition as much as I respected his.

And now, on Dad's first trip to Europe, he had the pain of seeing me reduced to a helpless invalid. I wished I could have kept the whole episode from both of my parents until I had regained my strength. On the other hand, it was a relief to have him here. I thought suddenly that I had great faith in his strength, and felt more reliance on it, now that I was without my own.

A conference that included Marge and Martha was soon convened. Since the summer term at Fontainebleau was coming to an end, Dad suggested that he move us all to a comfortable hotel in Paris. Marge was to spend the year in Paris; Martha had intended to go on to Vienna. But neither of my friends wanted to settle anywhere until it had been decided what to do with me. We knew Dad had come to take me home, and were just as determined to persuade him to let me stay in Europe.

The Hôtel Rond-Point in Paris was a great improvement over the d'Albe. We had rooms on an upper floor and Dad pushed my bed over to the window so that I could look out on the courtyard and breathe fresh air through the open window. Part of the day the sun streamed in and felt very healing as it warmed my back and shoulders and neck, where I still had constant pain. And this "private bath" really *was* a private bath and not a broom closet. I could walk the few steps to the bathroom by myself now, since I could lean against the foot of the bed, and then on the door frame into the bathroom. Once a day, usually in the evening, we went out for a meal. I could now walk a block, leaning on someone's arm.

When we went to the hospital to see Dr. Lipsitch, he asked me to walk a few steps by myself. I was still more than a little wobbly, but managed a few steps down the hall by myself. When I turned around and started back, he was smiling.

"Good!" he said heartily. "That's a great improvement!" Turning to my father, he declared confidently, "She'll be able to live a normal life."

My father nodded, looking at the doctor intently. "Her mother and I feel that she should come home with me. But Carol wants to remain in Europe."

To my joy, Dr. Lipsitch replied: "I don't see any reason why she couldn't stay in Europe as long as she has her two friends with her. Right now she should go somewhere like the south of France to recuperate for a couple of months."

My father nodded again, slowly, still fixing the doctor with his gaze. He wanted so much to do the right thing. And I wanted so much to stay.

My determination was based on the conviction that I would soon be playing again. Somewhere in the depths of my psyche I must have felt that to go home would be to admit defeat. I had come to Europe hoping for a glorious success. At the very least I could still find that cultural substance I sought. If I went home now, I would be doing what any invalid would do. If I stayed, I would be taking a step toward resuming my life as I wanted it to be.

"But I could study theory . . . with Mademoiselle . . . until I . . . can play again!" I had insisted at least a half-dozen times to Dad. "I can be learning a lot . . . while I'm getting stronger."

My father invited Mademoiselle to lunch, and the three of us discussed the possibilities. She was eager to help in any way, and assured him that, as soon as I felt up to it, she would devise some musically constructive things for me to do. She, too, was in favor of the recuperation period in southern France and suggested a *pension* in the little town of Menton that would be comfortable and reasonably priced.

Dad's flexibility came to the fore. Staying in Europe had

begun to look like something that would keep my morale high, and the doctor had said there was no medical reason to oppose it. Dad agreed to let me stay.

He and Marge and Martha went hunting for an apartment to rent. Sometimes they would let me come along in the back seat of the car, where I could lie down when my back tired. I saw the tops and roofs of much of Paris through the rear window. During these rides I discovered something else I couldn't do. I was already aware that I couldn't turn my head to the right or left. While sitting up, if I wanted to see someone or something just out of my range of vision, I had to push my whole torso around. But once or twice I tried to twist around quickly to see something we were passing. Both times the muscles in my rib cage cramped so severely that the cramp lasted for the rest of the trip. I soon learned not to turn quickly, and not to turn very far.

One day I stayed behind in the hotel room and decided to order some tea. The waiter poured me one cup, and I managed to drink about half of it, spilling the other half in the process. This was a good average at the time. I always tucked thicknesses of towel around me before attempting to pick up a teacup. Then, bracing my elbow so my arm would tremble less, I could get the cup to a certain point where I had to hurry the movement so that the cup wouldn't fall again. It was at this point that I usually spilled some tea. I had gotten used to the warm, wet feeling as the liquid seeped through the towel.

But this afternoon I had done fairly well, so I decided that there must be a way to get some more tea into the cup. The tray was on the dresser, and I braced both elbows and got hold of the handle of the teapot with both hands. I was sure I could tip the teapot and slosh some of the tea into the cup. It sloshed everywhere but into the cup—all over the tray, the patisserie, the napkin.

That moment when I stared at the teapot in dismay is one of the most vivid memories of those first months after the acute attack of polio. There was no one to help me; there was no way I could accomplish such a simple act as pouring a little tea. I had a terrifying insight into my true position, one shockingly clear opening in the fog of protection and denial that enveloped me. I was to have many variations on this experience in the years to come.

Dad and my two friends came back with good news that helped to push this recognition back into a corner of my mind. They had located an apartment on the rue Donizetti that seemed right for the three of us. I was sure that an apartment on a street with a musical name must be a sign that I was meant to stay in Europe.

Now that he was satisfied that I had a place to live in Paris, Dad was ready to make arrangements for the recuperation period. Marge and Martha would go along, and stay until my mother could come.

Dad left the day before the three of us were to take the train to Menton. I was excited at the prospect of the Riviera, and waved goodbye to my father with a smile, but he had scarcely left the room when I began to cry uncontrollably. I wasn't quite sure what was wrong, but I couldn't seem to stop. My abdominal muscles were still very weak, and the kind of sobbing I was doing made it almost impossible for me to breathe, but still I couldn't stop.

Marge and Martha tried to calm me, and at various intervals I heard one or the other say, "Carol-ie! Carol-ie!" They had never called me that; but somehow it must have seemed to them that the diminutive might be soothing. I couldn't say anything in return; I just continued to sob.

I was overwhelmed by my father's generosity, by his concern for me. I now felt empty, as if a vital part of my vicarious strength had been cut off. I wanted to go home with him, to be safe and protected somewhere. I was afraid for my future—even afraid for the next few months. I was terrified at the prospect of coping with the world from a dependent and weak position. I was frightened because I hadn't been able to pour the tea. I was gasping with fear because my hands and arms and shoulders and back weren't mine anymore.

Chapter Five

❦

Dreams, Sun, and Pain

The next day we boarded the train for Menton. I was exhausted from the emotional upheaval of the night before and, as I tested my berth, wondered out loud if I'd be able to sleep. Marge dug into her suitcase and brought out a bottle of cognac.

"Haaaaaaaaaaa!" was my response. "I'll be well in no time . . . now that we have . . . all the ingredients . . . essential to . . . a French cure!" We all laughed. What more could anyone want besides cognac and an imminent holiday?

The cognac was helpful, because lying in the berth was difficult. The slightest pull of motion in either direction made my muscles grab to try to stay in the same position. Since the muscles wouldn't hold, everything began to ache more than usual.

"I'm all tired out . . . from trying to lie down!" I told my friends the next morning, with a laugh-wail.

But I soon forgot about pain as I looked out the window at the fabled Côte d'Azur. I had long imagined it as the ultimate in beauty. I was sure it would offer up its scenic glories and history, and give me back my health—all in the next two months. No wonder my insides were leaping with excitement.

As Mademoiselle had described, the Hôtel du Parc was

old, spacious, and comfortable. We loved it instantly. Our room had two balconies, and I was almost too excited to breathe when I stepped out onto one of them. Below was the hotel garden, with lemon and palm trees, and flowers everywhere. I could see the blue of the Mediterranean beyond. Everything within my view seemed to promise me wholeness in its brilliant light.

I turned back into the room and said to Martha, "Let's walk down . . . to the beach . . . before we unpack!" She frowned, assuming I was tired.

"It's only a block!" I added. By now I could walk that far without much help. It was still slow, but I could take Marge's or Martha's arm for balance. I couldn't wait to see for myself that the ocean was within my reach.

The surf was splashing on the rocky coastline. Water of any kind—ocean, lake, waterfall, stream, or fountain—had always made me catch my breath with delight. The glistening water, the slow rhythm of the tide seemed to be telling me not to be so anxious. It told me to breathe with it and know that its timelessness would sustain me. It was an assurance of life—the ocean's continuity could help me to find my own.

Every day after breakfast we walked down to the beach. Martha bought me an orange air mattress, which she nicknamed The Bug. I would either lie on The Bug or on the sand, craving the sun's warmth on my aching muscles, feeling certain that every bit of its energy was healing and strengthening. The warmth seemed to be telling me that the pain would soon be ebbing away.

I wanted to go into the water, but Marge and Martha had been uneasy about that the first day. Even though the tide was gentle at that moment, my balance was none too good even without the tidal pull. That had been the inspiration for The Bug.

My two friends would pull The Bug to the tide line, and I would lie on it. Then they dragged it over the pebbles and launched it, one of them holding onto either end, and took me for a "ride" in the water. I could trail my hands and feet, and almost pretend I was swimming.

Martha was an expert swimmer, and Marge, with her Hawaiian background, had practically grown up in the water. I, too, had been a good swimmer "BP," as we had begun to call my before-polio self. Once we were in three or four feet of water, I would slide off The Bug and swim a few strokes. The saltwater was so buoyant, and I had always floated so easily, that I found it was less effort to swim than to walk, though of course my arms tired very quickly.

I knew swimming was supposed to be good exercise for polio patients who had paralyzed legs. Why wouldn't it be equally good for damaged arms? As soon as I was tired, I would hang onto The Bug and be towed in to land again.

On the way in, I could look up at the old part of the town on the hill—the Place de l'Eglise, with the tower of the Cathédrale Saint-Michel against the French Alps in the background. There in the distance was the aesthetic and the historic I had come to Europe to find. Here was the water and the sun. And two devoted friends willing me back to health. How could I not recover quickly?

I found it remarkable that I could lie out in the sun so long without feeling burned, and kept commenting to Martha and Marge on this phenomenon. I was using suntan oil, of course, but even so, I had never been able to lie out in the sun for very long. Wondering if it was the time of year, or perhaps something about this particular part of the world, I kept referring to the miraculous "no-burn" suntan of the Riviera.

Finally, Martha could stand it no longer. "For heaven's sake, Carol," she exploded. "I don't know what you're talking about!" I looked at her in bewilderment.

"You keep talking about the 'no-burn' tan. You are burned to a crisp every day!"

I argued with her for a while, but Marge backed her up. It

was true, I conceded, that my tan had a reddish cast, but surely I'd feel it if I were burned. As we talked, however, it began to emerge that the distortion of perception must be my own.

"You know, I try . . . to forget . . . about the pain . . . most of the time. . . . But maybe it keeps me . . . from noticing . . . if I'm sunburned." As I thought about it, I realized that I was trying to shut out any awareness of pain, no matter what the cause.

I have since learned that such masking of one pain by another is a common neurological phenomenon—one that I might have expected had I been more medically aware.

The paradise of Menton told me that recovery must be taking place. Also, I was gradually able to walk farther, swim a few strokes, drink my tea with fewer spills. I noted every tiny centimeter of progress as if it were a major victory. My prevailing mood was hope bordering on ecstasy.

No doubt related to my hopeful mood were dreams that first appeared in Menton—glorious Technicolor dreams, in which I would be performing a piano concerto. The soundtrack was always richly scored. Sometimes I would be playing long passages of the Brahms B-flat Concerto or the first movement of the Beethoven Fifth Concerto, "The Emperor," which I had been working on at Fontainebleau.

It was always music of grandeur and strength. I would awaken in the morning or from a nap, still hearing a golden passage from Brahms or Beethoven or Rachmaninoff, still feeling myself playing the piano effortlessly, bringing the musical message to life with all the skill and imagination I had ever possessed. Although the dreams were in extreme contrast to my actual physical state, I chose to interpret them as signs that I would indeed be playing that way again in no time.

Much later, I learned to equate these glittering fantasies with those of the bereaved who dream of a dear one who has died recently, or even someone long gone who was closely woven into the dreamer's life. The glorious dreams faded over time, gradually replaced by anxiety visions as my subconscious began to absorb the immensity of my loss.

Every evening after dinner, I would walk through one of the comfortable sitting rooms in the hotel and look longingly at an old upright piano in the corner. Nobody ever played it. I wanted to touch it—and yet was afraid to do so. The suspense grew, and one morning I could hold out no longer.

I went downstairs by myself and peeked into the sitting room. There was no one there. I walked over to the upright piano and sat down on the bench. I put my hand on the keyboard and pressed one of the keys. It took a lot of effort to push it down. Maybe it was a sticky key. I tried another. It, too, seemed to go down only with the greatest of effort. As I tried one after another, it seemed more and more odd. I had never come across a piano with such a resistant action. It must be through lack of care of the instrument, I thought. I had played a lot of uprights in my years of piano playing, and they had always seemed to have comparatively loose, easy actions.

How could I not have known instantly that the problem was my extreme weakness rather than a piano's strange condition? Though I had every indication that my hands and arms were scarcely capable of the smallest, easiest of normal movements, let alone the complex and demanding motions involved in piano playing, I couldn't make the connection. I could admit that I wasn't yet able to brush my hair, drink my tea with security, hold a book for any length of time, or perform a long list of other simple actions. But I couldn't yet admit that my piano playing, too, was gone.

My lifelong bonding with the instrument, a kind of organic fusion, was too ingrained to comprehend a rupture. The piano was at my very core; it meant life itself to me. To admit that my playing had gone the way of my hair-brushing or tea-drinking ability would have been equivalent to admitting to myself that I had died.

It was ironic that I should have sat there, continuing to play one note at a time, using my whole arm to accomplish what had been the most natural of movements to the pre-polio me. I had practically started out life playing one note at a time. My mother had told me that before I could even walk, I would crawl over to the piano, pull myself up with one hand on the keyboard, and play one note after another with the other hand. When I found one I particularly liked, I would play it over and over. Evidently I spent long stretches of time "playing" the piano as I grew, started to walk, and could crawl up onto the bench from behind.

My father took snapshots of me at about eighteen months, "playing" with an expression of total ecstasy and absorption. I must have assumed the piano was mine, and preferred it to any toy or other amusement. It had been placed in my parents' living room by fate—in the form of a friend who was moving from a house to an apartment and no longer had room for his grand. Little had my parents known that the piano would be the greatest source of both pleasure and pain, of meaning and despair, for their firstborn.

They had been pleased and a little mystified at my fascination with the instrument. One evening when I was three, a family friend who taught piano to young children had come over for dinner. Naomi watched with great interest while I "played" with my usual preoccupation. She offered on the spot to give me lessons.

At first my parents protested that I was surely too young. But Naomi had seen something that intrigued her. Such a fascination, she explained, told her that I was not too young. She volunteered her time if my parents would let her come to the house and start my lessons. They gave in, and another fateful step was taken.

Once I had found out that all the sounds I had come to love so much had names, I immediately wanted to know the name of my favorite. It was called B-flat, Naomi told me. B-flat:

the key of the Chopin sonata I had been playing immediately before the attack of polio, and the key of one of my first piano pieces, "Mr. B-flat."

It was a measure of Naomi's sensitivity that she found such a "masterpiece" for me, in my favorite key. I played it in my first recital appearance, at age four. Naomi told me beforehand that the audience would applaud as I walked onstage and after I had finished playing. But something very strange happened. The applause swelled as I approached the bench in my usual way: right knee onto the back of the bench, then up over the top to sit facing the keyboard. I couldn't imagine why the people were applauding so much. I hadn't played yet.

"Mr. B-flat" went off without incident, and there was more applause when I finished. Then Naomi took me out into the auditorium so that I could listen to the older students. I watched while one after another came out, walked past the bench, and then slid between it and the keyboard and sat down. At first I thought that was a strange way to begin the performance. Why was no one climbing onto the bench? Then the truth dawned on me: Theirs was the grown-up way; my way was wrong! That was the last time I climbed onto the bench from behind—in public, anyway.

One day during a lesson, Naomi called excitedly to my mother, who quickly came running from the kitchen into the living room.

"Billie!" she exclaimed. "Carol has perfect pitch!"

Naomi's laughing voice and the brisk movements of her tall frame radiated enthusiasm. I knew from the tone of her voice that whatever perfect pitch was, it was good for me to have it. She instructed me to walk across the room and stand with my back to the piano while she played notes and asked me to name them. Then she asked me to sing other notes she hadn't played yet.

She and my mother both seemed to be excited about something; my mother, I noticed, had tears in her eyes. I was puzzled when Naomi explained that not everyone knew those notes by their sounds, especially when she told me that she couldn't do that herself. How could that be, when she was the one who had taught me the names?

Later, Naomi would say that I "just seemed to mushroom"; that she was less aware of teaching me than of coming every week to listen to me play.

When I was six, I overheard one of my parents' friends, an amateur pianist, say, "Someday I'll be paying to hear Carol play in Carnegie Hall." I could tell from her tone that Carnegie Hall must be the ultimate in places to play. I never questioned that someday I would play there.

The first time someone mentioned the phrase "concert pianist" to me, I was eight, and playing my first solo recital. I knew it was an important occasion because Grandma and Grandpa Rosenberger had come all the way from their Iowa farm. Grandma went for a walk with me the afternoon of the recital, and I was bouncing a large rubber ball as we walked. She wanted to know how I could remember all the music that I was going to play that evening. I thought the question strange. I couldn't imagine *not* remembering it, but wanted to reassure her.

"I have it all right here," I told her, pointing to my chest. I thought that was the center of memory, for didn't one say, "I know it by heart"? But Grandma's question was my first indication that perhaps such memory was something unusual, like perfect pitch.

Naomi laughed and shook her head that evening, and said she had never seen anyone so calm and collected before a performance. I couldn't understand why this was so remarkable. I loved to play for people; I did it all the time, whenever anyone asked me. Why worry about something one knew how to do?

After the recital, someone had asked me if I wanted to be a concert pianist. I thought it over. A concert pianist must be someone who played the piano for people in a concert hall on a regular basis, especially in Carnegie Hall. What could be more natural for me than playing for people? And I already knew that everybody seemed to think my playing was something special. So I said yes, that's what I wanted to be.

How many years of hard work and exhilarating performances there had been since that evening! But now I sat playing one note at a time, as if I were once again that baby who had intertwined the piano so inextricably with her very core. I played a B-flat, the magic key. It was as hard to push down as the others. I decided I'd better go back upstairs. Once I had returned to Paris, we could rent a piano that had a more normal action.

Marge was leaving for Paris, but Martha would stay with me until my mother arrived. Marge said she had had a wonderful holiday. We all agreed that my getting sick had at least enabled all three of us to see a little of the south of France.

My mother arrived shortly after Marge left, and Martha and I went in a rented car to the airport to meet her. Mom said later that she didn't recognize me until she saw Martha standing next to me. Her voice quivered a little with emotion, but she laughed and said that she had never seen me so tan or with such a lovely haircut. She had also never seen me so thin.

Mom was dark-haired and slender, with a beautiful face and exquisite bone structure—a happy blend of her Polish, Czech, and English heritage. Her appearance was gentle, but everyone who knew her well was aware of the strong-as-steel interior. I, in contrast, had always looked my strength with the blond hair, sturdy frame, sometimes on the heavy side, and the Germanic facial features of the Rosenbergers. Now I was no longer sturdy, and I was thinner than my mother.

Mom was thrilled, she said, to see me walking, but noticed what Martha had pointed out, that I threw my right leg when I walked—pointing my right foot to the side. My balance wasn't good enough for me to look down at that foot myself, but it felt as if I were going to fall if I tried to straighten it any more. I was just walking the way it felt safest. I already knew the extreme back and abdominal weakness was the problem—the same thing that made going up or down a step frightening, as if I might fall at any moment.

Mom seemed to love being in Menton, and I was happy that she, too, could have a vacation after the worry and strain of Nana's illness. She invited Martha to stay for a while longer.

We kept the rented car and drove around Menton and the vicinity. I could lie down when my back was tired and sit up to see something particularly spectacular. We marveled at the inspiring views from the celebrated Grand Corniche cliff road "where Mediterranean meets sky," and such wonders as the medieval walled towns of Eze and Roquebrune. I wrote to Nana in the slow and careful hand I had developed since leaving the hospital: "Eze is built on top of a mountain, and the first time I saw it from a distance, the castle seeming to be rising from nowhere into space, I knew that story-book castles are real, after all!"

Later in the same letter, I summed it up: "This must be the most beautiful spot in the world!"

Mom seemed delighted with my physical progress, but, as I found out later, her letters home were a little less enthusiastic than mine. After assuring Dad that I was walking better and that my back was stronger, she wrote: "Carol's skin is clearing up nicely—just a few marks left from the nervous rash . . . She is anxious to start practicing but shouldn't do that for a while yet. We played a little bridge, and she seemed to enjoy it. There is so little she can do, but her spirit is fine."

And from another letter: "We had a nice talk at dinner tonight. She hasn't been very talkative—is very quiet, almost vague at times, which is so unlike Carol. But tonight she seemed a little more like her old self."

Mom and I had always talked a great deal. She was used to a lot of energy behind my words as well as my physical movements.

She told me later that it had been painful to see me devoid of either one.

Martha soon left for Paris, promising to have a piano in the apartment by the time I returned. I had been talking to Mom about the Italian Riviera, suggesting that we should go down there for a change of scene. She was reluctant to leave Menton with me in a semi-invalid condition but, against her better judgment, agreed to go.

I don't remember much about the train trip to Viareggio, but I do remember being disappointed in the hotel. It was less comfortable than the du Parc, the staff didn't seem unduly concerned about my welfare, and our room was damp and cold. Nevertheless, I wasn't about to pass up an opportunity to visit nearby Pisa, with its Leaning Tower, and persuaded Mom to take the bus tour from the hotel.

The trip was moderately bumpy, which meant that it took all the muscular exertion I could manage just to stay in my seat. My back was already tired by the time we reached the town and started out on foot to see the cathedral with its Michelangelo door. I insisted we find a medal for Nana, which took us another few steps.

About that time, my back progressed from being simply tired to being unbearably tired. It was the kind of fatigue that had become all too familiar since the polio attack. I can only describe it as similar to the way your arms can ache when you're holding something heavy up in the air, and it becomes too agonizing to hold it another second.

I put my hands around in back and tried to give my back muscles the illusion of support—a gesture that was to become familiar in the coming years. But it didn't help.

"I've got to lie down," I muttered to Mom, who glanced at me with a frightened look. My tone of voice sounded tense with a tinge of desperation. I hadn't meant it to come out that way, but the extreme physical ache left me without a margin for voice modulation. I had reached the point where it didn't matter where I was or who might be watching. I had to lie down.

Mom looked around hurriedly, but there was only the sidewalk. She took on her emergency attitude—quiet resolution, betraying her inner turmoil only by a slight tremble in her voice.

"You'll just have to lie down here, then," she said, steadying me while I flattened myself on the sidewalk. She squatted beside me, trying to shield me from passers-by. We tried to explain to the few who stopped that I was not dying, just fatigued. But our Italian wasn't good enough, and we attracted a lot of puzzled stares.

After about twenty minutes, I felt ready to walk back to the bus. Fortunately, we didn't have long to wait. On the trip to the hotel, I tried every possible way to brace myself, but my back muscles had given their all for that day, and we alternated between Mom holding me in my seat as if I were a toddler and my leaning over with my head between my knees.

Back in our room at the hotel, Mom ran a bath while I lay down. Warm water was a great kindness to my muscles in any state of pain or fatigue. It felt particularly good that evening; but as I lay soaking I suddenly began to cry. I didn't even know what it was about, but the more I tried to stop the more the sobs came.

Mom had never witnessed one of my post-polio crying bouts, and came running into the bathroom. She bent over the tub, asking me what was wrong, telling me it would be all right, trying every way she could to calm me. I felt ridiculous; but there was no way I could get enough breath even to tell her that it was about nothing at all. Or that perhaps it was about everything.

Afterward, when I could talk again, we agreed that I had not been ready to leave the cocoon, even to make a short bus trip. We decided to go back to Menton as soon as I felt able to travel on the train.

The manager of the du Parc welcomed us warmly and gave us our old room back. A letter from Mom to Dad at that time, in an attempt not to worry him, mentions very little about the Pisa incident, but does say, with understatement and humor: "It is a little difficult trying to get around with a gal who doesn't have much strength but who does have a lot of luggage."

We stayed until the weather began to chill. By that time, I was eager to get back to Paris. I had been "on vacation" for almost two months and felt that it was time to attempt a modest musical pursuit with Mademoiselle. Martha wrote that she and Marge had rented a small grand piano, and I was itching to begin trying to play again. Mom and I said a fond goodbye to paradise and set out for Life as Usual.

Chapter Six

❦

"Household Gods" and
the Oracle of Paris

We were greeted by the crisp air of fall in Paris and noise and activity everywhere. It all seemed to be telling me that important things would happen—things that could help restore my pre-polio strength and offer me priceless treasures. The treasure I sought above all was a greater understanding of Life and Art. If, in contrast to "free-floating anxiety," there is such a state as "free-floating ecstatic anticipation," then the latter describes my return to Paris.

Our rue Donizetti apartment was on the sixth floor of a massive yet graceful building and could be reached by a birdcage elevator. From inside the elevator, you were suspended in space as you were drawn very slowly upwards, past receding floors, stairs, and walls. You could see everything you were leaving behind and much of what you were approaching. It gave you the feeling that there was no hope of ever again reaching solid ground. The cage looked delicate as it rocked slightly to and fro. My still shaky sense of balance and the rocking of the little elevator combined to make me feel dizzy. "Just don't look down!" Marge advised.

The building rules stated that one must not ride down in the elevator, only up; but my father had made sure that an exception would be made in my case before he had taken the apartment. In my months at rue Donizetti, I was to incur everything from puzzled to wrathful stares from the other tenants, who were not allowed to ride down in the gilded cage. With my Riviera tan, I looked healthier than anyone who had to walk down the stairs. It was my first experience with the embarrassment of having special treatment when the reason for it wasn't obvious.

The apartment itself looked modern after the Old World charm of the Hôtel du Parc. The focal points for me were the couch-bed in the living room, where I was to sleep and rest and lounge; the grand piano against the far wall of the living room; and the fireplace, which was almost constantly in use.

"The fireplace is a necessity," Marge explained, with a twinkle that told me she was about to explore some point of French logic. "No matter how cold it is outside, the heat will not be turned on until the first of November." It was still October.

Marge's Hawaiian wardrobe was not especially suitable for Paris weather, and she had decided to go to London for a couple of days "to buy some warm clothes." Did my mother and I want to come along? I thrilled to the idea, but Pisa had taught me something. I suggested that Mom should go with Marge, and I would stay in Paris.

It was not only caution that guided my prompt decision; it was the presence of the piano. I wasn't looking at it but I could feel it. I could hardly wait for my back muscles to recover from their insistent ache so that I could sit down and establish contact with the keyboard. I felt I had spent enough time recuperating. Now I could get to work.

"How's the action?" I asked Marge.

"It's moderately light and very responsive," she assured me.

I had been lying on the couch-bed only a few minutes when I found I could endure the suspense no longer. I walked over to the piano and sat down, hands shaking a little as I felt the smooth keys under my fingertips. I put my hands over a chord and willed it to sound in that natural, lifelong, built-in process. It was as unconscious as walking. Your legs and body move automatically. You know you're walking, but you don't think about it. That's the way piano playing had always been. I had heard sounds in my head, or read them on the page and then heard them in my head. My hands had then done on the keyboard what I had heard in my imagination, and what I had, in the same instant, willed them to produce.

But as I willed this chord to sound, my hands didn't feel like my hands. It wasn't only that the keys were hard to push down. They didn't strike simultaneously, which is the most basic feature of a chord. It felt, and sounded, as if I had tried to play the chord with my feet. I tried another chord, but it was no different.

I decided to try an arpeggio. Almost unconsciously, my hands fell into the position of the opening arpeggio of the Beethoven Fifth Concerto, which I had been working on at Fontainebleau and had been playing so gloriously in my dreams since the first days in Menton. But what came out wasn't an arpeggio. It was a series of unconnected sounds, uncoordinated with each other or with me. There would be a little thump followed by a weak brush of the key followed by another little thump followed by something that didn't sound at all. The thumps and brushes and spaces were not rhythmically spaced but sounded as if someone were hitting them at random. It simply bore no resemblance to piano playing or to the arpeggio I heard in my head.

But almost worse was that when one of my fingers *did* press down a key, it was not done with the right muscle group. I could press down a key only by doing something that I knew was wrong. It was a little like not being able to swing your leg in a walking stride—as if you had to reach down with your hands, pick up your leg, and put it in the next position. That's what I was having to do with my fingers: pick up each one by means of a jerk of the elbow or arm or shoulder and set the finger down with a thump or a weak little collapse.

I tried one pattern after another, with the same result. It seemed unreal. These weren't *my* hands. I couldn't be producing these strange, unconnected sounds. It was as if a house you've lived in all your life had suddenly turned into a fun house, one of those carnival features that might more aptly be called a house of horrors. You look in a mirror that has always reflected your image, and it has turned into a concave or convex distortion. You are walking up and down crazy stairs that suddenly move from side to side or up and down, causing you to lose your balance, almost. The floor slants where you don't expect it to, and nothing is what it seems. You are totally disoriented, in a nightmarish way. And yet this is your only house. It was too much to comprehend.

As if I had been in a fun house and would soon, with a sigh of relief, reach the exit door, I told myself that the nightmare at the keyboard would soon be over. I just needed to work regularly, though my hands were shaking so much that I had to stop even trying to find patterns. After all, hadn't Dr. Lipsitch said that I would be playing before "too long"? And hadn't I been away from the piano for almost three months? It was only reasonable for my hands to feel strange.

I kept telling myself that soon I'd be going out into the light again, where everything would feel normal, and I would be *me* again. Meanwhile, there was no choice but to try to live with the horrors so that my muscles would strengthen and my hands would feel like mine. How do you accustom yourself to living in a fun house? I didn't know. But it may have been crucial to the retention of my sanity and optimism that I saw the phase as temporary, and thought I'd be out the exit door in no time.

"I must practice finger exercises as much as I can stand it," I vowed. Once upon a time, such exercises had added strength and control to my natural approach to the keyboard. Now I needed something to help simulate those qualities. I placed my hand in the simplest five-finger position and tried to do the exercise in which you raise one finger and strike the key quickly, then wait, relaxing all the muscles, then strike the key again. But even here, I couldn't move the finger up and down except by using my whole arm. The smallest joint, at the fingertip, kept collapsing, and wouldn't even support the force of pressure applied from another muscle.

How many years, I thought, had I done such exercises? And now everything felt disconnected: the finger disconnected from the rest of me. The insistent ache in my neck and back and the breathless anxiety that welled up as I sat there seemed to echo the fun house's eerie noises and weird laughter. How could I steady myself? Was there anything to hold onto? Any starting point at all? I looked as if for guidance at the pictures Martha had propped up on the table beside the piano—the men who had guided the talent they had found in me and helped me to develop it.

"What do I do now?" I silently asked my "household gods."

The man in one of the photos was looking downward and to his left. It was a good likeness: the long face, the aquiline nose, and heavy, horn-rimmed glasses. His blond hair was in place, however; usually it was falling over his forehead. I couldn't read the inscription on the photo, but knew it from memory: "To my dear pupil, Carol, with all good wishes for a bright future. Edward Bredshall."

Naomi had sent me to study with Edward Bredshall when I was ten years old. He was the finest piano teacher in the Detroit area, and my audition with him was one of the most vivid memories of my childhood. He was the director of the Art Center Music School, housed in a dingy gray building behind the Detroit Art Institute. My parents had driven me there for an audition one evening, so long ago, and we had all been excited and a little nervous.

We were greeted by Mr. Bredshall's secretary, Miss Smith,

a round-eyed Scotswoman with a brogue I could scarcely understand. She showed us into a waiting room that smelled of stale cigarette smoke and coffee. I will never forget the moment when the rear door of the waiting room swung open and in strode one of the tallest men I had ever seen. He was pushing his horn-rimmed glasses up with his left hand as he strode toward us, and extended his right hand to my parents. He bowed as he shook hands, first with my mother and then with my father. I had never seen anyone do this. His voice was low but sharp, almost rasping, and he spoke in a slightly clipped manner. I was awed by his speech, his height, his bearing.

As Mr. Bredshall showed us into his studio, I looked around me in wonder. Two grand pianos, scratched and dusty, were piled high with music and books. Bookshelves, a desk, all available surfaces were piled high as well. There was a bouquet of dried-up flowers on the piano. As he motioned me to one of the pianos, I noticed that the white keys had black ridges on the sides. I had never seen piano keys that dirty.

As I played the first movement of a Beethoven sonata, Mr. Bredshall strode to and fro, smoking a cigarette, his heels clicking on the floor, the floor creaking with each step. I wondered if the pacing meant that he liked it or that he was bored. I tried to make it as beautiful as I could, but he kept on walking back and forth. When I had finished the first movement, he signaled me to stop. He turned to my parents.

"She's very talented. Very talented." He strode to the other piano and played a chord.

"Can you tell me what notes I'm playing?" So he wanted to know if I had perfect pitch. That was easy.

"A, C, D-sharp, F-sharp (or E-flat and G-flat)," I clarified, since on the piano the pair sounds the same. He played some more complicated chords, but I sorted out the notes. He nodded at me and smiled. His smile was kind, but his eyes were intense and his voice sharp—an awe-inspiring combination.

"She has an excellent ear," he informed my parents. "Absolute pitch." I wondered if that was the same as perfect pitch.

Mr. Bredshall asked me to sit on the couch with my parents, while he sat down in a leather armchair facing us.

"She will have to work hard," he began, almost sternly. "We'll work mostly on technique for a year or so." As he explained what my playing needed, he gestured widely with both hands, alternately pushing his glasses up with an extended middle finger. He seemed unaware of the long ash on his cigarette, which would fall onto the floor or onto his suit. Occasionally, he would brush off the front of his jacket.

"Her playing is quite mature for her age," he said at one point. I wondered if he had that impression because I had tried to play the sonata as beautifully as I could.

"Can you have her here at eight o'clock on Saturday morning?" he asked my parents. "I want to teach her when I'm fresh."

I thought that was a curious statement, not realizing that he had just committed himself to getting up an hour earlier so that he could give me his utmost concentration before starting one of his long and tiring teaching days.

Mom and Dad gave me a reddish-brown music case, with my initials on it, to herald the beginning of my serious study and to hold the volumes of Hanon, Pischna, Cramer, Czerny, Dohnanyi, Clementi, McFarren: the five-finger exercises, études, scales, arpeggios, and velocity studies that Mr. Bredshall assigned to me during the first years of my work with him. He had said we would work on technique for the first year, but I wondered a little, later on, at his confidence in asking a ten-year-old to practice exercises and études three hours a day.

Somehow, though, he got the idea across to me that my technique was lagging behind my musical ability. My fingers needed to be stronger, more independent. I needed to be able to play more cleanly and with more control at greater speeds and with more endurance. I had spent hours a day at the piano ever since I could remember, but this was something entirely different from my self-directed self-expression. It was like being plunged into an athletic training that I never knew existed.

I began to worry that I had never practiced this way before. I wondered if ten-going-on-eleven was too late to develop the agility and strength Mr. Bredshall thought necessary. I felt anxious every time I sat down at the piano and opened my exercise manuals. Mr. Bredshall's heavily penciled directions insisted on the ideal. I was afraid I could never reach it.

"Two slow beats to each note."

"Keep steady tempo."

"High, clean finger stroke."

"Very flexible wrist, loose arm."

"Fingers well curved, nail joint very firm."

"Relax hands between measures, raise each finger high, wrist down, fingers up."

"Fast and clear."

"Firm and strong."

"Slowly and solidly, 10 times each, then faster, forte and piano, 10 times each, changing accents, 5 times each."

He wrote metronome markings; at first, slower than I had ever imagined playing, then moderate and hard to control, then exhilaratingly fast, almost faster than I could play. It was rigorous training, but its effects were meant to last a lifetime of piano playing. Neither Edward Bredshall nor I could have dreamed that years later I would be faced with something that made this effort literally look like child's play.

Toward the end of my first year with him, Mr. Bredshall let me begin a concerto, the Haydn D Major, and I found out what he considered to be the proper kind of work on a piece of music. Every phrase, every articulation slur, every detached tone, every legato line was shaped and worked out with the greatest of care. Almost every measure of my sheet music had something written over it, or underlined, or circled.

Our work was hard and rigorous; the bad habits were disappearing, and reliable ones were taking their places. I played my first Bach Prelude and Fugue, controlling every finger and clarifying each voice. I played my first virtuoso concerto, the Mendelssohn D Minor, with octaves and sweeping arpeggios and thrilling romantic melodies. I began to find that I could handle more difficult études and exercises with greater ease.

As time went on, Mr. Bredshall not only assigned more and more difficult repertoire, but spent more time talking to me. By the time I was thirteen, our lessons were two hours long: one hour for work and one for talk. It was a brilliant education: I drank in the exotic world of his monologues. He told me about his radical political and social beliefs, which were usually in opposition to anything I heard at home or at school. He told me about books I should read, especially those that told one something grim about life. He would quote long passages from memory; he was cursed with total recall, he said. Sometimes when he opened a book or a piece of music, a ten-dollar or twenty-dollar bill would drop out. Money seemed to mean so little to him that he would use it as a bookmark and then forget about it. He once said that if he ever got hard-pressed for cash, he had only to look through his books.

Cigarette dangling from one corner of his mouth, he would play passages from the opera that was to be broadcast from the Met in New York the following Saturday, translating as he went along and calling out unusual instrumentation. Sometimes he would put the cigarette down on an ashtray perched precariously on a stack of music and begin singing all the roles in rasping voice or hilarious falsetto.

He would pause dramatically on a chord: "Here . . . Salome kisses the severed head of John the Baptist."

I took very seriously his analysis of the absurdities in the concert field and laughed at his imitations of other pianists and their mannerisms. He told me what recordings I should listen to. He described his days in Europe with bitter humor and sharp detail: the bookstalls along the Seine in Paris, the opera houses in Germany, his teacher who had played the Strauss *Burleske* magnificently and who had committed suicide. It became evident that he spoke fluent German, French, and Italian.

It was then that my dream of going to Europe had formed. Mr. Bredshall had found something there that his musical soul needed. I wanted to find it, too. As soon as I had arrived in Paris for the first time, I dragged Martha to the bookstalls along the Seine, which I was happy to see were just as Bredshall had described them. We had spent hours picking out some yellowed, browned, and ragged scores. It didn't matter if I was actually saving money by buying music that was timeworn and clothbound rather than paperbound and new. It was part of a ritual that made me feel closer to that mysterious source Bredshall had drawn upon.

I was fourteen when he discovered a trick he used on me many times. I had wanted desperately to play the Saint-Saëns Second Piano Concerto and had secretly bought the sheet music and learned the piece. When I finally played it for him, I confessed that I had been afraid he would say I wasn't ready for it. He looked at me with an amused expression.

Many times after that incident, when I would mention a piece that I would like to learn, Bredshall would frown, hesitate, and look out of the window.

"Well, I don't know if you're quite ready for that," or just, "Well, I don't know . . ."

I would of course rush out to buy the sheet music, and work on it with a secret intensity until I felt I could prove him wrong. When I would bring it to my lesson for the first time, he would raise his eyebrows high over his horn-rims and say, as if surprised, "Well, I guess you *are* ready for that, after all!" It was only much later that I caught on to what he was doing.

Increasingly, by then, Bredshall was letting me do things my own way. He was writing in my music less and less. The first time I had played through the Saint-Saëns for him, he laughed and said to me admiringly, "You are an excellent faker!"

I knew what he meant: that when I wasn't yet quite up to achieving a musical effect I wanted, I was able to get my idea across anyway, without quite knowing how I did it. He was letting me pursue my own way and develop it to the point where I didn't have to fake anymore. Every so often he would say, "How did you do that?" about a particularly difficult passage that I had managed to play before he thought I was ready for it.

Another moment I'll never forget was the first time I played the Chopin G-Minor Ballade in public with Bredshall present. Afterward he embraced me, beaming and pink-cheeked, and said: "I've always listened to you as my student, but tonight I found myself listening to you as a pianist for the first time. It was very convincing."

I kept repeating those words to myself on the way home, trying to extract every bit of meaning from them. I also wrote them in my diary.

Mr. Bredshall thought of me as his star pupil when I was in my mid-teens, but a couple of years later he decided it was time for me to move on. I gave a marathon recital before I left, a strenuous two-hour virtuoso program. Our final performance together was the Rachmaninoff Second Piano Concerto, with Bredshall playing the orchestral part on a second piano.

"This is our swan song, Carol," he had said to me with a little laugh, but with a sad look in his eyes. Until that moment, it had seemed as if our relationship would go on forever. It was a test for both of us that we could get through the concerto that evening, and to this day I can't hear it without my throat tightening.

Just a year before I had left for Europe, Bredshall had died very tragically. He had been in an automobile accident, had recovered, but was found dead beside an empty bottle of sleeping pills. I had dreams about him every night for months after that, and awakened in the morning with the same shock that he was gone. I wished I had told him that he would always be one of my gods. I hoped that he knew anyway.

I went on to study with my other "household god," Webster Aitken, in Pittsburgh at Carnegie Mellon, where he was teaching at the time. At my audition, I encountered a tall, slender man with a deep tan and very blue eyes, wearing a Western shirt and well-fitting pants, a turquoise bracelet-watch, and cowboy boots. Added to his stunning appearance was his bearing—self-possessed and so straight that he looked almost stiff. I had wondered suddenly if I could play at all for this magnificent creature.

His studio was the opposite of Bredshall's. Instead of comfortable chaos, Aitken's was clean-swept and impeccable: two pianos, two benches, a few chairs. Instead of Bredshall's flow of commentary and information, Webster Aitken was a conversational minimalist, at least in the studio. He asked me a few pointed questions, which I stumbled to answer. I had already fallen hopelessly in love, complete with watery knees and elbows, and a sudden inability to find words. He asked about the repertoire for the solo recital I had just played, and upon learning that I had played Ravel's *Gaspard de la Nuit,* wanted to hear the "Ondine" movement. Fortunately, I was on familiar ground with the piece, one of whose treacherous passages Bredshall had once pointed to and asked, "How did you do that?" Aitken's response was impossible to read.

Much later, he told me that he had been very impressed with my playing from the beginning, but I would not have known it at the time. What I did find out very quickly was that from Webster Aitken I would learn to find the musical reason behind every note I played. I searched every phrase for meaning and contour. I sharpened my ear so that I could listen to myself objectively enough to tell if I were reflecting that in my playing. In the years under Webster Aitken's guidance, I refined my art.

He would sit very straight-backed on a chair across the

room from me and listen to something I was playing for him for the first time.

"Thank you," he would say, almost tonelessly, after I had finished. Then he would stride over to the piano and go through the score, thumping the page for emphasis.

"What were you trying to do *here?*" he would ask in a voice that was like fine sand. On he would go, pointing out the places where my expressive intention had not been clear or where I had failed to dramatize a musical point. The emphasis was always on *my* ideas. Because I had fallen in love with him, I hoped for his approval, but that was the last thing he was offering. A touch of praise or encouragement was nowhere in the equation.

On the other hand, I was being treated like an independent musician. Aitken was expecting me to come up with something original. It seemed a little like being actor and director, dancer and choreographer all in one. When I had expressed my own musical ideas in the past, I had been following my natural instincts. But now that the natural facility Bredshall had nurtured was fusing with the refinement of my work with Aitken, I was experiencing a musical coming of age.

Aitken and I gradually became friends, a friendship carefully controlled by a man who could exchange *bon mots* and barbs with the best of them. I had become adept at dodging his retorts, and we could laugh together, especially at the inadvertent word variants produced by his closest friend in the Carnegie music department, Maria Malpi, an Italian-Swiss voice teacher with an outgoing personality and casual demeanor. Some of Malpi's mixed-up words amused Aitken so much that they remain in my vocabulary: "disturbtion," for example, which meant an interruption of one of her voice lessons.

The last time I met with Aitken before leaving for Europe, I had just played a solo recital in Pittsburgh to a standing ovation and much excitement. I had worn a white dress, and he had turned up in a white suit. On some level, it felt as if I had finally achieved a form of togetherness with him. And Martha, whom I had met in Pittsburgh where she was studying voice with Malpi, had said the white garb was symbolic, that I was Aitken's "white hope."

In the recital, I played the same Chopin B-flat Minor Sonata that I had been practicing in Fontainebleau when the strange pain shot through my hand. The Chopin had earned me some special praise from Aitken, who rarely gave any. "Carol, you're like a small figure in a giant room, surveying the splendid techniques at your command," he said. "You have more than you need to do *whatever* you want to do at the piano."

He seemed to be saying that I had scarcely begun to make use of all these techniques: "Now it's up to you to go out and do something of consequence with it."

I realized that we were discussing the process of a lifetime, as the "small figure" would continue to grow. "From this point on, Carol," he declared, *"you* are in charge."

Hearing these words, I felt a considerable sense of responsibility, a tinge of anxiety, and much exhilaration. Then he gave me a photo of himself, with the inscription: "To Carol Rosenberger with every good wish for a happy and brilliant future–Webster Aitken."

But there was certainly no "happy and brilliant future" in sight as I sat at the keyboard in Paris and looked down at hands that no longer felt like mine. The piano had always been part of me, an extension of me, and I an extension of it. Now suddenly it felt like something alien, as if my best and most beloved friend had turned on me and said "I don't know you." What would my two "household gods" think if they could see me now, after their years of investment? They had taken my raw, exuberant talent and helped me develop it to the point where I could "do anything," as Aitken had said. Now, in contrast, I could do nothing. Could this be true? The question was too staggering to consider.

They say that human beings have surprising abilities to adapt. Perhaps that's what I was doing those first few days in Paris as I went to the piano for a few minutes at a time and forced myself to look in the fun house's distorting mirrors, to walk up and down the crazy stairs, and to stand with one finger on a treadmill that went one way and another on a treadmill going the other way. I went on trying to "practice." I set up exercise patterns for myself. As I sat there, making distorted and awkward movements to get the keys down somehow, I told myself that soon this would pass, that soon I would have my hands back again. Dr. Lipsitch had said "weakness," hadn't he? And weakness was dealt with best by exercises, wasn't it?

Mom and Marge came back from London with some warm clothes for Marge and happy memories for Mom of her first glimpse of London. She had bought me a few things, knowing that none of my clothes fit me now. I talked incessantly about my "exercise program," but I don't know what Mom or my two friends thought about it. They simply expressed pleasure that I was working again. We all talked enthusiastically about my getting stronger now that I could "practice."

Mom asked what I would like to do on my birthday. Since that was the same day the heat was to come on in the apartment building (November 1), I said jokingly that we should have an appropriate ceremony at home. But we ended up doing something much better: taking a trip to Chartres Cathedral. I lay down in the back seat so I could have full back-strength to walk around the famed edifice. I had read about Chartres and pored over pictures of it for years. But to be in its presence was so moving that I was trembling with more than muscle weakness. It wasn't only the grandeur, the reaching out and touching an earlier age, the history and aesthetic achievement. Somehow I wanted the Gothic to help give me perspective on the fun house. As I sat quietly, my eyes drawn up to the vast arch, up to the Rose Windows, I thought of American historian Henry

Adams's tribute in his *Mont St. Michel and Chartres*, a book I loved so much:

> *Of all the elaborate symbolism which has been suggested for the Gothic cathedral, the most vital and most perfect may be that slender* nerveure, *the springing motion of the broken arch, the leap downwards of the flying buttress, the visible effort to throw off a visible strain— never let us forget that Faith alone supports it, and that, if Faith fails, Heaven is lost. The equilibrium is visibly delicate beyond the line of safety; danger lurks in every stone. . . . The delight of its aspirations is flung up to the sky. The pathos of its self-distrust and anguish of doubt is buried in the earth as its last secret.*

How inspirational these words would turn out to be for my own struggle to maintain an equilibrium in the structure of my life!

We had planned to go out to dinner that night but I, as usual, was too tired. So I lay, and everyone else sat, in front of the fire. We enjoyed some excellent wine and delicacies from the charcuterie, topped off with fruit and *petit-suisse*, for which I had developed a passion. There were all kinds of cheerful toasts to the speedy recovery just around the corner, to the valuable things I would learn and experience here, to Mom's first trip to Europe, to Nana's recovery, to Martha's vocal career and Marge's year of grace in Paris before she would have to begin teaching.

As we clinked glasses—mine trembling and spilling a little, as usual—Mom's eyes misted as she smiled at me. I thought I knew what she was thinking: At least I was alive; I was not in an iron lung; I had walked around the cathedral unaided; I was sitting here clinking a glass with her. Surely the rest would follow. We drank to the next November 1—by which time I would be strong again.

Though the magnificence of Chartres pervaded our mood and conversation, Mom was leaving the next day. I was already steeling myself for the separation with as many optimistic thoughts as I could gather together. I was determined not to repeat the crying bout that had followed my father's departure.

I waved Mom off as cheerfully as I had Dad, and managed to control the weeping marginally better. But I felt nauseated and anxious almost immediately, feelings that prevailed for several days.

It was time, I decided, to plunge into what I was here to do—resume my sessions with Mademoiselle. She was delighted to hear from me, and we set a time for the following week. Martha and Marge both rode with me in the taxi to 36 rue Ballu. The celebrated Great Lady of Music welcomed me as warmly as if I had been one of her many beloved godchildren instead of a student who, as I saw it, had made a lot of trouble for her during the summer.

First, she made sure that I was comfortable, carefully arranging cushions so that I could be in a semi-reclining position. Then, while Martha and Marge went out to explore the neighborhood and find a good café, Mademoiselle and I talked of many things—music and meaning and life and perspective. She talked of her beloved younger sister, Lili, a composer who had died tragically at a tender age. Throughout our conversation, she seemed to be telling me that she considered me worthwhile, even in my present invalid state. Somehow she knew, almost more than I did, that I needed such reassurance.

Then she sat down at the piano and asked what I would like to "work on." It was clear that she wanted to know what music would mean the most to me. When I told her that I would find late Beethoven particularly soul-satisfying at present, she suggested that we analyze one of the late piano sonatas. As we started exploring the Opus 109 together, we both forgot everything but the music.

I wrote to my family later: "During the middle of our session

I put my hand behind my back to support it for a minute. When she looked up and saw this she jumped up from her chair and brought over another cushion for me. She said she had forgotten for a moment that I had been sick, and had been conducting the lesson as though I were just a regular student. Isn't that great?"

I added that the session's content had been so profound I couldn't even describe it. Then I bubbled a little about Mademoiselle's vast reservoir of knowledge: "It's marvelous the way she calls forth so much music in the course of a discussion—for example, playing a recitative from a Bach cantata to illustrate a melodic principle found in Beethoven!"

I spent the next few days happily "hearing" the Opus 109 in my head, jotting down thoughts and questions about its structure, and luxuriating in an imaginary performance of it in my fantasy.

Mademoiselle also gave me a musical exercise to try. She suggested that I memorize a Bach fugue away from the piano, one voice at a time, and that I then put the voices together from memory away from the piano. That sounded exciting.

I began Mademoiselle's exercise enthusiastically, but found that my enthusiasm was greater than my concentration. I had noticed this with other things: my mind seemed to trail off and lose the train of thought. And then, of course, there was the ever-present fog. I began to realize how much effort I was spending just to concentrate on simple things. The complex seemed beyond me. I talked it over with Martha and Marge one day.

"You know," I said to them, "it's as if I ran a marathon . . . and then had very upsetting news about something . . . and then ran up a few flights of stairs too fast . . . so I couldn't quite catch my breath . . . and sat down with all the aches and pains . . . and then tried to memorize a fugue one voice at a time."

After absorbing this, Marge suggested, "Well, wait a while before memorizing the fugue, then. Just enjoy analyzing the Beethoven."

"But Mademoiselle will be disappointed in me if I can't do it," I argued, my mind fixated on the more difficult goal.

"*You* are the only one who would be disappointed in you if you can't do it," Martha corrected, in her most precise diction.

They were both shrugging off what they saw as a small compromise, but it was the first time in my life that I was unable to respond to a challenge of my musical-mental abilities. Besides having hands that weren't mine anymore, my brain wasn't working well either. No matter how I tried to excuse my inability to play on my physical condition, I was now taking a first step toward undermining my confidence in yet another area.

I was losing confidence in my emotional control, too. I could burst into tears at the slightest provocation, especially if taken by surprise. Once when I was walking slowly along the rue Donizetti, a hurrying pedestrian bumped me enough to upset my balance, and I came close to falling. To my horror I started to cry. There were people all around, so I tried to shake my head a little as if I had something in my eye. I felt ridiculous but couldn't seem to stop.

Another time I had volunteered to go to the bakery down the street and get a loaf of bread. Very pleased that I could do something useful, I walked into the shop and waited my turn. In my best French I asked for the kind of bread Martha particularly liked. The baker answered rather abruptly that he was "out of that bread today." I couldn't say anything. I couldn't bring myself to order a substitute loaf; all I could do was turn quickly and stumble out of the shop. And I couldn't hold back the tears.

Friends from Fontainebleau and friends that Marge and Martha met in their studies in Paris came over to the apartment from time to time. I was always torn between the desire to sit up like everyone else or to lie down to relieve the aching muscles in my back and neck. Usually, when someone was coming to visit us, I tried to rest most of the day so that I could appear as "normal" as possible and participate in the conversation. Even though almost everyone knew I had been ill, I was becoming self-conscious about it.

Worse than the urge to lie down was the urge to cry. I could ignore the aching back or neck, but I couldn't seem to stop the tears. Sometimes I would get up and stumble off to the bathroom, from which I would emerge after I had pressed a cold cloth on my eyes to hide the traces. I was always sure someone must have noticed, and I felt uneasy and embarrassed. It seemed I couldn't trust myself on any front.

The Fontainebleau group decided to have a Christmas Eve party at our apartment, and I realized that I had nothing to wear. Since I was not in any condition to shop around for a dress, Marge came up with the solution. She had heard of a dressmaker not far away who did beautiful work. My friends went with me to Myriam's shop on the momentous occasion of choosing fabric and color. Myriam and her assistant listened sympathetically while Marge and Martha told her that I had been very ill, none of my clothes fit, and I couldn't stand for any length of time. Could she design a simple dress that wouldn't require much fitting time?

I loved Myriam's sketch and the dark green wool we all picked out; but what I remember best about the creation of The Paris Dress, as I called it for years afterward, was Myriam's understanding of my condition when it came time for the fittings. She had a comfortable place for me to sit down, cushions for my back, and had her assistant standing by. When it was necessary for me to stand up, they both helped me up, and one of them supported me while the other pinned or measured, or whatever needed to be done.

"Would you like to rest for a little?" she would ask me every minute on the minute. If I indicated that I would, we would all sit down and talk in an unhurried fashion until I felt able to stand again. I believe she would have sat there all day if necessary, even with customers waiting. Whenever I wore the dress, and I wore it for many years, I felt another kind of warmth besides the wool and the lining. Myriam's understanding and patience seemed to be woven into the garment. In the years to come, I would find out just how rare such qualities were, as I became more and more isolated from other people.

I wore The Paris Dress for the first time at our Christmas party and managed to get through the evening without any bouts of tears or major spills of wine. I did tire before the guests left, however, and had to retire to Marge and Martha's room to lie down, like a child who joins the grown-ups for a while and then is put to bed among guests' coats and purses for the remainder of the party. Even so, I felt the dress had helped me through the evening.

Earlier in the evening, while I was still upright, a young man who had spent the fall in Vienna told us about the wonderful opera and concerts there, which students could attend for practically nothing. Rooms and meals were also amazingly cheap—a fraction of Parisian prices. As he talked about the marvelous singing one heard in Vienna, and the famous voice teachers at the Academy, Martha and I began to ask questions as fast as he could volunteer information. Neither of us felt particularly happy about Martha's current voice study, and we had both become uneasy about the cost of living in Paris. And now here was someone talking about a musicians' city that would solve both problems.

I knew that Webster Aitken had spent many years in Austria and Germany, and I had a strong desire to learn German and acquaint myself with Central European culture. I also wondered somewhere deep inside if making a clean break with the city where I had fallen ill might catapult me from the ranks of invalid to the almost-well. The next day Martha and I could talk of nothing else, and I decided to ask Dr. Lipsitch how soon I could leave Paris.

"You can do anything you feel like doing," he assured me. "You'll tire easily for a while, though." I told him I had noticed that.

"There's something else that bothers me," I hesitated, ashamed to mention it and yet wanting to know. "I seem to be easily upset by things."

"A little jangled?" He nodded understandingly. "You will be for a while." He didn't sound particularly worried, so I felt relieved.

"My hands are still . . . weak," I went on. "I wonder how long it will be . . . before I can play?"

"Just keep working at it," he advised me cheerfully. "I had polio and I play the violin."

This was news to me, but it didn't tell me very much. I had never heard him play, before or after polio. And had his hands been affected by the disease?

"Just keep *trying* to live a normal life," he advised me. I nodded. That was my direction for the immediate future. *Keep trying*.

Chapter Seven

❧

Kinship with a Damaged City

The only thing that made it difficult to leave Paris was my prized series of sessions with Mademoiselle. During the two months since I'd returned from Menton, the weekly trips to 36 rue Ballu had helped me feel that my horizons were expanding. Many who had studied with Mademoiselle saw her as a musical disciplinarian, but to me she was a kindly, wise, even grandmotherly figure.

In our sessions, she focused on the musical and spiritual values I needed most at that point: something deep, lasting, solid—something I could hang onto. She made me feel that I was a worthwhile artistic personality, only temporarily handicapped, rather than someone no longer worth bothering about. I would never have admitted feeling the latter, but those subconscious processes had already begun. In succeeding years, as my confidence eroded steadily, one of the few things I had to hang onto was Boulanger's regard for me, as expressed in those post-illness sessions.

Nevertheless, I wanted to leave. Although I had once worshipped Paris from afar, it had become the scene of my lost health and lost self. It was a city in which I couldn't cope. I had begun to recognize that my recovery would take longer than anyone had predicted; and I wanted to stay in Europe as long as possible. If what little money I had would go farther in Vienna, then that was a powerful argument in Vienna's favor.

It was sad to be leaving Marge, but she had two friends who were looking for a place to live and would jump at the chance to move into the apartment. Another of Marge's many friends told us that we should also spend some time in Salzburg on our way to Vienna, and gave us some people to look up. It all sounded exciting.

The prospect of a new adventure somehow mingled with the hope that my health would return along with it. Maybe I would find my old self in Austria. I would have denied having such feelings if anyone had asked me just why I wanted to move on. But I was too foggy and desperate to analyze the reasons.

Martha and I said a fond goodbye to Marge, who promised to visit us in Vienna when we were settled. Then we boarded the Orient Express to Austria. We got off briefly in Salzburg—just long enough to be enchanted by its atmosphere.

We had heard that living in Vienna would be cheap. We soon found that "student accommodations" were also primitive beyond anything we had seen in Paris. Our first "hotel room" was a cold, dank, closet-sized cubicle up a flight of winding stairs from street level.

"Well," I said cheerfully to Martha, "it'll be good for me to climb the stairs."

Martha didn't seem to be concentrating on that, however. She deposited me and the luggage in our room and went out to look for a more permanent place to live, while I lay down with a hot-water bottle on my upper back—a typical pose in those days.

That evening, after Martha had come back tired and cold from her efforts, we ventured out to a small *Keller* not far from our little hotel. There, we ate lentil soup, dumplings, sauerkraut—hearty, steaming dishes that I had enjoyed on many cold winter evenings back in Michigan. They were some of Nana's specialties from her Central European background, and here they were again, staples of the Viennese winter fare.

The nuance and rhythm of the speech I heard from groups of people in the restaurant, that comfortable *gemütlich* feeling, reminded me of Nana's speech and her warmth. Her parents were Polish and Bohemian (Czech), and she had grown up speaking and understanding both languages. She had taught me a couple of phrases in Polish when I was a child and, just for fun, to count to ten in German. I even saw faces that reminded me of hers—the broad cheekbones, how the eyes were set. It suddenly felt as if I might find part of my roots here. Since I was looking for myself, that was a strong pull.

In the middle of the night, Martha and I were jolted awake by loud knocking on our door. Martha's year of college German and the few pages from the self-taught German book I had bought just before leaving Paris hadn't prepared us for dealing easily with an emergency when half asleep and unable to use gestures. While we were still deciding how to ask if there was a fire in the building, a male voice demanded—in German that even we could tell was quite slurred—that we let him in. While we whispered about what to do, he was joined by a second voice. We decided to pretend we were asleep. When the footsteps finally stomped down the hall, Martha said in a low voice: "Now you see why the room was so cheap."

The next night we went to the opera for the first time. The *Wiener Staatsoper* (Vienna State Opera House), which had been rebuilt after its war damages, had reopened just a few months before. Every night the house was packed with people who had loved opera all their lives, knew every aria and every singer's personal history intimately, and were filled with excitement at having their opera house back.

The evening's performance was Mozart's *Die Zauberflöte (The Magic Flute)*, with the great tenor Julius Patzak as Tamino.

A war injury had left him with one arm and one hook, and he was nearly sixty; but his exquisite singing gave me the uplifting message that music could triumph over all. In my teens, I had listened to the Metropolitan Opera Saturday broadcasts, and had bought some aria collections to play and sing for fun; but this, finally, was the real thing. My shoulders weren't up to applauding, but I shouted as best I could with my weakened voice support, and had enough foot power to give a few stamps of approval along with the audience. I told Martha I wanted to come back every night.

My letters to Mom and Dad from that period contain detailed descriptions of opera performances: who sang what, who was conducting, who had a cold or a fever that night, who had just been reworking something with a voice coach and/or changing roles. If I were to excerpt and combine those reports, the result would read like a newsletter from the Vienna Staatsoper. I'm not sure how much my family wanted to read all the professional and personal details I sent them, but that seems never to have crossed my mind. It *does* demonstrate how totally involved I became in the Viennese opera world. I had to rest in a horizontal position much of the day when I was going to the Staatsoper that evening, but I escaped into opera as a haven, and a distraction from the constant pain. The times I was able to remain upright through even part of a performance were the high points of those years.

At the Staatsoper, Martha and I sometimes watched the teenagers lining up for standing room with opera scores in hand. "Just the way American teenagers would line up for a baseball or football game," I commented.

"They think they're in paradise," she remarked later, as we watched them practically hanging by their toes from the standing-room rails way up in the gallery on the sides of the house, shouting and throwing bouquets down onto the stage. "Who knows," she added, thoughtfully, "maybe they are."

Martha was expressing what we both felt about the Staatsoper every time we approached the neo-Renaissance building. It was paradise to be living just two blocks away from the center where great opera performances took place throughout a ten-month season. Standing room was sixteen to twenty cents and was free to students; what we considered quite decent seats cost forty cents. If I rested most of the day, I could last through a performance without agonizing back pain. Perhaps my escape into opera also had a physical basis, since certain activities masked the constant pain better than others. Almost every night, from the first of September until the last day of June, there was something we both wanted to hear. A change of conductor, a change of cast, or even the repeat of a performance we had heard before. It made no difference. We had entered paradise, too.

Real life in Vienna, however, was considerably less than paradise. My parents were sending me $100 a month on a regular basis, with supplements when asked for. They couldn't imagine how I could live on that, but I kept assuring them that I could, since everything was so cheap in Vienna. What I didn't say was that I was living in a way I could never have imagined at home, and that I was helping Martha to stay in Vienna, too, as her monthly check from home topped out at $60. We were learning to live Austrian-student style, which is to say, at poverty level.

We had found temporary quarters that had no central heating, only a *Kackelofen,* a huge tile stove, in one corner. If you sat near the stove you were quickly roasted, and if you sat far away from it, you froze. That would have been fine for someone active, but it was hardly ideal for me. There was a communal WC (water closet) but no bath. Someone had mentioned something about a public bath, but the image of a large group of people in one big tub wasn't especially appealing.

One day Martha summoned her elementary German and said to someone we met at the opera: "I need a bath." The surprised recipient of this information managed to tell us that there was a public bath, offering individual rooms, called the Diana-Bath.

The next day, as we made our way to the facility, we saw the sign *Diana-Bad* on the front of a bombed-out building. Surely the operation must be housed elsewhere! As we got closer, we saw people going in and out. A bath in the open air in the dead of winter? But inside we found that the lobby was well heated and that one could buy tickets for a bath in a fully enclosed bathing room.

Soaking in a tub at the Diana-Bath for an hour was pleasant, but one couldn't make a trip there every day. Fortunately, Martha soon found quarters close to both the Staatsoper and the Vienna Music Academy, where she planned to enroll to study voice. The "suite" consisted of two small rooms flowing into each other, forming a space that was large and light and quiet. There was plenty of room for the upright piano I planned to rent.

The only catch was that we had to walk through two other people's rooms to get there. From the outer hall of the flat, we proceeded through a room with a purple curtain that stretched the length of the room and was meant to give a little privacy to the chemistry student who occupied it. But if his light was on, we could clearly see him and everything in his room, with the curtain only lending a purplish cast.

Beyond his room was a smaller room with a screen that was meant to shield the language teacher who lived there. Visually, it served its purpose, but this woman was a concentration camp survivor. Whenever we knocked at her door, the knock would set off her startle-reflex, and she would give a little cry along with several terrified gasps, "Oh, oh, oh, oh, oh, uhhh, uhhhhhhh . . ." before she could utter the words "Who's there?" as if she feared the worst, and we might be the Gestapo.

Once she knew who it was, she would calm down and beg us to proceed to our rooms. I started calling to her first, "Frau

Professor, it's Carol here," and following my announcement with a gentle knock. She came to know our voices, which cut down on the daily trauma. Sometimes she would open the door herself, with a warm greeting, and, I'm sure, relief that it was friend, not foe.

I soon became acquainted with Sieghart, the chemistry student. He was a thin, intense young man with a courtly manner and a deep voice. He studied in his room a great deal but was as eager to practice his English as I was my German. He usually won, as he had studied English for many years. In one of our conversations in English, Sieghart referred to our landlady, Frau Leber, as "Mrs. Liver"—a literal translation of her German name. The first time he did this, I couldn't stop laughing; so any time he wanted to make me laugh, he would refer to "Mrs. Liver."

Sieghart was in love with history and tradition and was a flesh-and-blood guidebook to Vienna. He wanted to show me everything about this city he knew so well—both in actuality and from the multitude of books he had read on every aspect of its history. By now, Martha had enrolled in the Academy and was out much of the time, so Sieghart invited me on his many expeditions. He never tired of planning, and I always had to cut his plan down to a fraction of what he had in mind if he wanted me to go along. He knew that I had been ill and was very solicitous, but couldn't quite grasp the limitations of my endurance. I saw only the first room of many museums in Vienna.

I was beginning to have episodes of feeling faint and breaking out in a cold sweat, while at the same time feeling ravenous. Sieghart thought it must have something to do with blood sugar. Perhaps I wasn't careful enough about my nutrition? I countered that I ate much better than he did. But after that discussion, Sieghart and I began poring over books on food content, making lists and tables of the cheapest ways to obtain the most nutrients. We began to eat many of our meals together. I had found my first new friend since my illness—someone who had not known me BP (Before Polio). It was curious to find someone who accepted me as I was now, a damaged person so unlike my former self.

Sieghart was in many ways more at home with his books and in his re-creation of the eighteenth and nineteenth centuries than he was in the present and in a personal relationship. There was always a certain distance, a certain reserve. But it was just this reserve that enabled us to be friends, although I didn't realize it at the time. He didn't find me strange, because he hadn't known many girls outside of his sisters. Anything American fascinated him. He didn't think of me as an out-of-commission concert pianist or as someone weak and ill. He thought of me as an American girl visiting Vienna who had been ill in some way and couldn't do much, but who wanted to learn all about Austrian culture. Sieghart wasn't someone with whom I could share my anguish at what had happened. But he accepted me as I *was*. Though I didn't like that polio-girl at all, I was grateful to him for accepting her with such kindness.

Meanwhile, Martha was reveling in her work at the Academy, convinced that she had found the greatest voice teacher in the world. Elisabeth Radó had trained, and continued to coach, some of the singers we heard all the time at the Staatsoper. In Martha's first few lessons, Radó already had pinpointed some of her vocal problems. I was fascinated, and followed every step of her progress.

I had rented an old upright with a mute on it so that, as I wrote to my family: "I can practice my ugly-sounding exercises in the morning without bothering anyone, including myself."

As part of these exercises, I used patterns from pieces I had once played, trying to recapture even the smallest vestige of coordination. As I labored away, I found that with a series of jabs with my whole body and jerks of the elbow and throwing of the whole wrist, I could push down a series of keys. The true neuromuscular channels were closed off. Gone was the old familiar open-handed feeling of being at home on the keyboard. It was as if I had to shut off any natural flow at all—almost shutting out the music itself—in order to deal with the situation.

The action on the old upright was feather-light, and that helped. My left hand was the more uncoordinated of the two hands, and since it was the weaker, it tired more quickly than the right. None of the snatches of music that I tried to "play" in this fashion sounded like music, but I felt I must persist. Surely I would be getting stronger any day now.

I wanted to attend the Baroque seminar at the Academy. I needed to learn more about Baroque style anyway, and decided that I might as well do it while I couldn't be playing the piano for real. One day I went over to the Academy with Martha, and found my way to the studio of the harpsichord and Baroque music professor, Eta Harich-Schneider. She was a lovely, kind-eyed woman with soft white hair and a gentle voice, and happened to have a little time in between lessons to speak with me. She spoke excellent English, and her manner was so sympathetic that I decided to tell her my story. By the time I finished I didn't have to explain to her what my difficulties would be in studying with her. She understood.

"You will have to audition in order to study with me through the Academy," she explained.

"But I can't play at all!" I said, immediately gathering my things for a hasty retreat as I felt the all-too-familiar, and still uncontrollable, tears coming perilously close to the surface. The "jangled" condition, as Dr. Lipsitch had described it, had not faded. Post-traumatic stress disorder was a term that hadn't yet been invented.

"That's all right," Harich-Schneider assured me quickly. "Just do anything at all and I'll accept you. It's just a formality."

One of the musical patterns I had been using to develop my push, jab, and jerk technique was the opening of the Bach E-Major Concerto. I decided that I would "audition" with that, and refuse to play more than the first few phrases, pretending I had forgotten the rest.

The audition was one of many nightmarish sequences that were becoming commonplace. Harich-Schneider and the president of the Academy were seated in a room that housed a piano and a harpsichord. I had played a harpsichord a few times in past years and knew that any harpsichord action would be considerably lighter than the piano. I also had a strategy.

I explained that I had been ill and had not played the piano for many months, and that I was still not able to work at the piano. I wanted to become acquainted with the harpsichord while I was regaining my strength.

"I cannot play the piano for you," I said in a shaking voice and with considerable understatement, "since it isn't up to my standard. But I will play a little Bach on the harpsichord."

The president of the Academy looked puzzled and said something to Harich-Schneider I couldn't understand. She responded with something that I couldn't understand and nodded at me encouragingly. I sat down at the harpsichord and began pushing, jerking, and jabbing at the opening of the concerto. It sounded, of course, appalling. I stumbled and had to start again, but soon Harich-Schneider stopped me.

I still wonder at the audacity—and willingness to be humiliated—on the part of that partially paralyzed creature sitting at a keyboard in front of the two expert musicians. I must have retreated from reality in allowing myself to get up in front of Harich-Schneider and stumble and thump around as if I were a total stranger to the keyboard. I must have been pushed into it by my own desperation. It seemed unreal, nightmarish; but then, everything seemed so at that time.

My excuse about being "thrown off" because I was unfamiliar with the harpsichord must have been at least faintly plausible, because the president of the Academy left it up to Harich-Schneider whether or not to accept this person who was clearly unfit for admission. She, as promised, accepted me. The whole episode had been so traumatic that I didn't even attempt to describe it in my letter home, knowing it would upset my family. I wrote only: "Yesterday was my audition for entrance into the Academy. I was, as you can imagine, feeling a little handicapped. However, I am accepted, so all is well. The harpsichord teacher is very nice and speaks excellent English."

My lessons with Harich-Schneider, unlike the audition, were relaxed. Her joy in the music itself, along with her sense of humor, prevailed. I loved her decision to assign descriptive titles to the Bach Inventions and Sinfonias. "Well," she said, "the French Baroque composers gave descriptive names to their short pieces, so why can't we do the same with Bach?"

Harich-Schneider had begun her career in Germany but left abruptly in 1940. She had been a professor at the prestigious *Hochschule für Musik* (Music Academy) in Berlin, but had been dismissed and threatened when she had refused to join the Nazi party. As she described it, a group of young storm troopers came into her studio and threw her music scores onto the floor, muttering contemptuously to each other *"Opusmusik!"* ("Opus music," i.e., classical music with opus numbers.) She had fled to Tokyo, where she had already been invited to teach. In 1949, she had moved to New York, where she taught privately, perfected her English, and pursued studies in other fields that interested her, such as sociology. When the Occupation forces finally left Vienna in 1955, she had accepted a teaching post at the Academy.

As it had been with Boulanger, our sessions were mostly paper-and-pencil study: suggestions from her and questions from me about registrations, embellishments, and ways of articulating this or that passage. She suggested that I participate in the Baroque seminar and assured me that I could come when I felt up to it. After the first class, I found that I couldn't sit up for the whole period in the stiff wooden chairs, so I would either come late and stay to the end, or I would leave when I was tired.

Many times, I didn't come at all, if my back was too tired or if I couldn't face the morale-lowering that I felt whenever I was around the other students. There was a hierarchy in the seminar, and those who were the best performers or who did the most interesting musicological research controlled the group. I had never seen a class from that diminished point of view before—I had always been on the other end of the totem pole.

I was not relegated to the usual European stereotype of "stupid American," at least to my face, but tried to intercede when it happened to others. One American girl in our harpsichord class had not been in Vienna long and was not used to German language protocol. She came from the South, so of course her instinct was to call Professor Harich-Schneider the literal equivalent of "Ma'am"—which would have been correct in French, but was hilarious in German. "Frau . . ." she addressed Harich-Schneider one day (that was the equivalent of saying "Woman . . ."). Snickers, giggles and laughs rippled through the class as she went on to her question, and I felt sure she had no idea what was wrong. After class, I explained that she should say "Frau Professor" or "*Gnädige Frau*" (honored lady) if the person was not a professor.

In general, I felt isolated among the other students in the harpsichord seminar, but stubbornly persisted in attending as much as my back would tolerate until one unforgettable day.

Each harpsichord student was allowed an hour per day of practice time on the instrument. I signed up for my time and went whenever I felt up to it, but the other students had found out that I often didn't use my time. When I did come to practice, I would usually find someone there who would then leave either reluctantly or graciously, depending on the person.

One day I arrived at the beginning of my hour and started working on a passage of a Bach suite for which I was trying to figure out registrations. Another student opened the door, frowned when she saw me there, and then came on in. I said that

I was using my time today. She said that she had been planning to practice this hour and sat down at the clavichord, which was on the opposite wall from the harpsichord. Was she waiting for me to finish, I wondered?

I felt I couldn't work with her sitting there, but was afraid of bursting into tears if I tried to insist on my rights. Maybe she felt that I was not a real student, someone scarcely worth noticing. I decided to brazen it out and started working at the passage I was trying to play when she had come in. Then, I heard another Bach piece being played on the clavichord. I couldn't believe it. She was ignoring me, and had simply started practicing.

I couldn't trust myself to ask her to stop. I couldn't do anything but gather my sheet music and get out of the room as quickly as possible. I managed to keep back the tears until I was out of sight. If she had told me that I was some substandard creature, I couldn't have felt lower. From having been an exciting new talent on the horizon a year before, I was now less than nothing. Even Harich-Schneider's special treatment was powerless to keep me from feeling almost subhuman. This was the "happy student life" I wrote home about.

I was starting to recognize that strength in my hands, arms, and shoulders was not going to come back easily. The "keep trying" motto, which I followed despite constant aches and pains, wasn't getting me very far as I worked at the muted upright in my room. I began making inquiries about a doctor who could help, knowing my parents would approve. I described the resulting treatments rather fully to them in successive letters:

> *Have finally found a doctor here—a Dr. Schmid. He examined me, and then next week I go to the hospital for muscle-tone tests. He thinks I need massage first. He told me that we can't begin with the treatments right away because the muscles can react badly if everything hasn't settled down. But he took a blood test, and thinks it is time now.*

*My tests at the hospital were not very pleasant.
They give you a series of stronger and stronger electric
shock type things; and then when you jump a bit from the
shock they tell you to relax and lie still. I could be sound
asleep, and if someone gave me an electric shock I'd jump,
wouldn't you? Dr. Schmid and I are going to discuss the
report on Thursday.*

*I'm having three treatments a week. Massage of
my upper back, shoulders, arms, hands, fingers by a wonderful masseur, Herr Wilhelm. He and I speak German
together, which is fun for me and amusing for him. He
recommended that I get a little ball and see how many
times a day I could squeeze it; so I am, and I think it's
going to help. It seems to be about time for such things.*

*Herr Wilhelm made a little contraption for me out of
rubber cord and a pulley. I attached it to a hook here in my
room, and just pull it back and forth. It's fairly high up, so
it exercises both the muscles that pull down and the muscles that pull out. He has me doing other exercises, too. The
rubber ball routine is wonderful. Every time he sees me he
asks how many times I can squeeze the thing in succession.*

*I'm having treatments galore. In the latest, my
hand is immersed in a basin of water, and then electric
current is turned on. This is known as galvanization. I
also have a pack-type thing strapped onto my back. That's
galvanization too. Then I take the thing I described to you
as in the muscle-tone tests and proceed to shock myself in
four places in my hand. This lasts for ten minutes. Fortunately, I only go for this treatment twice a week. My
massage and radar treatments are three times a week.
Dr. Schmid thinks these things will speed up progress,
and that it is time to do so. Even after all this time, some
muscles in my arms are sore to massage, though they will
strengthen now, I'm sure.*

The galvanization is from ten to twenty mA (milli-amperes). The "shocks," as I call it, are direct current. It goes to fifty V and lasts for half a second. I think that's right but I'm not certain, since my German is a little shaky yet, and I could have misunderstood. If that's enough to electrocute me then obviously I've quoted the wrong figures.

For the first time, I began to think and talk more about the immensity of the rebuilding process I felt compelled to undertake. Even though I was seeing only the tip of the iceberg, the mission was more frightening than I could admit. Every physical move I made at the piano was bewildering, since none of the usual impulses produced corresponding sounds or combinations of sounds. Ever. . . . Before polio, when I had a musical thought, that concept could remain in my imagination, guiding me to carry it out on the piano. But after polio, the moment I heard myself attempt to reproduce what I had just imagined, it would disappear. Soon the tears would come, and I would have to stop for a while.

It was hopeless doing much work on passages from my solo repertoire, but I found that I could be helpful to Martha. BP, I had often played song accompaniments with singer friends, in addition to playing chamber music with other instrumentalists. Now, I found that I could still work out some way to indicate the general idea of a song accompaniment. For Martha's purposes in learning a song or an aria, it didn't matter how much of the accompaniment I could play, as long as there was a general outline or approximately the right harmony. So I used her song accompaniments as my étude material—things to work out with my push and jab and shove-with-the-back technique. I welcomed opera arias, since the accompaniment was one step further removed from piano playing. Piano reductions of orchestral scores were often awkward, anyway. I could attribute some of my awkwardness to the reductions, rather than to my own almost-useless hands.

I was playing with everything but my nose in order to get some keys down at approximately the right time. In this bumbling fashion, Martha and I went through some opera roles she wanted to learn, as well as songs of Schubert, Schumann, Brahms, and Wolf. We went over the texts and discussed their meanings as our German improved. I knew that no matter how inadequate the playing was, the study itself was helpful to Martha and fascinating to me.

With my interest both in the opera and Martha's vocal repertoire, I began to pump her for details about her voice lessons, which were often in master-class form, so that students could listen to each other and to Radó's comments. One day a telephone call came for Martha, canceling an appointment she had immediately after her voice lesson. But I couldn't get through to anyone at the Academy who would guarantee to give her the message. I was going over to practice harpsichord anyway, so I decided to go early and stop by with the message.

As I neared Radó's studio, I heard a lovely, youthful-sounding voice full of light and sparkle, and listened, with chills running up and down my spine, until there was a break so that I could go in. I opened the door of the studio in time to see Radó finishing the last phrase. It was *she* who had been singing! She was in her late fifties at the time. I was awestruck.

After introductions all around, Radó asked me if I would like to stay and listen. I nodded and sat down. This was the first of many voice lessons I observed with utter fascination. I knew that she had taught many of the outstanding stars of the European opera houses at that time, and I found it a great privilege to watch and listen while this extraordinary teacher taught students to put light and ease, strength and support, flexibility and control into their voices. The Frau Professor was very kind and sometimes explained things to me that I otherwise would not have understood. She never asked what I was doing there, observing her class, or why I had the time to listen to singing. I never felt ashamed that I couldn't function. I was accepted with no questions asked.

It was comforting to lose myself in the world of singing and to feel at ease with a group of musicians—Martha's fellow voice students—who came from all over Europe. They seemed to accept me without asking what I was doing in Vienna. It was almost as if I could go to Radó's studio incognito. Sometimes I would join a group for coffee afterward. The talk, often in a language "mish-mash," as we called the mixture of French, German, Italian, English and other less familiar languages, would center on singing.

I knew there was some irony in my fascination with vocal art, as my own voice, even my speaking voice, was still high-pitched and thin due to losing such a large proportion of my abdominal strength. My vocal support was so shallow and non-existent that I couldn't even finish a spoken phrase without taking another short breath, let alone sing even a *sotto voce* fragment of song. So how could I stand to be reminded all the time of the glories of the human voice, when mine had weakened to such an extent?

The answer is that living vicariously in the singer's world was a welcome escape. My self-identity was as a pianist, and the loss of my own playing was a gut-wrenching reality. I had lost my pianistic voice, and listening to instrumental virtuosity of any kind had become an agonizing reminder of that enormous loss. But since I did not have a comparable stake in singing, I could throw myself into the world of song as a way of maintaining musical continuity. I knew that singing is at the very core of all music. I knew that immersing myself in the rich lore of opera and song could only add to my musicianship. Even in escape mode, I was thinking toward that time when my strength would return, and I would have all of this to bring back to piano playing.

We found that as registered students at the Academy (which cost approximately $16 per semester), we could obtain free standing-room tickets to the opera and to many concerts. Of course, standing in the standing-room sections was out for me, but there was a solution. I bought a tiny, featherweight folding stool that I could put into a lightweight bag, and smuggled it into the opera. Then, when surrounded by other standees or after the lights had gone out, I unfolded the stool and sat on it, leaning against the wall or against a bunched-up coat propped between me and the next step up. It didn't matter too much if I could see or not. I could stand up for a couple of minutes for a part I particularly wanted to see, then sit down again.

I said wistfully to Martha that if only I could get to the front part of the standing-room section, I could sit down, and also see the stage. But there was always a line for the front places. One evening I looked down at the front row of standees and saw a young man with glittering eyes and a strange way of tossing his head. He was talking to, or rather at, some other standees in the front row. They were laughing at everything he said, watching him as one watches some strange creature. They had left some space between themselves and him—not a whole standing space, but a good half space. I wondered why, but as I watched, no one filled in the space. I took a deep breath, picked up my folding stool, put my coat over it, and made my way down to the front row. I put my hand proprietarily on the railing and stood, looking straight ahead, shaking inside, wondering if anyone would order me to leave.

I could feel the strange young man to my right looking at me. "Well, who is this?" he asked the other standees. One of the girls giggled. They were waiting for him to order me out, I was sure. He seemed to have power. I said nothing, only stared straight ahead as if I had not understood. I knew that the Viennese could spot an American a mile away, so it was easy to pretend that I didn't understand him.

"Well, I wonder who this could be?" he tried again, to more

giggles. "Do you suppose it's Graahss Kell-lly?" (Grace Kelly in German, I thought to myself, trying to keep from laughing.) I couldn't help smiling a little, and he must have seen it. I tried to think of the best way to explain in German that I would be content with a half space because I would be sitting down most of the time, but my heart was pounding too hard for me to think clearly enough how to say this. One of the women on my left spoke up.

"This isn't a place here," she said. "You can't stay here." I glanced at her as if I hadn't understood, but she was looking at the "crazy boy," as I had heard someone calling him, for confirmation.

"Ah," he said. "But this is Graahss Kell-lly in our midst! If Graahss Kell-lly wishes to stand here, then Graahss Kell-lly may stay." The others laughed again and turned away from me. Finally, I found the words.

"Thank you very much," I said to him. "I'm going to sit most of the time anyway." I took out my folding stool, and he helped me set it up. Then he sat down on the step beside me and began talking to me about all manner of things. I knew that the others thought him crazy. But my German wasn't good enough to tell if he was making complete sense or not. He did have a strange look in his eyes, but I had the feeling that he was mocking himself at the same time.

"I am the leader here," he confided. "I must have power. I must be *first.*" I listened and nodded, thinking to myself that it was fortunate for me that he had taken such power for himself.

From that time on, the "crazy boy" was my protector in the standing-room section. If he was there, I always had a place in the front row and could see most of the opera while I sat on my stool and listened. During the intermissions, he talked of many things— philosophy, Chinese poetry, and the usual opera gossip. We didn't exchange much information about personal things or areas of music study. He knew that I had been stricken with *Kinderlähmung* (the German word for polio), but I tried to avoid any other talk about my illness. Besides, this way, I could remain Graahss Kell-lly.

Chapter Eight

❦

Struggling Forward in Vienna

My sitting-up time had reached a plateau of about four hours a day. I could stretch it for a special occasion, but the next day I would have to reward my back and neck muscles with some extra rest. I was still in pain most of the time. My shoulders, neck, and arms ached from the slightest effort, such as wearing a winter coat, so I sometimes called them the "coat-wearing" muscles.

Most days I also had insistent neck pain just from holding my head up. The ache or pain would shoot up into my head and make it difficult to think clearly. But I hated to mention this condition, because I didn't want anyone associating me with phrases such as "pain in the neck" or "headache."

One useful thing I *could* do was pick up Staatsoper standing-room tickets at the Academy before or after a harpsichord seminar. The main office had thoughtfully placed seating outside the door for students waiting in line. One day I fell into conversation with a charming, sturdy young American with strawberry blond hair, the resonant voice of a singer, and a slightly impish look in his blue eyes. I was surprised to find that he was from the same part of Pennsylvania as Martha, and so I mentioned her name and where she grew up. He looked at me with a shocked expression.

"She's my cousin!" he exclaimed, staring at me in utter amazement. He had been in the U.S. Army and was studying in Vienna on the GI Bill. He didn't know that Martha was in Vienna, and she had no idea of his whereabouts. By the time we got our tickets, Earl and I had exchanged information, and I had invited him back to our rooms to see his cousin. I was attracted to Earl, and he seemed to respond to me.

Martha and Earl exchanged family gossip and caught up on each other's singing careers and study. We arranged to have dinner together soon, and I thought Earl's long look at me when he left told me what I wanted to know.

Our dinner together at Earl's place started off in delightful fashion, especially when he asked casually if I would like to go to a concert with him. A couple of times he wanted to find out more about what I was doing in Vienna, but I brushed that off with a casual "I haven't been well, but I'm fine now and I'm studying harpsichord."

Soon, however, my spinal muscles began to show signs of their usual fatigue, and Martha asked Earl to find a cushion for me. I tried to say it didn't matter, but the search for a cushion opened a conversation about my condition, and soon Martha had told him the story.

There was no way to avoid it, but I knew everything was over before it had begun. While Martha was explaining carefully why my back was weak, I saw Earl's expression change. Martha told him to put his hand on my back, where he could tell how little muscle I had left. He did, but gingerly, as if the whole idea made him uneasy.

The faint beginnings of romance became lost in the aura of sickness around me—the first of many such incidents "AP" (After Polio) reminding me that I was unattractive because of my damaged body. It wasn't much of a surprise, as my self-image was already deteriorating. As a vital person, I seemed to have gone the way of my piano playing.

Earl stayed in touch with Martha and helped reassure us at the time of the Hungarian Uprising in October and November of 1956. The hostilities in the nation next door had brought back familiar anxieties to the Viennese and put the city on alert. At the time, World War II was never far from anyone's psyche. Bombed buildings—still unrepaired—were a constant reminder, while the triple and quadruple locks on people's doors were another sign of fear and distrust.

When the uprising broke out, Hungarian refugees began to pour over the border into Austria, and everyone we knew was taking spare clothing and food to collection points in the city. From there, volunteers took supplies to the refugee camps along the border. Martha and I made trips to one of the collection points, too, and it was touching to see so many people who obviously didn't have much in the way of material possessions arriving with bundles of clothing and goods.

The Viennese feared that Soviet tanks might return, especially since the Austrians obviously sympathized with the Hungarian rebels. The Soviets had left Austria in 1955, only a little over a year before. Many foreign students were opting to leave Vienna, feeling it was too risky to be so close to the turmoil in Hungary. Some Americans Martha knew were leaving for Switzerland. Although Martha and I were not inclined to leave, we consulted with Earl, who gave us a concise plan for what we should do if we saw any sign of escalation. Whenever either of us left the flat, we were to take along such basic things as our passports, cash, an extra sweater and scarf, some packable form of food, and other essentials. At the first hint of a crisis, we should try to find a streetcar heading west, and stay on it as far as it went. Then we should continue west on foot.

The thought of the streetcar made me nervous, as I couldn't ride one in safety. I had to sit down when the vehicle was not in motion, since my back wasn't strong enough to support me once the car had started up again. If I tried to grasp a handle while standing, it put too much strain on my arm and shoulder, since I always had to hold my elbows against my sides for support when using my arms. And yet to the casual observer I did not look handicapped, especially since I could walk to the streetcar and up the steps into the car. I was young and probably looked healthy from the outside, so I inevitably incurred resentful stares or actual complaints from other passengers when I tried to get a seat.

In a crisis, of course, those problems would be secondary; and Martha and I took Earl's instructions seriously. For months thereafter, neither of us left the flat without the essentials for a quick flight. But we also laughed at a bitter joke going around Vienna at the time: A fictitious telegram from doomed Hungarian leader Imre Nagy to the Austrian government asks, "Send tanks," to which the reply is, *"Eins oder alle beide?"* ("One or both?")

While waiting for Staatsoper tickets, I had another chance meeting that resulted in a delightful conversation with a piano student by the name of Dady Mehta. Dady talked a lot and laughed a lot. He was clearly of East Indian descent, but explained that he had grown up in China, attended music school in Paris, and was now in Vienna for graduate study. Ordinarily I would have shied away from talking with a piano student, but Dady chatted so easily about a wide range of things that he made me feel at ease. I thought that Martha would enjoy him, too, and arranged for him to meet us for tea one day. My chance meeting with Dady turned into something very special; the next thing I knew, he and Martha were dating. He was to become her future husband and the love of her life.

One day a letter came from my family, looking like the others that arrived regularly, with my mother's clear and flowing handwriting on the envelope. I opened it eagerly and read the first page, which was conversationally written about everyday things. But when I got to the second page, I suddenly realized that the first page had been a careful and thoughtful prelude to devastating news.

"Our dear Nana has gone to join my dad," my mother had written. "We are thankful that she went quickly and that her last day was a particularly pleasant one."

I was trembling in shock as I read the rest of the letter. Mom explained that Nana had been playing cards with some friends, and then had sat back in the chair for a few minutes, rested her head against the top of the chair, and was gone. She and Dad were thankful that Nana's heart had given out before the cancer became more painful. Cancer? Mom and Dad hadn't told me about that.

Everything around me was falling away, as I tried to comprehend that Nana, my grandmother and lifelong close pal, had died. Annie Wasielewski Gibson had been there when I was born, had lived with us always, and was my treasured friend and confidante. She had come to visit me in Pittsburgh when I was a student at Carnegie, and had charmed my friends there with her warmth, personal depth, and sense of fun. To everyone's delight, she even spoke Polish with one friend who came from a Polish-speaking family. We could all discuss our student lives and dreams with her over a traditional Central European-style supper she would gladly prepare for us. By the time she was ready to leave, everyone was asking how soon their new friend Nana could come back.

Now, I kept replaying something Nana had said to me at home in Michigan just before I left for France. She had told me, in a quiet moment, that she was sensing her late husband, Will, my grandfather, as closer to her than he had seemed for many years after his death. "He has always been slightly ahead of me," she had said, with tears in her eyes, "but now he is just at my shoulder." She told me that I mustn't be sad if she went to join him before I returned. At the time I wanted to interpret this as

Nana's general perspective: If the unthinkable were to happen, it is part of life. She was always saying, in one way or another, that we must savor the moment and know that loved ones are always with us.

But the possibility that I might never see Nana again was something I couldn't have imagined. She had talked often about Will, and my younger brother, Gary, and I felt almost as if we had known him. At age sixteen, young Annie had fallen deeply in love with thirty-two-year-old Will Gibson and had married him in the same year. Their only child, my mother, was born three years later. Both Mom and Nana had told me wonderful things about Will. He had taken on the task of supporting his mother and sisters when his father had died suddenly, though Will himself was only twelve at that time. He had met adversities with humor and resourcefulness, and had always put things into a perspective that made them bearable.

That last conversation with Nana began to haunt me as I attempted to process the fact that I would never see her again. Why hadn't I gone back to Michigan sooner? How could I have missed seeing her one more time?

Martha was understanding and supportive. Sieghart tried his best to comfort me, and during the weeks that followed, he went with me on walks to nearby churches. As a child I had accompanied Nana on some of the many visits she had made to St. Mary's, the Catholic church in our neighborhood. She had always maintained her Catholicism as something private, since Will had been a Presbyterian, and my mother, their only child, had been given the freedom to choose either or neither. As soon as I had come to Europe, I had begun to collect little souvenirs and postcards for Nana from the Catholic churches and cathedrals I had a chance to visit. Now, all I could do was look for the right church where I could have a novena said for her. I chose the small Baroque Church of St. Anne.

Everything seemed to remind me of Nana. I had been

helping Martha to learn Schumann's song cycle *Frauenliebe und -leben (Woman's Love and Life)*, but had to beg off for a while. Its story was painfully reminiscent of Nana's life: her adoration for her beloved Will; her treasured child, who looked like him; and her feeling that the one cruel thing he had ever done to her was to die too soon. Will had passed away when Nana had not yet reached the age of forty.

Nana had been strong, spiritually and emotionally. She knew how to get a lot of joy out of life and how to savor the simplest things. When I was still so weakened and seemingly without ballast, just the thought that she was there, even halfway around the world, had been sustaining. I had felt that I was discovering part of Nana's root system in Central Europe, and therefore part of my own. But now the flower of those roots had died. I wondered what I was doing in Vienna that was so important that I couldn't have gone home, that I couldn't have seen her once again. The "defeat" part of "going home in defeat" suddenly seemed less important. Nana and my mother had been very close, and I knew that Mom would be in a state of deep grief. Was my "keep trying" program more important than that? Maybe I should give up, after all, and go back to be with her.

But the letters that came from my mother, with added notes from my father, described wholehearted support from friends and neighbors. Thoughtfully anticipating how I would be feeling, they expressed ongoing interest in whatever was happening in Vienna. They were making it clear that they wanted me to stay if something there was contributing to my recovery.

One day in early 1957, as I was leaving Harich-Schneider's studio after the Baroque seminar, I saw an announcement for an analytical lecture on the Beethoven Piano Sonata Opus 57, "Appassionata," and decided to check it out. I sat in the back of the room, near the door, where I could leave unobtrusively if the sadness took over, or if my muscles started telling me that they'd had more than enough for the day.

The professor, Franz Eibner, was drawing an elaborate graph of the entire first movement of the sonata. This wasn't just a variant of the usual vertical analysis of harmonic progressions taught in typical music theory classes. Here, the professor was picturing horizontal motion representing the grand design, the overall tonal structure of the entire ten-minute first movement. In blueprint fashion, spare single tones represented the tonal direction. The lines representing horizontal motion intersected at the principal harmonic goal posts, so that the vertical harmonic events were also represented, but in the context of the horizontal movement. It was a dazzling view of the underpinnings of Beethoven's tonal architecture.

The professor's blueprint-after-the-fact of Beethoven's genius creation was thrilling and struck me as something of import, as Boulanger's sessions had done in Paris. The graph expressed the underlying tension, forward motion, and breadth I had always responded to in great classical music, and had tried to express when I performed such piano works.

Clearly, this architectural analysis was in tune with a performer's intuition. The graph of the first movement represented the tonal structure of the music as being in motion from the first note to the last. Traditional music theory analyzed classical structure on a mostly vertical basis and had always felt static to me.

Professor Eibner explained that this analytic technique had been devised by a great scholar-musician named Heinrich Schenker, and that he, Eibner, was one of Schenker's "disciples." The disciples called themselves *"Die Schenkern"* ("The Schenkerites"), and Eibner was spreading the word under the auspices of the Academy.

Schenker Theory courses were divided into three levels: beginning, intermediate, and advanced. Over the next few weeks I started to drop in, and stay as long as I felt up to it, during all three courses. It didn't matter which level I was auditing: Each discussion not only included something meaningful to me, but also resonated with my former life as a pianist. The discussions drew me back into that resonance. The graphs represented the glorious tonal events I had wanted to communicate. And if I couldn't be playing, at least I could be living some magnificent creations in my imagination. I could be feeling them acutely, from the inside, by a different means.

Eibner was tall and wiry, and radiated high intensity. His eyes filled with tears when he got emotional about his subject matter, which happened frequently. One day, when I had felt up to staying until the end of the class, Eibner beckoned to me as the others were leaving. He had noticed that I came intermittently to all three levels and wanted to know a little more about my own field. What was I studying?

"Harpsichord," I answered. Ah, so I was a harpsichordist. "No," I replied, "I am actually a pianist, but I'm not studying piano at the Academy." If that seemed a little strange, he evidently wasn't bothered by it.

"Well," he remarked, "you seem to be very interested in Schenker theory! Are you working on something that you'd like to analyze? If so, we can have a private session." As I hesitated, knowing that what I'd like to bring in would be a piano work, he added: "There is no cost for a private session."

"Yes, Herr Professor," I answered. "I'd like to work on the Opus 111." Beethoven's final piano sonata was almost sacred to me, and I could think of nothing I'd rather work on from this unique perspective.

So our private sessions started, as I saw it, at the top of the mountain. I ventured a graph of the first few pages and brought it to Eibner at our first session. This did not seem to be what he had expected, but it *did* seem to excite him. We sat with my manuscript propped up on the piano rack. He scratched his head, tousling his dark hair a bit, and erased some of my suggestions, writing in others. We went back and forth, considering the various levels of tonal importance, sometimes with Eibner erasing and rewriting what he himself had just put in.

From that point on, Eibner gave a generous amount of time to our joint graph creations. I had a private session once a week, on average. In between, I fiddled with the analysis, trying to get at and express the powerful architecture of whatever piece I was analyzing. We went through all three of the late Beethoven sonatas (all sacred to me in various ways), and a number of other works.

The Schenker graphing of important piano works was molding on paper the powerful musical motion I heard in my ear and wanted to recreate in performance, but could no longer attempt at the piano. I was drawing pictures of what I couldn't do! The graphs addressed the underlying beams and girders and powerful currents of the tonal world of evolved classical music. And "writing" graphs of Beethoven's music seemed especially satisfying because his structural underpinning has a unique power and dynamism; to me, it is the supreme architecture in tonal music.

Unlike most people I had met in Vienna thus far, Eibner did not speak any English, so my German was making considerable progress. One day a colleague of Eibner's stopped by his studio-classroom. After a brief exchange, Eibner introduced me and pointed to our joint graph. *"Wie das Mädchen schreibt!"* ("How the girl writes!") he said to his colleague. That was the first compliment in German I'd ever received.

At one point, Eibner asked if our work together was having any effect on my piano playing. This was a moment I'd been dreading, as I was afraid that he might dismiss me as someone unworthy of all this attention. I took a deep breath and began to give him an understated and abbreviated version of my story: the paralysis, the present incapacity. I presented these problems as *temporary*.

Tears came to his eyes as I started to tell him what had happened to me. He turned away from the music rack to face me directly, asking questions about how I was coping with such a devastating blow. After a while he began to talk about his experiences during the war, especially the year just afterward, when public services in Vienna had come to a halt and food was so scarce that many starved to death. He spoke of his beloved young daughter, Agnes, who had become desperately ill one evening. No streetcars were running, so he had no option but to carry her to the hospital in his arms. It was a considerable distance, and Agnes had died before he got there.

We both wept as he told me the tragic story, his devastating *"Erlkönig"* experience. "Her name was Agnes," he said, choking on the words. Tears ran down his face. "So close to Agnus . . . She was the Lamb, the innocent sacrifice to war."

It was a long session that day, a turning point in our relationship. Eibner and I both knew that we had spoken of things not often communicated with others. I was no longer just the American girl who did interesting graphs, but also someone with devastating life experiences to absorb and process. And he in turn felt comfortable speaking with me about major tragedies that he and his friends and loved ones had endured during the war, which they, too, were still struggling to absorb and process.

My relationship with Eibner represented in some ways my relationship with Vienna itself. The damaged person I had become felt a kinship with the damaged city that had been home to so much great music. Many of the Viennese were reeling from their wartime and postwar experiences, just as I was reeling from the effects of polio. Vienna was important to me symbolically—its damage and great beauty, combined with its passion for music, created a spiritual bond.

In a sense, nothing seemed truly whole except the glory of what happened at the Staatsoper. Martha and I continued to marvel at the consistency of its high artistic standards. Such celebrated music directors as Karl Böhm and Herbert von Karajan drew great and legendary singers throughout the company's season. We delighted in the citywide fascination with opera stars—what and when they were singing, if they were in top form, if they had recently been re-studying roles or techniques, and much more.

One of my favorite examples is the day a visiting soprano who was to sing the Marschallin in *Der Rosenkavalier* that evening suddenly fell ill. The Staatsoper office immediately placed a call to Hilde Konetzni, one of Vienna's resident star sopranos, who had sung the role hundreds of times and had been accorded the title of *Kammersängerin. (Kammersänger* and *Kammersängerin* are the equivalent of a British knighthood; in England, she would have been Dame Hilde Konetzni). When Konetzni did not answer her phone, the Staatsoper put out a news bulletin on the radio: "If anyone sees Frau Kammersängerin Hilde Konetzni, please tell her to call the Staatsoper." Within minutes, she was spotted at the hairdresser's and returned the call. Martha and I heard her sing gloriously that night.

On one of the first days of spring, I went for a walk in the Stadtpark, and sat down to rest for a few minutes on one of the park benches. As I looked around, I noticed that the woman who was sitting at the other end of the bench, just a few feet from me, was the great soprano Birgit Nilsson. She looked over, smiled, nodded, and said good day, as I did in return. Then we both just sat there quietly, enjoying the sunshine.

It was sheer magic to share that warm day on the park bench with someone who had inspired such joy and wonder as I had listened to her sing. Birgit Nilsson was supreme in her category; what she had accomplished was rare among generations of great singers. With her gleaming voice, she could make Wagner's Brünnhilde sound like an energetic, rambunctious youngster. It felt enormously comforting to share such a personal moment, as this magnificent artist relaxed with no incursions into her space. The great stars in Vienna knew that nearly everyone recognized them but would be respectful of their privacy.

As summer drew near, and things would be winding down

at the Academy for a couple of months, I decided to go home to Michigan for a visit. Since I was not giving up the struggle, but merely taking a vacation to rest and spend some precious time with my family, I reasoned that no one could consider this "going home in defeat."

My parents and I were happy and warmed to be together again, and we had a great deal to catch up on. A year and a half had gone by since we had seen each other in France. Transatlantic phone calls had been few and far between because of the expense.

One of the first things my mother and I did was to go together into Nana's room, our presence there a poignant mixture of tears and smiles. We looked silently out the window from the spot where Nana used to sit with her rosary in hand, gazing at the trees behind the house. While sitting in that spot, Nana had often talked about the flow of life, and in that sense the room was sacred. But my mother also knew that Nana would have liked it to be used for some practical purpose. As a compromise, Mom had brought some of her books and sewing projects into the room, where she could either read or work quietly and feel Nana's presence.

Dad missed Nana, too. Because they shared a strong, close relationship, I had never understood mother-in-law jokes as I was growing up. Dad had always insisted on Nana's being part of things and never wanted to start our family dinner until she had joined us. When Nana decided to clean up something in the kitchen before coming to the table, Dad would call to her: "*Pani!*" (meaning "Ma'am!"—the Polish term of respect he'd learned from his in-law family). That meant "*Pani!* We're not complete without you!"

My own room was pretty much as I had left it two years before, which was comforting, since so much else in my life had changed. If I had expected to be jarred by further reminders of the stark difference between who I had been and the damaged person I had become, I hadn't anticipated how soothing it could be to feel the bonds with my past. When I was in my teens, I would pack into every day an ambitious school curriculum, several hours of piano practice, and a schedule of teaching piano to neighborhood kids. Sometimes I would come up to my room before switching from schoolgirl to pianist or piano teacher and just stare out of the window, letting my mind go blank. If Mom checked to make sure I was OK, I would answer something like "OK! Just resting my mind!" Maybe staring out of that same window could help to "rest" for a few moments the constant stream of anxiety that had begun with the polio attack two years before.

Mom and I had long talks while we relaxed in the sun and took walks, sometimes with another friend from the neighborhood, Reta Simons. Reta's son, Jay, who had been my younger brother Gary's classmate in grade school, had paralytic polio as a child. He was one of the youngsters I had thought of the first time the doctor in Paris had mentioned the word "polio" to me. When Jay had returned to school after the attack, he had seemed shaky and easily upset. He would burst into uncontrollable tears at the slightest thing. It hadn't been general knowledge in the neighborhood that such nervous instability and personality change was a typical result of paralytic polio. It was painful for me to remember the little boy being thought of as a "crybaby," when I now knew only too well that those crying bouts were impossible to control. Jay's parents had been staunchly behind him, and I was thrilled to learn from Reta that he was by then doing very well in college.

On evenings and weekends I had good opportunities to catch up with Dad, too, and there were get-togethers with long-time family friends. Bob Schilling, a close friend and business associate of Dad's, had grown up in Germany, and his wife, Winnie, in England. Mom couldn't wait to hear Bob and me converse in German, and kept egging us on. It took me a while to figure out why. Yes, it was partly that she had grown up among maternal relatives who spoke Central European languages when they gathered together, but I think it was also partly that she wanted to highlight what the time in Europe was contributing to her daughter's life.

I had been afraid that getting back to my Steinway A grand, the instrument that had been part of my life for so many years, would be particularly painful. But after a few days I found that I had formed as tolerable a relationship as possible with any instrument at that point. Mom tactfully focused on the simple fact that I was once again able to work at the keyboard. This was a vast improvement from what she had seen and heard on the rue Donizetti in Paris.

She understood that the work I was doing was partly mental and partly a "keep trying" gesture. She also understood that the mental component drew me especially to the music of Bach. Bredshall had characterized the Bach 48 Preludes and Fugues as his clear "desert island" pick; and Aitken had once made a statement I'd often quoted to her: "Bach knew everything." I also showed her a couple of graphs of late Beethoven sonata movements, from my work with Eibner, which she found fascinating. She heard me working on little bits from those late sonatas and knew that they were a special goal for me, as I dreamed into the future.

Mom had found a highly recommended physical medicine center where we could consult with a Dr. Fleming, who had a fine reputation for his work with polio patients. When I met the doctor, all seemed to be going predictably as he and his assistant took my medical history and put me through the usual muscle tests. He asked questions that were by then familiar to me, and I showed him the exercises I was doing, recommended by Dr. Schmid in Vienna. Though he found the exercises appropriate, he seemed surprised that I was even trying to play the piano. He gave me the same advice that I'd heard from the doctors in Paris and Vienna—to be glad I could walk and do many "normal" things, and to focus on living a "normal" life. But he seemed to be saying more strongly than the other doctors that I should try to find an area of activity that did not require highly skilled piano playing. His assistant accidentally left the exam room door slightly ajar as they left, and I heard Dr. Fleming say, "The world is full of 'em. Somebody should tell her!"

Full of aspiring pianists? I wondered. But a moment later, I realized that his medical world overflowed with damaged people who were simply learning how to live the kind of lives they *could* manage. I had a sick feeling in my stomach. It was like overhearing someone say that your life is over.

My parents commented on the range of things that appeared visibly improved since they had seen me in France. I didn't have to pretend or write fantasy letters to them because they could see some tangible improvement, even though I clearly had a considerable distance to go. We had frank discussions of the pros and cons of my returning to Vienna for another year; and they left it up to me to decide what to do. Dr. Fleming hadn't come up with a treatment plan that looked as if it might make a difference, and I felt that I had more to learn from Eibner and Harich-Schneider. The three of us agreed that I might as well return to the Academy for one more year, in the "keep trying" mode.

Back in Vienna, I felt that the summer vacation with my parents had given me a good start, and I approached the Schenker study and Baroque study and seminar with renewed determination. Soon I was back to pushing my narrow limits—and beginning to feel the physical consequences once again. But I accepted the now-familiar pattern as a current fact of my life.

Martha had kept up a correspondence with some of our fellow students from Carnegie, and I would often add a note. One such friend was David Appleby, who had finished a two-year stint in the Navy, applied for and been granted a Fulbright scholarship, and wrote that he was planning to join us in Vienna to study conducting at the Academy. That was welcome news.

David was born into a Salvation Army family (both his

mother and father were Salvation Army ministers), and had grown up with the concept of service to others, along with the idea that music could enrich the lives of disadvantaged youth. While still in college, he had volunteered a substantial chunk of his time to Salvation Army centers, where he taught youngsters to play brass instruments and sing. David had fallen in love with Martha during their freshman year at Carnegie, but she had already begun what was supposed to be a secret affair with a dashing English professor who gave brilliant classes for the music and arts students. By the time that affair had come to a tempestuous close, Martha and David had become close friends, and I had joined their circle.

At Carnegie, David and Martha had started a madrigal group, just for fun, and I had joined as their "pitch pipe" and as a serviceable second soprano. David had gotten dates for our group to sing at senior centers and at other places where we were most welcome. It was one of my favorite recreational activities during those years; but after polio and its effect on my core muscles, I never again thought about joining a singing group. I didn't explain this to anyone; it was difficult enough having to acknowledge the damage to my shoulders, arms, and hands.

When David arrived in Vienna, he was shocked at my appearance and at some of the things I couldn't do. In our letters, Martha and I had been presenting the aftereffects of my polio as problems I was rapidly leaving in the dust. David thought our living arrangements looked somewhat uncomfortable, especially for me, and started looking around for something that would accommodate the three of us. He discovered that real estate in Vienna was amazingly cheap by American standards and decided to use some of the funds he had saved from his Navy years to buy an old flat that needed some fixing up. It was a fifth-floor walk-up on a short street called the *Köllnerhofgasse* (Cologne-Court Alley). There was a handy Julius Meinl coffee shop right across the street, and it was just a short walk to the

Staatsoper. If you leaned out of the living-room window, you could see the famed *Stefansdom* (St. Steven's Cathedral).

David was determined to do his own renovations to the "Köllnerhof," as we called the flat, and I offered to buy the furniture as my contribution, in addition to renting another piano. It wasn't hard to find used furniture, and my favorite discovery was something called a *Garten Sessel* (garden chair) in which I could lean back comfortably, with back and arms well-supported, right in the living room. Being able to participate in conversations without having to excuse myself to go lie down from time to time was remarkably freeing.

David thought that our lives would improve with a means of transportation other than a streetcar or walking—in other words, a car. My parents, too, thought it a fine idea, and Dad used his automotive connections to help us acquire a little blue Volkswagen. David and Martha were both excellent drivers, and I was happy to leave the driving to them. The "Blue Bug" enabled us to move our belongings into the Köllnerhof flat and to take a few refreshing side trips out of town, during which I could be reasonably comfortable.

One of our first trips was to visit Sieghart and his family in Grieskirchen, a little town just west of Linz and north of Salzburg. When I had first met Sieghart, he told me that his father had been assassinated by the Nazis; but as our friendship blossomed, I noticed that he spoke of his father almost as if his beloved parent were still alive. One day he mentioned that he wanted me to meet his mother and father. I answered very gently and carefully that I would love to meet his mother, but was under the impression that his father had been assassinated by the Nazis. "Oh yes," he said, "he was assassinated, but he escaped." Once we determined that his father, who had been part of the Austrian resistance movement, was alive and well, I explained to Sieghart, with enormous relief, that in English you would call that an *attempted* assassination.

David registered at the Academy, where he found the musical activities he had been anticipating with great excitement. He was interested in studying harpsichord in addition to conducting, so I introduced him to Harich-Schneider; and he signed up for both harpsichord lessons and Baroque seminar. And now, instead of volunteering for the Salvation Army in his spare time, he could attend the Staatsoper and explore Vienna. He was in heaven.

There were also times when David and I had the opportunity to talk seriously about personal matters, especially about troubling things he had observed. David had a way of joking, or making lighthearted comments, to relieve but not interfere with a serious atmosphere. This manner had probably developed from childhood, when he was sometimes brought into a serious rescue mission. He had developed a selflessness of service and an awareness of what would lift another person's spirit to help in coping with major loss.

David's earnestness in wanting to talk about what things he observed helped me to get through such discussions with fewer breakdowns into uncontrollable sobbing. He was distressed that in addition to the normal things I couldn't do, my manner and way of speaking had become much altered since he had known me at Carnegie. This observation forced me to admit that I still had to take more frequent breaths because of my weakened abdominal muscles and that I must still be using more head tone than I had pre-polio just to make myself heard. He also noticed the way I moved my head. He demonstrated how I would jerk it up and down, or to one side, rather than moving it smoothly. David and I held practice sessions in which we moved our heads up and down, or from side to side, *slowly* and *smoothly*.

Since David had a clearer comparison between Carol BP and Carol AP than anyone else among those close to me, he began to question the path I had taken. He took Martha aside for some private discussions that prompted her to look back at my trajectory since the onset of the polio. One evening at the *Köllnerhof,* they suggested that the three of us have a glass of wine and a serious talk. We started at the kitchen table, over supper, and during the long talk, moved to the living room where I could sit in the *Garten-Sessel.*

"Carol, you seem to be having more and more coat-wearing problems," Martha began. "That just hasn't seemed to improve and probably has even gotten worse."

"I don't have the history that Martha has with all this," David said, "but I can certainly see that you've been having increasing pain and stiffness in your neck and shoulders. At this point it just seems constant!"

Then they looked at each other and back at me. "We've been talking about it," Martha said, with her characteristic frown of concern, "and it's beginning to look as if you're not progressing at all anymore. In some ways, you even seem to be going backwards."

I will never forget that milestone conversation and how Martha and David confronted me as only close friends could have done. Up until that moment, I had managed to pretend to myself that I was making slow-and-steady progress. But when pressed by both of my friends—one with a fresh view, and one who had witnessed all the steps along the way—I couldn't back it up.

We discussed openly the enormous differences in my personality post-polio and pre-polio. We even talked about my "keep trying" work on the upright piano. I admitted to them both that I was willing to let my body scream at me, or at least moan and groan, to make any kind of progress. But David's gentle objectivity made me look at the whole and admit that I seemed to have come to a standstill.

"Carol, I think it's time for you to start looking for some help," David said, and Martha agreed. We had some more wine and began to discuss a change of direction.

First, I wrote a frank letter to Webster Aitken and his wife, Lilian, a respected physician in New York City. I figured she would have some perspective on my true situation once I presented an accurate picture. This time, it would not be my usual fantasy letter describing Vienna's music scene to my revered former teacher, but rather a communication that would address my current realities.

I told Webster and Lilian that I needed help, and summed up what Martha and David had said. I went on to describe far more honestly my actual condition, which I had been trying to hide, even from my family and myself. I told them that despite all the exercises I had attempted at the keyboard, most movements still felt "incredibly stiff and frozen, even when the muscles *are* trying—like there are two hundred-pound weights holding back the movement. . . . Some of the sounds *(thumps)* are conceivably raw material. *Aber wohin?*" (But where to?)

It was usually Webster who answered my letters. This time it was Lilian, who wrote back almost immediately. Since she was a department head at Bellevue Hospital in New York City, I had assumed that if she made a recommendation, it would be a doctor or a medical group in the United States. But after speaking with some of her colleagues who had up-to-date information about advances in physical medicine and physical therapy, she suggested a consultation with Dr. H. C. A. Lassen, a top specialist at Blegdam Hospital in Copenhagen.

Chapter Nine

❧

Clarity in Copenhagen

L ilian Aitken's research had ascertained that Dr. H. C. A. Lassen, professor of epidemiology at the University of Copenhagen and chief physician of the Department of Communicable Diseases at *Blegdamshospitalet* (Blegdam Hospital), was acknowledged in medical circles worldwide as uniquely qualified in the treatment of polio and "post-polio effects." I had never heard of the term "post-polio effects," nor had I known there were specialists who treated them.

Lassen and his team had come to international prominence for their quick thinking and innovative treatments during a record polio epidemic in Copenhagen in 1952. The team had refined a treatment for the acute stage of the disease and developed an outstanding physical therapy program. The many patients with lingering post-polio effects from that epidemic, and subsequent outbreaks in Copenhagen, were all treated with loving care by the Blegdam Hospital Physical Therapy Unit under Dr. Lassen's supervision.

Dr. Lassen himself welcomed me warmly when I arrived in early August of 1958. A tall, composed, kindly, but no-nonsense person, he spoke excellent British-accented English. We discussed various details of my medical history and general background, and he suggested checking me into the hospital for two or three days—partly because I had developed a slight cold on the journey from Vienna and partly to facilitate tests and follow-up. Also, staying in the hospital meant that I could delay looking for a place to live until I'd gone through my entire series of tests.

After we had talked for a while, Lassen brought in another specialist on his team, Dr. Snorrason. They put me through an extensive range of muscle tests, carefully noting neuromuscular responses to a variety of commands such as "push," "pull," "hold," "don't let me push," and "don't let me pull." It was the most detailed version of such tests that I had ever encountered.

Lassen and Snorrason also noted those places where they found severely over-contracted muscles, called contractures. They explained the side effects of my "keep trying" motto. I had evidently gone into daily emergency mode—an adrenalized effort that had allowed my muscles to perform almost beyond their true capacity for short periods. But since the damaged muscles were too weak to perform like that, my emergency-mode pattern had built up contractures, bringing additional fatigue and pain. This explained my increasingly unhappy "coat-wearing" muscles, for example, since they had clearly developed such contractures. Lassen and Snorrason were describing with eye-opening accuracy my pattern since the acute attack.

Their first objectives, Lassen explained, would be 1) to get me out of emergency mode and 2) to ease the contractures. Only then could any systematic rebuilding and retraining begin. This was familiar territory to them, and they presented it to me in a gentle and reassuring manner. Their whole description made so much sense that for a while I sat there in stunned silence while they explained it all. Then, perhaps predictably, I burst into tears. Thankfully, the Blegdam doctors well understood the emotional side effects of post-polio syndrome and were not taken aback.

By the end of this revelatory discussion, I began to recognize that the treatment would be intensive and extensive, requiring a long-range plan on everyone's part. I explained that my parents' insurance policy still included some coverage for post-polio care, but that it would run out in a few months. My mother was planning to be in touch with Dr. Lassen about the treatment and the financial arrangements. He nodded and said he would look forward to communicating with her.

Then he smiled broadly and leaned forward to look straight into my eyes. "*We* can do things for you here," he said emphatically, "that your own country will *not* do for you!" It suddenly dawned on me that Denmark had universal health care—the "socialized medicine" that had become a topic of debate in the United States. He wanted me to know that the cost to my family and me would be something we could handle.

Once I had settled into the hospital room for the evening, I wrote a report to Webster and Lilian Aitken:

> *Dr. Lassen was expecting me, and expended many kind words to make me feel at home. From the beginning, he had the idea—just from talking with me—that my breathing ability ("vital force," as he called it) might be defective. So he put me through some breathing tests, and he was right. He said that alone could account for my lack of endurance. This breathing ability or "vital force" affects many things, of course.*
>
> *We also had a discussion of the steps to be taken. The first step is heat—not the kind they use for bones and joints, which is evidently what I had in Vienna, but the kind they use for muscles—and massage.*
>
> *The second step will be relaxation exercises—that is, learning the difference between contracting the muscles and relaxing them, and practicing same. That means isolating certain muscles, or groups of muscles, to contract-relax, while trying to keep the others entirely*

relaxed. They noticed random areas, especially throughout arms and hands, where there is a significant lack of connection between brain and muscle.

They have other exercises we will start once the muscles in the upper back, neck, shoulders, and arms, which have developed contractures, have become relaxed. No one is sure how long that's going to take.

Toward the end of the letter, I wrote a paragraph especially for Webster:

The Professor suggested that the hospital piano be moved into a basement room in the physical therapy department, where I can use it every day if I wish. Also so that I can show them some of the things I can't do at the keyboard. They want as complete a picture as possible. Having even these polio experts watch me try to play something at the keyboard instantly raises my fear level, of course. The fear of sitting down at the keyboard again in front of anyone, including you, has been increasing steadily. And of course you're the only person alive who really knows what I had to work with before. . . .

I explained a few more details to my mother and father:

Lassen is the first doctor who has seemed interested in helping me to overcome the complex weaknesses or defects in the core muscles, shoulders, hands, and arms which keep me from keyboard work. Only after he does everything possible will we know what I can and can't do. He said that this treatment should go on for about six months.

From my descriptions of the therapy I've had so far, he says that none of it was systematic. I had begun to think that no doctor would ever be interested in my special

problem when they had life-threatening situations to deal
with. But here is the man, supposedly, and he is interested.
This could well be the difference between my being able to
be a pianist and having to reorient myself. It looks as if
this will be an all-out effort in every way.

The next day I met Lise Nybo, whom Lassen had described as the most experienced polio physical therapist on the team. She had twinkling eyes and a wide, expansive grin that turned out to be indicative of her personality.

It was "Nybo," as everyone called her, who explained that the first step would be "The Bath"—her amusing name for a good-sized, warm-water spa in the hospital basement. Eventually I would be doing exercises there, but for now I would be soaking and warming up every morning before Nybo began massage and stretching of the contracted muscles.

Nybo had a natural way of creating an atmosphere of ease and relaxation. When we first began working together, I asked her how to pronounce a couple of Danish words. She told me to be prepared to pronounce these words from the back of my throat, with the throat practically closed off. If I persisted, she said jokingly, I should be aware that many Danes had to go for regular speech therapy to alleviate the throat tightness brought on by speaking their own language.

It was easy to laugh with Nybo, and I immediately felt comfortable. She was not only familiar with the polio patient's struggle to adapt to a post-polio persona, but she was also used to looking at the world from the damaged person's point of view. And Nybo also knew her patients' serious, all-day-long physical limitations. She spent her time with people like me, who had to work very hard to do little, everyday things, while they were aching constantly. In our time together, we were aiming to alleviate some of those problems; and it was an enormous relief to be with someone who understood, and could discuss with me, the journey I had taken so far.

With the help of the Blegdam team, I soon found a place to live, about a block and a half from the hospital, on a street called Ryesgade. Mrs. Buttrup, a widow who lived in a comfortable flat with her ten-year-old son, Marcel, was willing to take in a boarder for a few months at a very reasonable price. This would not only include room and board but also easy access to the upright piano in her living room. When I moved in, I found that friends of hers who lived downstairs, the Holm-Jensens, had a grand piano in their living room, which I was also welcome to use. As I wrote to my family: "Suddenly I have three *piani* available!"

Mrs. Buttrup was a gentle, friendly person who spoke very serviceable English and seemed to enjoy sharing information about the neighborhood, the dishes she liked to prepare, and the activities of her friends and relatives. Her son, Marcel, was bright and full of fun. He, too, seemed to like having another person to interact with, even though we didn't share a common language.

I soon found that Marcel loved to read and that Mrs. Buttrup was delighted to let him go with me on excursions to the public library when he got home from school. Since my therapy treatments alternated between a strenuous day and an easier day, I sometimes felt ready for a library walk after one of the easier days. Once we reached the library, we would go our separate ways: Marcel to the Danish section, while I sought out the English or German section. Then we would meet at the central checkout for the walk back home. Marcel gallantly carried my books both ways, as we took our picturesque walks along the canal at dusk, enjoying the sparkling lights and pointing out things to each other along the way. The two of us soon developed an amusing and effective mime language, sprinkled with English and Danish.

As my Blegdam therapy sessions progressed, Lassen's team was educating me about what I was up against. I was learning more about the paralytic stage of the acute polio attack, the dreaded second-fever period, in which I had sustained what was called "neuromuscular scatter damage." In this stage, the virus attacked and killed motor neurons, the neurons that activate muscle tissue. As I read about the scatter-damage principle, I began to understand why a polio patient could lose anything from a tiny to a large part of any one muscle. I had lost small parts of some, larger parts of others; the net result was great weakness and lack of coordination. In general, with polio patients, the relearning process involves building up whatever is left to compensate partially for what is no longer usable.

One of the books Lassen gave me to read emphasized that the motor neurons targeted by the virus were dead and could never regenerate or be brought back. The polio patient could only try to train neighboring motor neurons—those that had escaped the attack—to jump in and help with tasks they were never meant to do. That was a lot to absorb.

The book also explained that the most vulnerable motor neurons were the ones most strenuously in use during the few days between the two fever periods of the polio virus. The virus is already in one's system during the first fever period; then it either fades away during the days after the fever has gone down—in which case there will be no second fever period— or it gathers momentum for the paralytic stage. This explained the "flu" epidemic that had hit so many of us at Fontainebleau. As the Lassen team agreed, that epidemic was undoubtedly the first fever period of the polio virus. What identified it as the polio virus were my own symptoms resulting from the second, paralytic, fever period, since no one else at Fontainebleau had experienced that second fever period and the resulting paralysis.

The vulnerability of the most active motor neurons during that key interim between the two fever periods made enormous, stomach-churning sense to me. What would children have been doing before they contracted polio? Moving around on their legs—running, jumping, hopping, skipping. Hence the typical after-polio picture: children with lower trunk and lower body damage; many patients needing a wheelchair, although most could still effectively use their upper bodies.

And what had I been doing between the two fever periods at Fontainebleau? Practicing the piano strenuously, many hours a day. I could easily trace the heaviest damage, and it was chillingly accurate. If I were to draw a detailed map of the muscle tissue I had used most intensively at the piano just before the paralytic stage of the virus had hit, it would be an exact map of the heavily damaged areas.

The parts of my hands and arms developed most painstakingly in many years of piano playing had been hit the hardest. Since I was right-handed, I had always worked harder on the left hand to make it equally strong and flexible. Hence the entire left hand had sustained considerably more damage from the paralytic stage than had the right. Since a pianist often balances chords and melodic content with the top voice leading in strength, which frequently calls on the fifth finger of the right hand, that finger had been singled out by the virus as a prime target.

I had strenuously used my core, back, abdominals, and breathing muscles while playing virtuoso repertoire at the piano. I had constantly used my right foot in handling the "flutter pedal"—a damper pedal technique that gave extra resonance to the strings without muddying fast passagework. That explained why I now had to turn my right foot out for balance while standing or walking. My left foot had not been similarly engaged in piano playing, so the motor neurons in my left leg and foot had been almost untouched.

As Nybo and I worked every day with stretching and trying to retrain simple and complex movements with my hands and arms, it became ever clearer that the virus had been diabolical in its targets. It had knocked out—unevenly—key muscle function in both shoulders, arms, and hands. Because of this uneven damage, we had to isolate and customize treatment for each shoulder, each arm, and each wrist.

For the hands, the problem proved to be even more complex. The virus had damaged each side of each hand differently. It had killed differently in each of the ten fingers. A compensatory movement for one finger that Nybo and I might be working on would not help its next-door neighbor or its parallel on the other hand.

I was taking my first unsettling steps toward recognizing that I would have to learn different ways to do everything. I would need to use different muscle tissue and develop new neural pathways to compensate for what had been lost. It was my first glimpse of the enormous undertaking it would be to build a new set of complex reflexes. No wonder other doctors I had seen had told me to just keep trying to live a "normal life"—without high-level piano playing. No wonder Lassen was saying that he'd never tackled a case like mine, where the goal was to rebuild a network of neuromuscular movements so complex and finely coordinated.

Lassen was already telling me that he would like help from an expert in the piano field—someone to watch our various exercises and demonstrate how a normal pianist would do what I couldn't. He also felt that we would need help in making assessments and decisions when we got farther along. At both stages of our work, that ideal expert would be Webster Aitken, since he knew my playing "BP" better than anyone still alive. One day I decided to bring Webster into the discussion. I wrote to him, adding a P.S. that summed up my doubts: "Am I worth it? By now an old question, of course."

His answer was immediate:

Your letter came, disturbing in its vivid picture of your physical and psychological problems, but at the same time heartening and even satisfying with its implication of having at last got to the bottom of this purgatorial state you have been inhabiting for the past three years. I am so glad Lassen can and will help to see this through; my own first impulse was to hop a plane and be with you Monday morning! Perhaps I could help, but let us see how things work out first. You ask me if you are worth it; I can only give you a flat affirmative."

After that exchange, I tried to keep Webster and Lilian up to the minute on what was happening. My next report went into more detail:

I think I am finally getting the point about the overall difficulty—that it is not brain but reflex. As long as it all goes through the brain, the movements cannot be coordinated. If every time you took a step you had to think which muscles pull your leg and foot up; how and where you put it down; when and how to shift the weight, when to relax which muscle again, etc.—your walking would not be normally coordinated. So before I can really begin to work with the hands, those back and core muscles— which together should feel like the central control point— must take over. As they explained this in child's language to me, I finally see what they mean about the "dead end" of working on my own, of being forced to think too hard about every movement. I am now in the odd position of trying just to peek over my own shoulder.

In doing very simple relaxation exercises, we have found another problem: you know how people drum on a table with four fingers—one after the other? Well, do that in the air and you have the exercise. At first I could almost do it, though awkwardly, with the right hand, but the left would get hopelessly confused. Fingers would sometimes go the opposite direction; that's a good example of what I mean when I say that my left hand doesn't seem to belong to me anymore. Now, today, I am actually starting to do it—not fast or smoothly, but that's not the point! I could have gone on trying to do that exercise for months, years, and probably never arrived at any way to do it.

But here, somebody sits with me and rehearses it over and over, and I am beginning to get it. I am just starting to see why Lassen thinks I am expending way too much effort in my attempts, and that at least part of what I had thought to be lack of strength is lack of reeducation.

Although I was beginning to understand that the process could take a long time, the true meaning of that "long time" was—perhaps mercifully—nowhere in sight.

During my rehab work, I experienced many revelations that encouraged and at the same time distracted me. We worked on other significant things affecting everyday life rather than just focusing on my piano playing. It was exciting to find that my voice was becoming more resonant and that talking became correspondingly easier as we worked on the core muscles.

Walking down steps was another of those "everyday life" problems. Even though my legs had been the least affected part of my body, a great fear of descending a flight of stairs, first evident in Paris, had stayed with me. As Nybo and I worked on exercises for the core muscles, I found that descending a staircase was gradually becoming less frightening.

A different test came up at Mrs. Buttrup's, as she, Marcel, and I were having dinner one evening. She explained that she needed to go into the hospital for a few days to have some surgery and was hoping that I would be able to take care of Marcel while she was away. I was eager to help; the main difficulty would be preparing the evening meal. But Mrs. Buttrup assured me she would have several dishes prepared in advance and that it should be relatively easy for Marcel and me to manage.

True to her word, she left the refrigerator well stocked, and Marcel and I were determined to run everything as smoothly as possible. One day I put some soup on to simmer shortly before he got home from school. It seemed a little bland, so I looked around for peppercorns to add to the broth. An obvious jar sat close to the stove, and although the peppercorns seemed a little different in texture from what I had expected, I proceeded to sprinkle a few into the mix. When Marcel came home I showed him a puzzling thing about the simmering soup—a strangely abrasive feel and sound was coming from the bottom of the pot. When I pointed to the jar from which I'd taken the peppercorns, he burst out laughing—too convulsed to speak. He pointed to a birdcage on a high kitchen shelf. Aha! What I had thought to be a jar of peppercorns was a jar of bird gravel! We laughed all evening, having of course fixed ourselves something else for supper.

Mrs. Buttrup came back to the Ryesgade flat in good shape, and we resumed our accustomed patterns. After our evening candlelight dinners, Marcel would settle down to do his homework and read, and I would retire to my room to lose myself in one of the books I'd brought from the library.

The books were a refuge from the reality that was emerging from the treatment program. That reality required constant adjustment, not only to the daily breakthrough-letdown patterns, but also to the physical fatigue. By the time I had done my exercises, including core exercises for the muscles involved in breathing and speaking, I was spent, emotionally and physically. It was more restful to avoid talking, and the reading allowed me to forget about my own journey for a while.

I found a way to prop up a book so that I didn't have to hold it. My arms, of course, had to be supported so that I could turn a page without a repetitive strain on my shoulder. I had this technique down to a science, so that both elbows could be supported, and I could flick over a page with a relatively good finger. I just had to make sure that my back, shoulders, and neck were well supported and wouldn't undergo any extra strain.

An excerpt from a letter to my family gives the picture of the refuge that had replaced Vienna's Staatsoper, Baroque Seminar, and Schenker graphing. I could rave about what I was reading, instead of continuing to subject my family to the seesaw of the daily search for neuromuscular breakthroughs:

> *If I read something absorbing in the evening, it helps me to get to sleep at a decent hour. I've just discovered Karl Jung's* Modern Man in Search of a Soul—*fascinating in the way a great psychologist blends Western and Eastern thought. Speaking of which, I've also been reading the Taoist philosophers (Laotse and Chuangtse) and wondering why I never read them before—so delightful, and of course helpful.*

It's not hard to understand why I was drawn to philosophical material at that time, at least to the authors whose writings I could interpret in a hopeful manner.

I was beginning to see my therapy goals in clearer perspective. In the first year or so after the polio attack, I thought that I was making good progress, and that I would surely keep on at that rate. I had no idea of the distance I had to travel. What appeared to me as, say, a distance of three miles, was really more like three thousand. Feeling that I was moving at a good pace along the first mile, I expected to reach my destination—where I would have full strength again—equally fast. That proved to be an extremely unrealistic vision.

When we began the Copenhagen program, I felt excited again after having gradually become discouraged in Vienna. I was thrilled over every minor breakthrough Nybo and I made. Each one felt major; and in reports home or to the Aitkens or to Martha and David, I would describe it as such. But after each breakthrough came a corresponding letdown, as that tiny gain would take its place in the larger picture. My excited "breakthrough" reporting was simmering down, as I began to glimpse a long road that was uncharted, even for Lassen.

It became ever clearer that we weren't finding a magical path to my "real" reflexes: to the way my movements were supposed to produce sound. Instead we were finding artificially created "work-arounds" that allowed me to do similar movements through strenuous repetitions. In a sense, I had already given up looking for my former "real" pathways. I wanted to find *some* pathways, *any* pathways that would lead me back to the keyboard.

The only bearable outcome for me was based on this assumption: If I could get enough movement to return to my hands, arms, and supporting muscles, eventually I could find my way back to a more "real" partnership with the piano. For that transition to happen, though, Lassen thought I would need help from a professional pianist. He and I were both counting on Webster.

As my birthday drew near, I couldn't resist reporting to Webster on one of my breakthrough moments, though I knew I should try to put it into the bigger picture:

> *"On Saturday I reach the quarter-century mark—had been dreading it—but now what a birthday present I've been given! A perceptible part of my left hand! The most precious thing to me is feeling the beginning of some life in both hands. I've been working with so much dead tissue that I hardly know what "life" in either hand feels like anymore. I've long since gotten used to their feeling like somebody else's hands.*

A few weeks later I wrote to my family:

> *Lassen and I have had another of our important talks. He has set January as the time we will estimate what*

is possible for me and what is not. He thinks there will always be certain deficiencies, at least in the left hand, which I'll have to work around in some way, if a way can be devised. He isn't sure about it yet, or about the fifth finger of my right hand, but that is the way it appears. He said again that he thinks I should start working with a pianist as soon as possible after leaving here, so I hope that I can work out something with Webster. I'll want to do a few things back in Vienna, and then hopefully be on my way home!

Lassen's original estimate had been for six months of therapy, which would take us until the beginning of February 1959. But early in January he invited me to his office for a meeting with the team, to discuss everyone's view of where we were. Lassen, Snorrason, and Nybo were all smiling warmly.

We discussed in detail the positive gains we had made together, and some of the attitudes they hoped I would always keep in mind. All three felt that they had done everything they could for me, and they held optimistic hopes for continued progress as I worked at the piano, hopefully with some professional help.

In Lassen's opinion, backed up by his team, the next step should be his long-anticipated session with Webster Aitken, me, and a piano. Webster had let me know that he had reasons to come to Europe in early March, but that he could come a little earlier if necessary, and would adjust his schedule to accommodate Lassen.

I was surprised and grateful when Lassen said that he was willing to travel to Vienna, rather than asking Webster to come to Copenhagen. He felt that Vienna might be the best place for the three-way conference "at the piano." That way, he said, I would have time to get my bearings first, back in Vienna, and then he and Webster could coordinate their time there.

Toward the end of the meeting, after Nybo and Snorrason had left the room, Lassen stated a conclusion that would echo in every corner of my consciousness for many years to come. He led up to it gently, but there was no way to cushion the words. "In my opinion," he said, "whatever neuromuscular function hasn't come back in another year's time will probably not come back at all."

Another *year? Only* a year? But how could my continuing effort and progress be restricted to such a short time, when there was still so far to go? Even as I was shaking inside, however, I knew that Lassen—with characteristic compassion—was humanely trying to protect me from a lifetime of disappointment.

Nevertheless, since I couldn't truly accept what he was saying, I soon began to shift his assessment into a positive direction. After all, I still felt changes almost daily that surely indicated progress. By the time I wrote the news to Webster, I had progressed faster than anticipated:

> *Lassen believes that they have done all they can for me, so I will be leaving shortly!*
>
> *Every so often I feel as if one of my many heavy chains is dropping away. I start feeling a little more emancipated, and cannot keep my imagination from leaping ahead. . . . I can almost sense, at times, what it would be like to be able to play the piano again—indescribable! I had completely lost that sense, and now that I can imagine it once again, even just a little bit, I am almost too anxious and excited to sleep.*

Webster responded with considerable enthusiasm:

> *We have both followed the process with keen interest, but this news is really more than we dared hope for; I thought we might have to wait months and even then have to make*

do with less than has already been accomplished. So I think
we are every bit as excited about it as you are! How well I
can understand your sense of urgency to get back to keyboard
problems! Whatever I can do to help is yours to command.

Martha and David welcomed me "home" to the Köllner-hof, and it felt good to be back in Vienna with them both. I soon adjusted to working and experimenting on my own rather than having almost every movement guided by the physical therapists. I didn't resume Baroque studies or the Schenker study with Eibner, as I wanted to spend every possible bit of physical and emotional energy continuing the search for neuromuscular connections at the keyboard. And, at all times, I was nervously conscious of Lassen's "one year" deadline.

I found that I could rent an hour's worth of time every so often with a beautiful Bösendorfer grand piano at the company's piano showroom just a few blocks from the Köllnerhof. Since it occupied a practice room of its own, I felt comfortable that no one could hear me. Instinctively I hoped that the beautiful, singing sound of this instrument would inspire me to think positively about whatever bits of music I was working on—and that, I hoped, might encourage more neuromuscular breakthroughs.

Martha and David were both excited at the prospect of Webster's visit in early February and made sure that the guest room was as ready as possible. Webster had spent a substantial amount of time in Vienna during his own student days, so we were sure that he knew what to expect in the way of living conditions.

The day he arrived felt like high drama. Here on our doorstep, to spend some time with me, was the man I had been hopelessly in love with for some eight years.

"God, you've been through a lot," he said, after one penetrating look—before a hug or even a hello. That first look made it clear that he saw shocking changes. As he was to tell journalist

Evan Wylie several years later, once upon a time he had considered me "one of the genuine new talents" of my generation. Now he saw a person who was much thinner, more fragile, "but the real differences were other than physical. Where she had been self-possessed and confident, she was now uncertain. Where she had been exuberant and outgoing, she was now withdrawn. In place of the dynamic energy that used to overwhelm us all, there was now a nervous preoccupation. I saw an entire change of personality. She was shattered."

He greeted Martha and David warmly and was soon talking with all of us about having a *gemütlich* time together. He said he was looking forward to experiencing Vienna again, but I knew that his main goal was to create a pleasurable backdrop for what would be a painful joint effort at the keyboard.

Webster and I went on some lovely walks, and the four of us drove to a few spots that he didn't want us to miss. One high point was a quick trip to Venice that Webster and I took together in the Blue Bug. He wanted to pay a visit to Arnold Schoenberg's daughter, Nuria Schoenberg Nono, whom he had known from Los Angeles, and to meet her husband, Luigi Nono. In Webster's opinion, Nono was one of the more interesting contemporary composers. For me, it was a dreamlike experience, traveling with my hero to Venice, meeting his friends and even taking a canal trip in a gondola.

Back at the Köllnerhof, we set up a routine to tackle the real reason for Webster's visit. In some ways, his presence made the awareness of my condition more painful. Here was Webster, who had once insisted on perfection, sitting with me at the keyboard, racking his brain as to how best to help me. He was trying to help me find some way—*any* way—to use what I had left in my hands. And some of the problems I had experienced by myself were more acute when I was trying to "play" for someone else, especially for someone of his expertise.

A phenomenon occurred more frequently with Webster by

my side—probably because I was trying that much harder with even one person as an audience. When a message from my brain wouldn't get through to my fingers, I would be seized by what I had come to call a "nerve shudder." It was as if something had gone haywire inside me, and I would begin to sob. Even without a "nerve shudder," we considered it a good day if the necessarily short session ended before frustration and fatigue overwhelmed me and I would burst into tears.

When I was not at the keyboard, however, I was less agitated, and therefore emotionally better off, than when I had first gone to Copenhagen several months before. The constant anxious thoughts rushing through my head ever since the hospital in Paris would turn off for a while. Sometimes I experienced an absence of thought that felt almost comfortable.

But one day, after Webster had been there for a couple of weeks, he confronted me: "Carol, you haven't finished a sentence since I've been here!" he said, almost in exasperation. That was bewildering and, I first thought, unfair. But when I queried Martha and David, they backed him up. As the four of us discussed the matter, it was clear that Martha and David were so used to my silence that they didn't notice it anymore.

Evidently I had taken refuge in the blankness whenever possible, and even though it felt like a relief to me, the "normal" world did not see it that way. Webster wanted me to talk about serious things, and I went blank when I tried, at least with him.

One evening he invited me out to dinner and the opera—a special occasion that he had probably designed to put us both into a relaxed mood. Sitting at a table in the Sacher restaurant, across from the Staatsoper, we had some wine with our schnitzel and basked in the warm atmosphere. Still, Webster was obliged, as usual, to do most of the talking. When the waiter brought our coffee, my brain must have registered that the opera was about to begin. Perhaps because I knew that I wouldn't have to continue for very long, I finally started to talk.

And once I had started, a lot came tumbling out. Webster never looked at his watch, though he must have known that we were missing the opera. He let me lose all track of time. At last I was talking to him about the pain of the past three-plus years and about the discouraging picture Lassen had given me toward the end of my Copenhagen treatment. At one point, I finally gave voice to the feeling that had been forming during the last part of my work in Copenhagen: that I was probably no longer worth any special time and effort on Webster's part.

"What is really important, Carol," he responded, "is that you reestablish some kind of belief in *yourself.*" I didn't know how to answer. "*That* is the reason I'm here," he added. He said that he agreed with Lassen's limit of one year. "Above all," he continued, "I want you to be a happy person!"

Maybe because of the wine or because it was finally the time, I spoke the truth that shocked even me the way it came out: "But I don't want to be a happy person! I want to be a pianist!"

There was stunned silence on both sides. After a long pause, Webster leaned forward and locked eyes with me. "I don't want you to end up with *just one dried-up flower,*" he said slowly, weighting every word with emphasis, trying to counter-act the shocking thought I had just expressed. I was to replay this exchange countless times in the months and years to come, especially when grim thoughts crossed my mind.

Fortunately, Lassen arrived in Vienna after my conversation with Webster had taken place. We had set March 23rd as our approximate meeting time, and Lassen mentioned that he would fly in the day before. Webster and I met him at the airport, took him to his hotel, and had a get-acquainted talk over dinner.

The following day, Lassen came to the Köllnerhof. There, we got serious, as I did numerous demonstrations for him at the piano, and Webster showed him in detail the kinds of motions and move-ments that were beyond my capability at that point. Lassen asked questions, and explained to us what he saw in our demonstrations.

The conference was exhausting for me but evidently enlightening for both Webster and Lassen. Afterward, we went out for dinner, some wine, and warm-hearted conversation with toasts to Lassen's team, to Webster's expert participation, and to my recovery. Webster and Lassen agreed that another year would be a fair and reasonable time in which to draw further conclusions about my prospects. I still found it frightening that they agreed on the one-year deadline, but accepted it for the time being.

All three of us thought it was time for me to go home to the United States, so that Webster and I could continue working together more easily. In fact, Webster was already talking about a six-month stay in Santa Fe, where he and Lilian had their summer home. I could have a little guest house for sleeping and practicing, and Webster and I could spend some time in his studio every day, at an unhurried pace.

I was sad that Martha and David would be so far away, but there was no question as to what I should do. Webster's offer of continuing help might be my only hope. I would have some time in Michigan with my family and then head for New Mexico. Webster left soon after our conference, and I stayed a little longer, working in a few last visits to the Staatsoper, a couple of summary sessions with Eibner, and a last Baroque seminar.

Shortly before I was to leave, Luigi Nono—"Gigi" to his friends—came to Vienna for a conference of contemporary composers who favored twelve-tone style. When Webster and I were in Venice, I had told Gigi that he could stay at the Köllnerhof with us. I was excited to meet his friends and fellow composers, including Pierre Boulez and Bruno Maderna, during a couple of café breaks and a dinner, but soon realized that they were seeing me as Gigi's "squeeze."

This was upsetting for two reasons. Gigi was married to a wonderful person, and though he seemed to be drawn to me, I would never have entertained anything beyond friendship with him. Clearly, his friends couldn't see any other reason for him to hang out with me, as I was a nobody. As it happened, I had been looking at the score of Pierre Boulez's First Sonata for some months, fantasizing about playing it someday, and was eager to ask Pierre a couple of questions about it. But the discussion was short-lived, for whatever reason, and it was all too easy for me to retreat from further conversation.

If I had been on more solid ground personally, the episode with the composers' group would never have bothered me. But since everything about my life was up in the air at that point, it felt like proof that my contemporaries had no reason to accept me. It reinforced the feeling that I was, after all, "going home in defeat."

Chapter Ten

❦

Webster, Santa Fe,
and the Move West

After a couple of catch-up weeks with my parents in Michigan, I got in touch with Webster about his Santa Fe plan. He and Lilian were indeed inviting me to spend the entire summer there so that we could make as much "piano rehab" progress as possible. We didn't know it then, but that rehab program would stretch through two long summers in 1959 and 1960. It was a remarkable commitment for anyone to make, but the Aitkens presented the plan as a foregone conclusion, and so I accepted it without question.

Webster and Lilian, at that time in their mid-fifties, were both career-minded professionals. Lilian's "children" were the countless young tuberculosis patients she had helped in her work at Bellevue Hospital. Webster, a concert pianist admired in music capitals such as New York and London for his sophisticated solo programs, taught piano only on an advanced level. He was used to working with pianists who already had well-developed technique, and mainly needed guidance in refining the expressive content of their playing. For example, his main approach to me at Carnegie Mellon had been, "Whoa! You can do something more subtle in this phrase." And yet here he was, someone not naturally inclined to give encouragement or praise, taking on a completely different role from any he had assumed before. And here was Lilian, who had met me only a few times prior to that summer, accepting me into their household, where I would be spending the better part of each day.

The little studio-guest house near the Aitkens' home seemed perfectly comfortable, and a rented piano arrived shortly after I did. Their house on Camino de la Luz, which would be our mutual home base during the next two long summers, looked out toward the mountains from their living-room picture window and up the hillside from their patio. This was my introduction to the Southwest, to life at seven thousand feet above sea level, to the beauties of the high desert and its vistas. My memories of what followed—the painful work, the closeness with these two remarkable friends—are intertwined with that rarefied atmosphere.

Webster knew all too well—from working with me in Vienna—that our predictably distressing sessions together at the piano should be short. So he had designed a daily plan with the best potential for progress. We were to get together twice every day for a brief session in his studio: one in late morning, after he had finished his own work at the piano, and another later in the afternoon. Before the morning session, while he was practicing, Lilian and I had an open invitation to go for a swim in a neighbor's pool. That ensured that I could do my Copenhagen water exercises regularly.

Webster's studio was located on a second level, built into the hillside, affording us the privacy to work without sound leaking into the main part of the house. The studio was a good-sized room with lots of finished wood that allowed a lovely resonance for Webster's Steinway grand. The room was sparsely furnished, in Webster style, with a few chairs and an ornate, soft-voiced

Baroque clavichord in addition to the grand. The studio's generous windows framed a beautiful hillside view. I drew on that view before and after our difficult sessions and many times between the frustrating moments in our work.

Since Webster anticipated that many of our piano sessions would end abruptly with one of my emotional upsets, he and Lilian had planned for the late-morning sessions to segue into a leisurely lunch.

In Lilian's many years as a pediatrician, she had developed simple techniques for distracting young patients from discomfort or pain. Each day, when Webster and I came down the stairs from our morning session, she would look out the picture window and exclaim, for instance, "Oh, look over there! You can just see . . ." or "Look! I wonder what that is! Can you tell?" These distractions, or redirections, worked every time and made me chuckle at their transparency even as I was being coaxed back from despair over what had just happened in the studio.

After lunch, with the Aitkens carrying most of the conversation, we would all take an afternoon siesta—a local custom—for which I would return to my little guest house. Following our siesta time, I would reappear at the main house for afternoon tea, the prelude to a second run at pianistic problem solving.

The siesta break involved more than simply local custom. Lilian knew that my damaged spinal and upper body muscles needed horizontal positioning in the course of each day, to cut down on overworking the muscles. The Aitkens also encouraged me to stretch out, or get into "the horizontal," as they called it, at any time that I felt the need.

After our late afternoon session, Lilian would prepare her "prescription" for muscle relaxation and low-stress conversation: a generous Jack Daniels and soda, presented with a warm smile. The three of us would talk about a broad range of topics as we sat around the patio fireplace, eventually moving inside for dinner. Webster and Lilian both read widely and had interesting world experiences, so I found their general conversation fascinating. I began to view Webster's piercing bon mots—which some of his Carnegie students had come to dread—in a new light, once I saw how they amused Lilian and inspired her humorous retorts. Those were memorable evenings, warmed by the glow of the fire, the "prescription" cocktail, and a conversation as relaxed as I could manage.

It was clear that Webster and Lilian were doing everything they could to counteract the feeling of doom that arose often during our piano sessions. Lassen's one-year deadline was hanging over us all.

During those first months in Santa Fe, I temporarily abandoned any attempt to play with the "right" muscles or to rediscover any "right" pathways. We concentrated on finding something—anything—that worked, which usually turned out to be compensatory "work-arounds": minute approximations of the small, reflexive movements that make up a complex piano technique. I might even call some of these approximations microscopic. I made each one consciously rather than reflexively. The problem was that a work-around could look right, and sounded better than I had done on my own, but didn't feel right. The work-arounds felt all wrong.

This lack of connection between the musical image and the mechanism I needed to carry it through was deeply frustrating. I was being forced to work against my natural reflexes. When I *did* reach for a reflex that had been built in for many years BP, it usually resulted in little or no response—the brick-wall effect— or the dreaded "nerve shudder," or a combination of both. At first, we set a goal to build my tolerance of this distressing process past fifteen minutes at a time. If I lasted for half an hour, it was a good session.

I had hoped that Webster could "teach" me how to make some of the more subtle movements and could help me open some of my pre-polio pathways. But I gradually discovered that he could only *describe*—in as many ways as possible, and demonstrate at the keyboard—what the natural movements looked and felt like. Only *I* would ever be able to find an elusive needle in such a messy haystack.

When working on my own, I knew that the best plan was to alternate my vision of the musical ideal with my ongoing attempt to find neural pathways. BP, piano playing had felt like one continuous flow: imagining the sound, feeling that musical impulse flow through my body, through my arms, through my fingertips, through the keyboard, through the instrument itself, and out into the room or the concert hall.

I would go back and forth between trying to recall that way of playing and calling on whatever work-around response I could find for a tiny part of a musical passage. I could only hope that this technique, on a microscopic level, would help to break through some part of the blockages in my neural pathways. Among the "nerve shudders" and the bumping up against brick walls, I found places I could almost break through—but then would be stopped short. Since the musical material itself is complex—as the combination of reflexes must also be—my task turned out to be a constant search for many needles in many haystacks.

If each piece of music, or section of a piece I tried to play, could be called a house, I needed to know every nook and cranny of every room in it. But I had to accept the fact that, post-polio, I no longer felt comfortable inside *any* house, or piece. I could trip so unexpectedly; I could get cornered so easily; an unforgiving demon could stop me on a whim; and any of these things could happen if I hesitated for an instant. As a result, I had to know the inside of each complex dwelling so well that I could turn on a dime, or a fraction of a dime; so that I could quickly hop over a place just meant for me to trip on; so that I could regain my balance—again in a split second, during a complex passage.

When practicing a piece of music, I had to think the movements from different places in each hand/arm/side of the body.

Neither side worked properly, so neither could serve as a model. But because the right side was less handicapped than the left, I kept trying to let the right be the guide, where possible. I learned that I had to shift multiple times—instantaneously—during even a short, simple musical passage, to come even close to some kind of musical approximation. As soon as I made one mistake in which "technique" I was going to use for even a split second, the whole thing would fall apart.

The musical material I chose for my own practice and for our sessions was usually drawn from parts of complete works. Early on, within the Beethoven Sonata Opus 109, for instance—a work I loved, revered, and had studied mentally with Boulanger and Eibner—I found a few almost-accessible passages that I could explore, even in this painful mode. The gentle opening, the serene theme of the third movement, the lovely arcs of the third variation on that theme, for example, allowed me into their dwelling places. A few Bach preludes and fugues beckoned to me, as did a few Chopin and Debussy preludes. Later, parts of Schubert sonatas, passages from the Beethoven Sonata Opus 110, and even parts of the Beethoven Sonata Opus 111, along with a few of the Bach "Goldberg" Variations, let me come in to explore. Since each passage required heroic efforts, I needed to choose the music I most valued in the literature, and inhabit it as thoroughly as possible.

In Vienna, as I had learned and experienced other aspects of music, I believed there would be a magical time when my playing would all come back if I just "kept trying." In Copenhagen, I could tell myself that once we were through with the treatment, I could start getting back to being *me* again. But now in Santa Fe, in the discouraging search for work-arounds and breakthroughs, I had to admit I was nowhere near being able to walk hand in hand with the piano again.

In between the two extended summers, the Aitkens went to New York for a few months and thought it would be better if I didn't join them. Webster felt, probably rightly, that being in the center of American concert activity would be a discouraging contrast with my own condition, now that I was trying to address that condition realistically.

He suggested that, instead, we might continue our sessions in Los Angeles during the winter, since he had plans to visit there. If I went to LA, he explained, I could stay with his sister, Margaret, and her family. The Aitkens both felt that the warm Los Angeles climate could be soothing to the damaged muscles I was trying to encourage.

This plan gave me time to visit with my family for a couple of months. It was good to be home in Michigan for my mother's birthday in December. I had some precious catch-up time with my brother, Gary, and a lot of discussion with Mom and Dad about future possibilities.

In Los Angeles, I received a warm welcome from Margaret and her family. It was a comfortable atmosphere in which I enjoyed friendly conversation with Margaret and her husband, Herman, a physician. I also enjoyed getting to know their children: Susie, an outgoing youngster who had had polio as a small child and knew its after-effects all too well; Janet, her accomplished older sister, who was close to graduating from high school and was focused on becoming a journalist; and Donald, the youngest, a handsome young boy, trying to find a way to assert himself in a household where his older sisters could already express themselves effectively.

In my LA sessions with Webster, it became clear that, since Santa Fe, my rate of progress had not increased. With the perspective of more time in between sessions, the picture seemed even more discouraging. We explained our frustrating efforts while visiting Webster's beloved Aunt Agnes, who seemed most empathetic. As we were trying to describe our working process, she said that it sounded as if we were putting things together with pins. The metaphor struck me immediately, as images flashed through my mind of childhood sewing attempts. If I had failed to put in enough basting stitches, or enough pins, the material in between would sag, and you couldn't tell what the shape was going to be. You also could never wear the item in that condition. Because my shaping of musical substance felt precarious and unwearable in a similar way, Webster and I started referring to my playing efforts during those years as "put together with pins."

During Webster's stay in Los Angeles, he introduced me to his longtime, close friend Dr. Carolyn Fisher, a retired UCLA psychology professor. Carolyn was a great music lover and a friend to performing artists and composers. Some of the first performances of Arnold Schoenberg's string quartets had taken place at her home. Distinguished touring artists stayed with her and practiced in her living room when they were in Los Angeles to perform. One didn't have to be in her presence very long to recognize that she lived and relished an intellectual life, and that music was woven all through it. Since she was in some ways "family" to Webster, we told her about my illness, but she also understood that we did not want it mentioned to most people I would meet. She invited me to come over and practice at her house any time I wished, and I met a few of her psychologist friends. She introduced me as one of her "house pianists," which I found heartwarming. Though I instantly braced for awkward questions, none came up.

Back in Santa Fe for the second summer, as I worked more on my own in the mornings, I became increasingly aware of an emerging pattern. I would wake up saying to myself "Maybe today's the day!"—the day for an important breakthrough or for finding some way to merge paths a little better in whatever piece or musical passage had my focus. Hope would surge in that early part of the day, before reality would gradually crowd it out. But I knew that recurring hope was still my best chance.

Then as the day wore on, and fatigue set in despite a siesta, despair would prevail. In the evenings, I relied on the Aitkens' company and good conversation, along with Lilian's "prescription," to help mask that part of the syndrome.

One welcome diversion was looking through the treasure trove of piano scores in Webster's studio. Especially fascinating to me were the scores with notes from pianist Artur Schnabel, who had been one of Webster's major teachers. My favorite discovery was Schnabel's notation at the end of the Beethoven Sonata Opus 111: *"ins Himmelreich angekommen"* ("arrival in heaven")—the final perfect chord, the quiet "amen" after the turbulent first movement gives way to the second movement, which begins quietly, becomes joyous and ecstatic, and finally attains a transcendent serenity.

The Opus 111 had already become a kind of life reference for me, as I had clung to it in Paris with Boulanger and in Vienna with Eibner. It seemed to express my determination to keep great musical essences in my life. As I fought every day for my pianistic existence, I could see my tragedy reflected in Webster's eyes, constantly reminding me how precarious that existence had become. The downward leap that began the Opus 111's first movement—the leap into space—symbolized my own leap of faith, against all odds.

I wrote to Martha about the ongoing emotional seesaw: "Webster admitted that we were back to the same kind of work that had to be done last summer. Somehow I seem to get lost in the mess, and still cannot bring forth a coherent whole to stand in for reflex."

The Aitkens and I celebrated August 9, to mark the fifth year since the polio pronouncement of August 9, 1955, the day that had changed my life forever. Our daily sessions were going to end in a few weeks, since Webster had accepted an offer to teach at the University of Illinois for the upcoming school year. I would go back to Michigan and visit him from there.

Toward the end of our second Santa Fe summer, Webster broached the subject of the Lassen deadline, reminding me that the one year Lassen had set for maximum neuromuscular return was now approaching *two* years. I had no need for the "dried-up flower" speech again; I was clearly nowhere near being able to play at a level that either of us found acceptable. I begged Webster not to write me off yet, to give me just one more year. But even the people who wanted most to help me were questioning the wisdom of doing so.

A nudge in a different direction appeared soon after I had moved back to Michigan in the early fall. Mom and I were on a walk with our friend Reta Simons, who wanted to know if I would be interested in taking on her daughter, Cheryl, as a piano student. Reta remembered that I had taught piano during my teenage years, and that my young students in the neighborhood had done well. When I brought up caveats about my own post-polio keyboard problems, she was undeterred. She had seen her eldest son, Jay, through his recovery from paralytic polio and figured that I could draw on my inner resources, just as he had.

Reta's vote of confidence was all it took to reopen that door. In Cheryl's and my first session, we tackled her habit of glancing at the teacher every few seconds for approval. Her delighted chuckle marked a moment of recognition that it was *her playing*, not someone else's approval, that would be our focus. My overall approach would be to help Cheryl build her confidence and strengthen her connection with the piano. As we went along, we had a great time. Her playing improved at a good clip, and it felt to me as if I had never stopped teaching.

I had started giving piano lessons at age twelve, when a substitute teacher at my school asked if I would help her re-approach the piano. She hadn't played for some twenty years, and evidently felt less embarrassed to ask questions of a student rather than an adult teacher. I sensed immediately that her main problem was fear, and I did my best to make our sessions natural and nonthreatening.

By the time I was thirteen, I was teaching several of the neighborhood children; some were beginners, and others had had unproductive experiences with adult teachers. I was closer to their ages and open to an individualized approach for each child, since each one clearly had a different set of needs and learning abilities. Once I had watched and listened to a young person's approach to life, I could help find pathways into the music. Of course, I taught them all some good ways of using their hands and fingers and arms, along with exercises to strengthen their fingers. Sometimes my individualized approach for a student was focused mainly on a matter of pacing or on which element should come first.

Debbie, one of my first students, was hyperactive, and viewed by her classroom teachers as a problem. She was extremely bright but prone to compulsively interrupting people with some irrelevant comment or question. In one of our first lessons, she interrupted something I was saying with the comment, "You wore that same blouse last week!" When I asked if she remembered what we were discussing before she noticed my wardrobe repetition, she repeated almost word for word what I had explained to her about the music. After that incident, I just went with the flow. I found that we could make a lot of progress if I let her vent when she needed to. If she wanted to get up and run around the room in the middle of working on a musical passage, that was fine with me. When she settled down afterward, her concentration was usually better.

I'll never forget the day I invited her mother, Jane, to listen to Debbie play a Clementi sonatina we had been working on. Debbie dug her fingers into the figuration with gusto, and when she came to the end of the piece, turned to her audience of two with the most excited expression I had ever seen on her face. Her mother was thrilled to tears.

Two other first students at that time, Bonnie and Philip, were both fearful at the beginning. Bonnie found it difficult to talk to anyone except her older sister; Philip was disheartened after working with one of the adult piano teachers and was afraid to try again. My job was to encourage them. Philip needed to discover that he could indeed play a musical passage successfully; Bonnie needed to find out that it was safe for her to come out of her shell expressively. For both, in different ways, I first put the focus on smaller sections, so that they could experience shaping a phrase or section and bringing it to a successful conclusion. Then they could build on and extend those experiences. It had been a joy for me to see them emerge and develop some self-confidence at the piano, even with relatively simple repertoire.

When I had talks with parents, I asked them not to order their children to practice, and not to insist on a set amount of practice time. "Let me do that," I suggested. "They get enough of that kind of scheduling at school, and I'd like piano playing to be fun at this stage." I described the value of "see if you can do this" challenges, rather than telling the kids they had to practice some prescribed amount of time. The parents I spoke with were willing to go along, and happy with the result.

One day when I was about fourteen, I had gone to the local sheet-music store looking for repertoire for my young students, when I came across something I knew instantly to be a treasure: a volume of children's pieces by Dmitry Kabalevsky. I also found a volume of fascinating children's pieces by Prokofiev. Neither of these wonderful creations for the young had been part of my own childhood experience, but I was determined to bring them to my students. The Kabalevsky pieces were perfect for beginners through intermediate, and I enjoyed playing each of them through as soon as I brought the volumes home. They introduced a beginner to musical patterns in a charming and imaginative way. The melodies were instantly appealing and playable by almost anyone.

I had continued teaching through high school and then acquired some students during my college years in Pittsburgh—a total of about nine years before leaving for Europe at age twenty-one. It seemed natural to Mom and Dad to trust a young teenager to be capable and responsible. They both grew up on family farms, where the children participated in the real work. My father had developed great body strength through pitching hay and handling hay bales as a kid. My cousins were given serious responsibilities as youngsters; the youngest, Jay, had been driving a tractor since the age of nine. To my parents it seemed normal that, at age fourteen, I had my Michigan driver's license and an entire class of students.

Since I had been earning money as both a teacher and a babysitter, I could save some of it, splurge on candy bars and movie magazines, and buy myself sheet music or books, all at my own discretion. Allowance money was available from my parents, without the need to know what I might be spending it on, but often I told them I simply didn't need it. I knew that they had skimped and saved, having made their way through the Depression, and was happy to be making some income on my own. Self-reliance, to me, seemed a most desirable quality.

But at twenty-six about to turn twenty-seven, I was far more dependent on others than I had ever been in my teens. Since the polio attack, I had felt the opposite of self-reliant. I usually felt fearful and uneasy, and it was something of a miracle that I suddenly felt capable of teaching again.

Soon after Cheryl and I began our sessions, I had a message from Celia Merrill Turner, director of the Will-O-Way Theatre in Bloomfield Hills. Will-O-Way was both a summer stock company and a year-round community theater, founded and directed by a family with a long theatrical history. I first met Celia when I was fifteen and had enrolled in Will-O-Way's Apprentice Theater Program for a fun summer. I had met some interesting students in the class and had a wonderful time, which included playing Juliet in the Apprentice Evening of theatrical scenes. From the time we first met, Celia and I had felt a special bond, since she was also an accomplished musician. As a violinist and conductor, she had graduated from Juilliard in both specialties, and was one of the most energetic and positive people I had ever known.

After my Apprentice Theater summer, I had brought a neighbor friend, "Georgie" Scott, to Will-O-Way to audition for Celia and her brother Bill, the stage director. Georgie, about seven years my senior, had been in the Marine Corps, after which he went back to school to study drama. I had a crush on Georgie and looked forward to those times he visited his father and stepmother, when he would talk with me at "eye level" about serious matters. Georgie had done some impromptu readings for my mother and me that had revealed his stunning dramatic talent, and I hoped that Will-O-Way would accept him for some of their regular productions. They accepted him enthusiastically, and George C. Scott, as he was called formally, had been an instant hit at Will-O-Way before New York, Hollywood, and the rest of the world discovered him.

When Celia and I got back together after so many years, we had a delightful reunion, catching up on major events that had happened to each of us. She also had an idea she wanted to discuss with me: a plan to add music study to Will-O-Way's Apprentice Theater Program. When I had worked with her at Will-O-Way years before, her daughter Robin was barely a year old. Now Celia and her husband, Ken, had two more children, and twelve-year-old Robin was playing the piano. Would I teach Robin and work with Celia on the projected music study program?

Although I felt compelled to repeat the caveats I had given Reta, I knew in advance that they would fall on deaf ears. Celia had always believed that the thought, the idea, the will was stronger than anything else and can prevail. Young Robin had grown up with music around her and had evidently inherited a musical gene as well. She responded instinctively to the material I gave her, and made rapid progress at the keyboard. So with

Cheryl and Robin both onboard, I was off and running once again as a teacher.

Mom and Dad were delighted that I was still able to teach and was enjoying it as much as ever. They had been somewhat worried about my financial prospects. Dad had given both my brother and me portions of his family's Iowa farm, from which we derived a modest income after each year's harvest. But he knew that I was using my share as I went along, whereas Gary could save most of his.

During the next months, my own slow work at the piano continued the seemingly eternal search for breakthroughs. There was no "Aha!" moment. There was no time when something suddenly started working again. There were countless times when I had a fraction—or tiny hint—of a response, and I would immediately jump to the conclusion that one of the many channels I needed might be opening up. Far too often "maybe this is it" turned into "well, maybe not, after all."

But I did have many moments that marked important progress. No matter how small it was, I treated each moment as if it might be *the* breakthrough. And it was these small, scarcely detectable gains that would eventually add up. I wrote to Webster at one point during that winter: "Occasionally I find some response out of the distant past, timid and rusty, being awakened as I try to put a couple of these newly acquired movements together. I grab onto it like mad where possible; sometimes it's so fleeting that I can only recognize that a spot was somehow less wooden, or whatever. When that happens, I feel like a different person for a few hours."

I continued to alternate that experience with thinking through a piece of music at a very slow tempo, so that every detail got built in, as well as thinking through the material as I'd ideally want it to sound—as a flowing piece of music. Both modes were necessary to allow my musical intent to direct my hands and fingers as much as possible.

As the months went on, when I was away from the piano I was thinking ever more clearly about what I wanted a passage to sound like; then I would go back to the piano and try to find paths to make it sound that way. I needed to keep going back and forth—to keep refreshing the musical idea in my mind. Otherwise, I was afraid I might accept a solution of lesser quality, just from being worn down by the process. It was still all too easy to collapse in tears. But in some ways, the back-and-forth technique kept me in better emotional balance.

I visited Webster a few times in Illinois but found it discouraging to be around his students, who had normal bodies and normal piano-playing equipment. He said he wished we could find someone else to work with me, as he'd exhausted his ingenuity.

That was the winter (1960–61) when I learned the entire Goldberg Variations, a major work for both harpsichordists and pianists. Each variation is somewhat complete in itself and satisfying to memorize away from the piano on its own. The variations went deep with me; I built my life around them for about two years, along with the three last Beethoven sonatas.

One evening my parents invited a couple of friends over and asked if I would like to play something for them. I had reached a tentative pact with my beloved Beethoven Opus 109, and could make my way through the entire glorious work without breaking down completely. I had mentally prepared myself to be able to restart at any place along the way, in case I encountered a blockage or a nerve shudder. In other words, I had studied the entire work in such minute detail that I could walk into a room and start cold on any note or chord during the entire twenty-minute piece. That may sound like an extreme precaution, but for my condition, there was no such thing as being over-prepared. I was fearful of outside ears, and yet was aware that if I could manage to play Opus 109 in front of an audience, that, too, would be a milestone. Dad was experimenting with a tape recorder he had rebuilt and asked if he could try it out for the occasion.

The "performance" was frightening beyond description; but at the same time, it felt like a miracle that I could get through it at all. Later, when the three of us were by ourselves, Dad hit the "play" button, and I was amazed that the musical message had come through, despite everything. I heard some technical unevenness, but it was not glaring, and the musical ideas had come across. It was an indescribably emotional moment for all of us, recognizing that I was still *there* somewhere, way beneath the handicaps and technical problems.

While I was at home, Mom and I talked a lot about other important matters, especially the fact that my onetime classmates, and other friends my age, were all married or in committed relationships. I knew that she didn't want me to end up alone, and though she didn't use the "dried-up flower" metaphor, she had a similar concern. I did go on a few dates with a friend who was also home visiting his family, but we soon agreed that we should just stay friends. I was twenty-seven, headed toward twenty-eight, and recognizing that some potential relationships might already have passed me by while I was in rehabilitation.

Life was changing for my Köllnerhof friends, too. David had moved back to the United States, where he was soon to marry his sweetheart, Eileen. He plunged immediately into teaching public-school music and volunteering at the Salvation Army center in Harlem, where he directed a young people's brass band and a young people's chorus, and even helped youngsters with homework. I loved the stories about David's recognizable Volkswagen being sacrosanct in Harlem; evidently he could safely leave it on any street, as the word had gone out that it was not to be touched. Martha and Dady were very much together, and David gave them the Köllnerhof flat as a wedding present.

In late spring of 1961 I received an invitation to visit Carolyn Fisher in Los Angeles, along with word from Webster that he would be in LA at the same time. Since I would be staying with Carolyn, any session with Webster would take place at her home. One Sunday, after I had settled in for my "resident house pianist" role, Carolyn had an informal party for some of her psychology friends, former colleagues, and a couple of onetime students. It started in the afternoon and extended through the evening. I had a particularly good time talking with the two former students: Sam, who was now a psychiatrist, and Phil, a psychologist. Both were in their late thirties, considerably younger than the rest of the group, and both seemed attracted to me. I responded and found the conversation engrossing. By the end of the evening, Sam had invited me out to dinner, which I readily accepted. After everyone had left, I asked Carolyn some questions about both men. She explained that Phil had been married for several years, but that the relationship was currently rocky. Sam had never been married and had recently broken up with a longtime girlfriend.

What happened over the next few months was not what I had anticipated when I had come to visit Carolyn. A romance with Sam developed very quickly, and I was aloft with expectation and excitement. The relationship put everything into a different light. I found a modest little bungalow, about the size of a small apartment, on a hill behind the Hollywood Bowl parking lot and sent for the things I hadn't brought with me, including my Steinway A.

Before long, we seemed to be an engaged, or nearly engaged, couple. Sam talked first about "our" restaurant, and then about "our" life together, and "our" plans. Here, finally, was the romantic partnership I'd hoped for. I felt as if all that was missing was a ring and a ceremony.

During our time as a couple, Sam and I had shared a few evenings with Phil, and the three-way conversations were warm and engaging. After those evenings, I sometimes wondered what would have happened if Phil had been available and had asked me out before Sam did. But the growing closeness with Sam felt "right" and seemed to have all the ingredients for a long-term relationship.

Then one day, out of the blue, Sam said, as if thinking about this for the first time, "Well, you want a career, don't you? You wouldn't want children—you want a career."

I was shocked. Sam knew that I had had polio, but he evidently didn't understand its consequences. I answered that I had always enjoyed my relationships with children and assumed I would have my own someday. I went on to explain that I wasn't thinking of—or, for that matter, fit for—any career besides teaching. I probably didn't spell out to Sam just how remote a "career" was, as I was still downplaying the severity of the polio's aftereffects.

But as we talked, I began to realize that this was the beginning of the end. It didn't matter what I said; Sam had already decided that our relationship had run its course. Later, I found out that he had gone back to his former girlfriend, whom he eventually married.

Perhaps the main problem in my relationship with Sam was that, at the time, I was so uncertain about my life. Until he talked about having children, I had just assumed that at some point I *would* have children, an assumption based on a selective awareness of my post-polio condition. But if I could only with difficulty take care of myself and my own daily needs, how could I realistically have had children and continued any kind of piano pursuit? Although Sam didn't express that question sensitively, or even correctly, he *did* see the inconsistency.

Despite my hurt and disappointment, when I was honest with myself I was not surprised at the outcome. I had had an affair the year before in Michigan, but on both sides it wasn't meant to be more than that. I was farther along than I'd been in Vienna, for instance, when I'd met Earl; but the aftereffects of my illness were still turning out to be the game changer in the romantic realm.

After the breakup with Sam, I stayed on in LA, mainly because I wasn't sure what to do next. Fortunately, my tiny bungalow was a short walk to Carolyn's house, so I could easily continue that friendship and remain one of her "house pianists." And because I was always looking for ways to improve my physical capabilities, I signed up for a movement class (a kind of ballet class for women who were out of shape). Among the class members were two people who asked if I would give them piano lessons. Once again, teaching appeared as a bright spot in otherwise uncertain territory.

Chapter Eleven

✑

Amelia and the
Death-Defying Leap

L ater in the fall of 1961, Dad needed to make a trip to the West Coast, and Mom came along. It was great to share some time with them in the LA atmosphere. They enjoyed the warm Southern California climate and recognized its benefits for my polio-damaged muscles. They also approved of my little bungalow and went on walks with me up and down the hillside and through the pleasant, low-key neighborhood.

Mom and I talked about my romance with Sam, but she mostly wanted to know how I was moving forward with my life. She found part of that answer when we attended a party that Carolyn Fisher had planned with her circle of friends to coincide with my parents' visit. Although everyone seemed to enjoy meeting each other, when Mom and I were alone after-ward, she asked, "Honey, do you ... uh ... have any friends under sixty-five?" It was a fair question. Carolyn was in her early seventies, and her longtime friends and colleagues, mostly connected with UCLA, were also in that age range. I was heading toward my twenty-eighth birthday, and had no friends in the area any-where near my own age.

Carolyn had encouraged me to practice at her house anytime I wished. That gave me a chance to vary the often-discouraging work—on my own piano in a small room and on her piano in a larger room. Practicing at Carolyn's house also provided a sense of connection with another person close by. She had given me a key so that I could come and go whether she was home or not. Carolyn often went to lectures and events, and friends or former colleagues would come by for her while I was there practicing. If the events interested me, I occasionally went along, but I usually elected to continue my explorations at the piano, during which I still required frequent periods of "horizontal" rest.

One day, after my parents had gone back to Michigan, I was at Carolyn's house, practicing Schubert's great B-flat "Opus Posthumous" Sonata, which had become another of my "homes"—music that I found welcoming and comforting to live inside. Carolyn was going to a psychology lecture with a onetime graduate student of hers, Amelia Haygood, who was by then a practicing psychologist, and whose husband had died recently of a sudden heart attack. Douglas Haygood had been a well-known psychologist and former president of the California Psychological Association.

I was making my way through the Schubert while Carolyn was getting ready to go out. A few seconds after I finished, the doorbell rang. I got up to answer, but Carolyn had already opened the door to a woman standing there with a wide, friendly smile that lit up her face. On her head she wore a "baggie," as large plastic storage bags were called then, and we all laughed about the unusual headgear. It had begun to rain, and the plastic bag had been the most serviceable "rain hat" to be found in Amelia's car.

After informal introductions, Amelia told me that she had been standing outside the door for a while, not wanting to inter-rupt the Schubert. Standing outside, when it was raining? And she knew what I had been playing? She told me that she had several recordings of the work and that my treatment of certain elements in the final movement were intriguingly different from any she had heard.

I was stunned by her comments, amazed that a stranger who knew nothing of my struggle could hear some of what I was trying to express. Carolyn's friends tended to be sophisticated about arts and literature, but this woman was obviously a classical music connoisseur. She told me whose recordings she had listened to and made interesting observations about my interpretation.

Even more surprising, my conversation with Amelia led from the Schubert sonata to Schubert lieder—German art songs—of which she also had an extensive recording collection. She and her late husband, Doug, had been avid fans of German and French art songs. Doug's mother had been a pianist who often accompanied singers, and Doug grew up knowing the repertoire, playing the piano, and singing, since he'd also had a lovely tenor voice. We talked about some of their favorite lieder singers, including such artists as Elisabeth Schwarzkopf and Dietrich Fischer-Dieskau. I hadn't had a chance to talk about singers and art songs since I'd left Europe. Amelia was fascinated to know that I had lived in Vienna, where I'd heard most of the great singers perform many times. She and Doug had heard some of these same artists on tour in California. Carolyn joined the conversation for a few minutes and, since they needed to leave, invited Amelia and me for brunch on Sunday.

It was a beautiful day for Carolyn's brunch on her outdoor patio. Our three-way conversation was wonderful, as it followed many interweaving strands. When I asked Amelia about her musical background, she said that she had studied piano for a few years, but that her major influence was her father, a great classical music and opera lover, who had been a law professor at the University of Florida in Gainesville. Every weekend they had listened to Metropolitan Opera broadcasts and to treasured "classic" recorded performances. Amelia's father had come from a family of doctors, and felt that music could be an important ingredient in a balanced life. He had taught Amelia and her younger brother some classical Greek and Latin when they were children, and it had seemed a natural extension of that study when they later pored over texts of arias in Italian, French, or German. Although her father had died when Amelia was only fifteen, he had clearly contributed significantly to her interests and her outlook on life.

I felt immediately comfortable around Amelia, who was in her early forties but seemed to have a generous amount of wisdom and life experience. She had an open and welcoming gaze, enhanced by her large, soft-green eyes. Her way of speaking sounded especially friendly, and was softened by what a musician thinks of as legato—a flow brought about by a slight elongation of vowels. When Amelia wanted to know about my musical background, I was more open than usual about my illness, rather than glossing over things I usually tried to hide. I also felt comfortable about discussing my polio experience once she mentioned working for the Veterans Administration as a bedside psychologist in a spinal-injury ward. It was the first time I had heard someone pinpoint the more elusive aspects of what a sudden loss of function means to a young person.

At one point in our leisurely afternoon, Carolyn went to her study to write some letters, and Amelia and I just kept talking. Much to my surprise, I found myself going right to the heart of something I was wrestling with: that I had become a different person since my illness. It was a subject I had occasionally touched on with a very few others during the six-plus years since the polio attack, but there had never been a response like Amelia's.

"You're still the same person, Carol," she said gently, "but most likely a depressed version of your former self." That seemed hopeful, but was also somewhat confusing.

"But I don't feel sad," I told her. She smiled encouragingly.

"In clinical psychology," she explained, *"depression* means depressed function. And as a depressed version of yourself, you probably haven't been allowed—or allowed yourself—to grieve for your lost magic." That made enormous sense.

As we talked about experiencing various kinds of loss at a young age, I learned that the year after her father's death, Amelia had gone to France with family friends—Douglas Haygood, his wife, Margaret, and their four sons. Amelia had graduated early from high school, and her mother felt that a change of scene would be beneficial. In France, sixteen-year-old Amelia met Ricky, a young British journalist who had been covering the Spanish Civil War for a British newspaper, and who shared many of Amelia's interests and ideals. Since Amelia was interested in international relations, she had begun writing articles for her hometown newspaper, encouraging her fellow citizens to look beyond their then-isolationist point of view. She and Ricky had fallen in love, become engaged, and planned to marry once Amelia finished college back in the United States. But when war broke out in Europe in 1939, Ricky enlisted in the Royal Air Force. His plane was one of the first to be shot down, and the whole crew was killed.

Amelia went on to study at Florida State University, majoring in history and international law. After college, her interests and abilities led her to Washington, D.C., where she got a job with a very long title: Editor and Director of Publications for the State Department Interdepartmental Committee for Cultural and Scientific Cooperation. While working there, she had fallen in love again, this time with a Navy captain whose ship was part of the Pacific fleet during World War II. On one of his Pacific missions, his ship was attacked and severely damaged. He managed to get his crew to safety, but as the last person left on board, he had been unable to save himself and went down with his ship. Amelia had been in her early twenties then, and again coping with major loss.

Shortly before the war ended, Amelia's friendship with Doug Haygood turned into a love affair. Doug's wife, Margaret, had left him, and once the divorce was final, he asked Amelia to marry him. This meant a move to Cleveland, where his psychology practice was based. Two of Doug's four sons were already in college, and two were still home with their father, so Amelia became both Doug's wife and a stepmother to his children.

Through their years together, Doug and others in the psychology field began to recognize that Amelia had a natural gift for working with people. Her new direction—studying and pursuing a career in psychology—followed. In the last years before Doug's sudden death, Amelia and Doug had been in private practice together.

The fatal evening had begun like many others. Doug and Amelia had gone out with friends to a favorite restaurant where a jazz combo played on certain evenings. Doug loved to sit in as a pianist with the group and had an open invitation to do so. On this evening, during one of the sets, he suddenly slumped over the piano. Some in the group at first thought it was a joke because Doug was also a talented comedian, who sometimes added unexpected twists to give everyone a laugh. But Amelia knew instantly that something was terribly wrong. Doug had suffered a massive heart attack and died at the age of fifty-seven.

Although Amelia's losses and reorientations had been very different from mine, I was beginning to understand some of the factors that had contributed to her remarkable wisdom and perspective. As we talked further, she described the concept of premature aging, which occurs when a younger person becomes infirm overnight and then is forced to make unforeseen life choices. At the VA hospital, she had worked with wounded veterans experiencing that syndrome.

Premature aging made a lot of sense to me, and I told Amelia about the ambitious number of tasks I had taken on as a teenager: being a scholarship student at school, teaching a number of private piano students, practicing the piano many hours a day, performing in public—all part of what had once been my normal life. But now, six years after the polio attack, it was difficult for me to do even simple, everyday things; I had to rest frequently and was still struggling at the piano to attain uncertain goals. And since I had chosen that struggle, I had to turn my back on many things that others my age could do easily.

The concept of premature aging resonated with me from another direction. When I was seven, I had learned in school about a hunter-gatherer custom: When an older and ailing tribal member decided that he or she could no longer keep up with the rest of the tribe, the elder would simply stay behind, indicating that the others should go on ahead. The teacher had explained that the elder had made that choice knowing that no one could survive alone. I found that horrifying. I couldn't help picturing one of my beloved grandmothers in that plight. The image had haunted me for a long time, and even gave me nightmares.

A few years after the polio struck, I had sometimes wondered if *I* had become useless far younger than those unfortunate tribal elders. That fear had been hitting me especially since I had come home from Europe "in defeat," feeling that I could be part of things only with someone else's help. On several levels, the "premature aging" characterization of my condition was a revelatory concept.

This discussion with Amelia enabled me to touch on some deep terrors of the past six years. I confided that, with very few exceptions, I had been avoiding any talk about my illness. Or if I mentioned it, I would gloss over the most difficult aftereffects. In Amelia's opinion, trying to keep the extent of my illness a secret had probably been isolating, and would eventually become too much of a burden for me. As we talked, I had a sudden insight: My feeling about the aftereffects had a lot in common with a sense of shame.

As I got to know Amelia better over time, whenever she

mentioned that she preferred to "get down into the well" with a patient, rather than sitting at the top and trying to pull the patient out, I always thought of that first extended discussion when she had been willing to do exactly that with me—the first time anyone had truly done so. I had a loving family and some good friends, but I had rarely let anyone go with me into the dark places.

Until I met Amelia, I had mostly felt alone in those dark places. This great new gift of friendship with someone who understood the psychological toll that my post-polio years had taken, and who could enable me to discuss it for the first time, was priceless—probably the single most important stroke of good fortune in my entire post-polio life.

Another startling aspect that emerged as I got to know Amelia was her view of my options—a view no one else seemed to share. I had told her where my change in direction was headed, since piano playing was going to be mainly for myself and as an aid to teaching. But against all conventional wisdom, she was convinced that I still had something to say as a performing pianist.

Although Amelia came from outside the music world, she listened frequently to the best of classical music performances with a keen ear that many top musicians were to comment on in the years to come. Here was the amazing truth: She heard in my playing some of the things I had carried around in my head and heart ever since those struggling days in Vienna, when I would imagine the music as I wanted to hear it and would will it to take powerful shape in my mind.

It was life-changing to discover that Amelia found those musical ideas treasurable, despite my handicapped playing mechanism. I already knew that the best plan was always to approach any passage—even one containing what appeared to be an insurmountable problem—as if it were about to reveal itself. And for that approach to be most effective, I had to anticipate the potential revelation as joyful, fun, or intriguing. I had to feel that I was *just about* to find the way.

As we discussed these concepts, I told Amelia the story of teaching in my early teens, and that I had known instinctively how to help the neighborhood children make progress at the piano. Because I had emphasized the joy rather than the time spent practicing, my young students had accomplished much more than anyone had expected of them.

We agreed that I now had to approach my *own* efforts not as "work" so much as anticipation of pleasure—the thrill of playing a beautiful phrase, total immersion in a short musical passage. Once upon a time, pre-polio, that feeling had come naturally, when I was able to do anything I could imagine at the keyboard.

But this long rehabilitation required mental and emotional work that was far more complex. Neurologists and physical-medicine experts looked at my hands, arms, shoulders, and upper body, and told me that what I was attempting was out of the question; I was wasting my time.

Amelia seemed to understand what I had been unable to explain to anyone else. She understood that tiny, almost imperceptible improvements came about partly because I was approaching them *in expectation* of discovering something positive, and being elated at the prospect. She believed wholeheartedly that the positive image was essential. If I could imagine myself doing this beautiful or exciting or joyous thing, I had a remote fraction of a chance of making some improvement—of taking one step among hundreds of steps that would be required. And she understood that I had learned to notice the tiniest degree of progress. I told her I knew I had miles to go, but that a millimeter of progress thrilled me.

It was wonderful to talk all this through. Amelia also suggested that I should start playing more, informally, for small groups, and see what might emerge. She mentioned friends and colleagues to whom an afternoon or evening of classical music—

played live for them by someone as devoted as I was—would have great meaning. These were colleagues who spent their working days with people who were in trouble, with youngsters gone astray, with devastated families—painful situations requiring agonizing decisions.

Amelia was sure these colleagues would treasure live, informal performances. To her, great classical music could provide "a shelter against the heavy weather which comes to us all," as she was later to write in a CD introduction. It wouldn't have to be a long program; she thought I should start small. The Schubert B-flat Sonata could be the "program," for instance. Or the Beethoven Opus 109, with or without a Bach prelude and fugue before it—a program I had done for my parents and their friends before moving to LA.

Amelia found it easy and natural to bring a few of her friends over to my little bungalow, where I could play through something, followed by dinner out with the group. Or sometimes the visitors would bring refreshments. Amelia continued to emphasize how much the informal evenings of great music meant to her friends, which in turn helped to ease my play-through fears.

Psychologist Craig Boardman and his wife, Helen, who was head of social work at Children's Hospital in LA, became "regulars" at these play-throughs. Craig was a wonderful storyteller, but when I complimented him, he said no one could match Doug Haygood for hilarious stories. Sometimes Amelia invited a beloved mentor of hers, psychologist Bruno Klopfer, and his wife, Erna. They had fled Nazi Germany, and Bruno had worked with Carl Jung in Switzerland before emigrating to the United States. Bruno radiated compassion in a quiet way, and I felt especially relaxed around him. After one of the play-throughs, he confided that if he had a close friend or family member who needed to talk through a problem, he would send that person to Amelia.

Another friend of Amelia's who became a "regular" was a French-Swiss woman, Jeanne Hansen, who ran the classical

Already in love with the piano—at about eighteen months.

Edward Bredshall in 1948.

Webster Aitken in the early 1950s.

Mom and Dad in Southern California in 1965.

Eve Brackett at home in Malibu.

Walking on the beach in Malibu. Photo by Richard Gross.

Amelia Haygood at home in Santa Monica. Photo by Millard Tipp.

Ms.

GIVE 'EM HELL!

Pre-concert note from Gloria Steinem and the Ms. *Magazine staff. April 1974.*

At the party after my UCLA performance in 1976—left to right: Mom, Whit Cook, Michael Kermoyan, Betty and Gene Ling.

Jimmy DePreist and I listen to a playback during the recording session of The Four Temperaments *at Abbey Road Studios, London. June 1976. Photo by Reg Wilson.*

Jerry Schwarz and I plan a recording session. Fall 1980. Photo by Johan Elbers.

Recording session of Dvořák Stabat Mater *with the New Jersey Symphony and the Westminster Choir. Front row left to right: me, co-producer Stephen Basili, conductor Zdenek Macal, recording engineer John Eargle. Back row left to right: co-producer Karl Held, Amelia, choral conductor Joseph Flummerfelt. February 1994. Photo by Arthur Paxton.*

With Constantine Orbelian, after a concert at Peterhof Palace in St. Petersburg. Summer 1999.

With Sean Hickey, composer and Naxos VP, Sales and Business Development. August 2013.

Recording session of Mark Abel's new opera Home Is a Harbor—*with co-producer Christopher Anderson–Bazzoli, left, and composer Mark Abel, right. July 2015. Photo by Tom Zizzi.*

department of the local record store. Jeanne's husband had also died recently, and when Amelia popped into the store from time to time, they had become close friends with a great deal in common. Jeanne, too, was particularly knowledgeable about classical music.

One day Louise Gretschel, another of Amelia's colleagues who came to some of the play-throughs and had a challenging job with LA County Juvenile Services, suggested that the three of us visit an acquaintance of hers, Eve Brackett, who lived in Malibu and had a fine piano in her living room. She was sure Eve would like to have some live music there, as well.

Eve's apartment overlooked the Pacific Ocean, and her front deck had a spectacular, sweeping view of Santa Monica Bay. Eve was a Bostonian in her early fifties who had moved to California recently, and was still marveling at life in Malibu, where she was now free to pursue her own interests since her two sons had become well established with families of their own. Eve's husband, Truman, a Boston businessman, remained on the East Coast, but would visit when he could.

Eve loved music and art, and was planning to write a book, which she confessed was going slowly. I played her piano for a bit, walked onto the deck to breathe with the tide for a few minutes, and then we all went out to dinner at The Sea Lion, a modest restaurant in a stunning beachfront location.

At one point Amelia mentioned nostalgically how much she and Doug had loved living in Malibu. She had not been able to keep their hillside house after he died and had moved into a rented apartment in LA. Suddenly Eve had a brainstorm. She had heard that the apartment across the hall was going to be available before long and would be happy to find out more, since she had become friends with the landlord.

From that point, things were on the move. Eve soon reported that the apartment, which also had a spectacular ocean view, could be rented for little more than the rent Amelia was presently paying in the city. As it turned out, the building next door would soon have a smaller apartment available with the same ocean view. That apartment included a nice-sized room over the garage that could be a studio for my Steinway and where I could do any kind of awkward practicing without bothering anyone. My Malibu Era was about to begin.

In all three apartments, the sundecks overlooking the ocean extended over the water at high tide. You could see large rocks under one of the decks and watch all sorts of seabirds, and even a seal from time to time. On a clear night, our view of the bay included a sparkling string of lights.

In my apartment, I had the back room over the garage converted into a studio, lined with cork to temper the sound, air-conditioned so that the piano strings wouldn't get too much salt air, and double-glazed as a buffer against the highway noise. When the piano was not in use, it was covered by what we called a "complete kimono."

A long, blissful walk on the beach every day helped to balance out my struggles at the piano. The ocean seemed to be giving me back something I had used up in my post-polio years—a perspective that could take some of the sting out of my uphill climb. I could go back and work at the piano after the ocean had dispelled some of the tension and discouragement. If you gazed at the water and let yourself breathe with the tide, everything else mattered just a little less, and that was an enormous relief. And right next door were two good friends with whom I could discuss anything and everything.

As I became close to Amelia and Eve, my limited existence was gradually enhanced and extended far beyond what I could manage alone. I felt as if I could become more a part of the world around me. Eve had the time to give dinner parties, cocktail parties, and tea parties, and loved playing hostess to doctors, psychologists, social workers, artists, and musicians. She had an elegant appearance and manner, and was always a lively conversationalist.

Amelia was genuinely interested in just about everyone she had ever met, remembered what they told her about themselves and their lives, and thus was always a magnet. She radiated an empathy that came from her very core. She always had many strands of thought going on and could express any one of them with naturalness and ease. When Amelia was around, there was never an awkward silence, and her encouraging manner brought out thoughts or feelings that others usually kept below the surface.

All I had to do was show up at these intimate gatherings, which always had lively conversation and often music. And during the play-through part, of course, I could concentrate on the all-important "performance."

Eve had volunteered in medical settings back in Boston, while her sons were growing up, and had begun to do some medical volunteer work at UCLA, so she brought in some interesting people from that world. The three of us became close friends with a highly respected neurologist, Margaret Jones, who took great interest in my situation and was helpful when I had strange side effects from various exercises or practice patterns. We also became close to a doctor of physical medicine and his wife, David and Sara Rubin, who were very helpful when my muscles got into trouble. And there were other new friends, all of whom enjoyed hearing me play something I had been working on, and who began to feel part of my many-year struggle.

Eve went back to Boston every so often to be with her husband, Truman, and their sons' families, but was always happy to get back to Malibu. Truman came to visit her whenever possible, especially in December and January. At those times her elegantly beautiful wardrobe would emerge, and inevitably Truman would glance over at Amelia and me, and anyone else present, and exclaim, "That's my gal! That's my gal!"

The strenuous efforts that I was putting into my work at the piano, and at the same time a little teaching, left me no energy to build other relationships on my own. But Amelia and

Eve had—and made—those connections, and I could be part of it all. When we went out in public, Amelia or Eve would casually open doors, pick up packages, move a chair this way or that, make sure there was an armchair for me to sit in—done so gracefully and naturally that only our medical friends would have noticed my disability. I felt as if I were emerging once again as a person—emerging from that very protective shell I had built for the first years after the polio attack. I no longer felt like just a struggling soul in rehab.

If my energy had been used up for the day, it didn't matter. The conversation was lively and enjoyable, and all I had to do was smile or add a comment here and there. If the three of us went to a concert or an opera or a play, Amelia and Eve would do the applauding and I would smile, exchange enthusiastic comments with them, and not have to tire my shoulders to show my delight. Instead, I could shout "Bravo!" and pound the floor with my feet.

My own informal performances became more frequent once Eve began hosting them, with Amelia's help. Thanks to these play-throughs, I once again became accustomed to the adrenaline rush, and learned to work with it. Play-throughs turned out to be the path—the only path—to redeveloping my piano playing.

Imagine that you were a circus performer, sure-footed on a tightrope, and then one day you'd suffered paralytic scatter damage all through your entire body, to the extent that you felt weak and unstable walking from your bed to the bathroom. Yet you were determined to get back on that tightrope—a tightrope without a safety net.

Extreme athletes say that in life-threatening situations, once the adrenalized "fight or flight" response kicks in, they can find the right solutions in "flow" state. British BASE jumper Shaun Ellison, who jumps off "big cliffs in beautiful places," describes this state as being "on a different plane," where he can find "channels that are closed in day-to-day life."

For me at that point, playing for even three or four people was terrifying, and therefore felt like that high-wire act with no safety net. The gradual gains I made must have been in some form of "flow" or I couldn't have endured the process.

I found ways, in informal performance mode, to connect dots that otherwise would have remained isolated. It took the actual act of presenting music to others to call forth neuromuscular responses beyond what I could work out consciously in practice sessions. It was a magic that could have happened only in "flow" state.

I had stumbles, of course, and terrifying moments, on a regular basis. But I also found windows into a gradually smoother, more integrated, more effective way of handling some of the musical detail. Those windows that allowed vision and discovery were found randomly among hundreds or, over time, thousands of prospective openings.

To function for the play-throughs, and get into flow state, I had to develop an entirely new way of preparing to perform—even for a piece of music I had "lived within" and memorized thoroughly. My old pre-polio "normal" way of preparing wouldn't have worked at all. In general, pianists who perform from memory rely heavily on reflexes developed in the process of building a piano technique over the years, and in practicing and memorizing a specific piece. But my normal neuromuscular reflexes had, of course, been destroyed by polio.

As I had found a way to do with the Beethoven Opus 109 when I had played it for Mom and Dad and their friends, I prepared every piece by creating "starting places"—many, many spots throughout each musical composition—where I could have walked into a room and started cold.

All musical performers are highly conscious of natural starting places. It's where you break the silence and start the music. Since these "opening" spots become unforgettable, the reflex needed to play them is the most reliable. It's the most solidly built-in detail in the entire piece. One always mentally rehearses a starting place. If it's the very beginning of the piece, you know exactly *how* you're going to start it.

What comes afterward should flow naturally from that beginning, if you have normal technique, and if you keep the musical whole in mind consistently, as well as the specific moment within that whole.

But what if the music *doesn't* flow naturally? Or what if the flow is unreliable? My solution was to make another starting place as soon as necessary after the beginning, so that the next step would also become highly clarified and highly defined, in both musical and neuromuscular ways. And each starting place had to be imagined and played expressively as if flowing from the previous material, or it wouldn't work.

To better explain what I mean, let's discuss a moderately paced piano piece that takes about ten minutes to perform. If you know the work well, you will have no problem coming into a room, sitting down at the piano, and playing the very beginning of the piece. There will also be a few places during the piece where you could restart "cold" because you are entering a different or contrasting section, and therefore you've had to be more conscious of that spot. Even so, most of the piece is a musical "fabric" that moves seamlessly forward, flowing and blending and creating a musical shape. But what if your reflexes aren't reliable, and you are stopped suddenly right in the middle of creating this beautiful fabric? Then you have to create a super-secure infrastructure for your performance.

As an example, now let's lay out the above piece of music in "swatches" that take an average of five seconds each to play in performance tempo. That would make about one-hundred-twenty swatches within the ten-minute piece. You'll want the swatches to make musical sense within their own small confines, of course, so the five-second length of a swatch is just an average.

Next you'll want to become acquainted with, and fix firmly

in your mind, the beginning of each swatch as thoroughly and deeply as you know the very beginning of the ten-minute piece. As a test, you'll want to come to the piano fresh, sit down, and start at the beginning of any one of those one-hundred-twenty swatches.

But it's not enough just to know the one-hundred-twenty starting places "cold." You'll need to think of each swatch as emerging from its predecessor in thoroughly musical fashion. Each swatch needs to be fixed in your mind as absolute in its own detail, but also as a natural musical continuation of what has gone before.

For my situation, a five-second swatch would sometimes be too long. Some were half that length. It would all depend on the complexity of the passage, along with my specific neuromuscular unreliability.

Another important aspect of preparing for my high-risk performance was slow-motion practice—both actual and mental. I would play through the piece in slow motion from memory and play each swatch in the same fashion. I would also make sure that I could *think through* the entire ten-minute piece away from the piano, in slow motion, from memory. Then I would make sure that I could think through *each swatch* in slow motion, from memory. I would confirm that I wasn't relying on reflex to fill in a complex chord, for example. I would think up and down that chord, away from the piano, making sure that I had fixed the entire makeup of the chord in my conscious memory.

I knew that, in performance, a disruption could happen at any moment. Some impulse would try to join in, and everything would go haywire. I would suddenly have a neural blockage or a nerve shudder; or I might unconsciously begin to put together one work-around with another one in a different way. There were incalculable neuromuscular unknowns and seemingly infinite variations on such events. I wanted to be so secure in knowing the material mentally that I could make a lightning-quick judgment as to how to recover, or how to take a slightly different neural path, in the heat of the moment. Almost anything could happen at any split second as I played a piece of music.

Presenting complex musical/pianistic material that required neuromuscular complexity of impulse, reflex, and strength in this way was indeed comparable to a death-defying act. And this is where the adrenaline from "performance nerves" came in.

In the heat of performance, with adrenaline flowing, time seems to slow down. That is why inexperienced performers tend to play a piece of music faster than they've practiced it. Or if they try to keep to the same tempo they've practiced, even those with normal reflexes can find themselves in a frightening position. What comes next? Too much time to think!

But if you are keeping to the intended tempo during the performance, you can also welcome the adrenaline-induced sensation of having much more room between successive notes, even between microscopic movements. From my detailed slow-motion and "swatch" practice, I knew exactly what should come next. That knowledge gave me life preservers that could rescue me from any neurological hiccup, nerve shudder, or sudden neural blockage.

Since I was so well prepared, I could welcome the extra time the adrenaline gave me. I could even take chances. In the adrenalized slowdown, there were times when I would suddenly try to call on an old, rusty reflex or some new, dangerous-feeling connection that I wouldn't have dared to try while practicing, or that wouldn't even have occurred to me post-polio. If I did try it in performance mode, and it didn't feel possible, the adrenaline time-stretch gave me a chance to recover quickly and go back to what I had so carefully prepared.

In the play-throughs, I also tried to maintain a sense of joy in sharing the music with friends, despite my limitations. I didn't sink or swim right away. I took all kinds of neuromuscular wrong turns and steps-too-far. But after every few performances under these circumstances, I was clearly finding paths in the only way paths could be found for someone in my condition.

I'm describing split-second, microscopic things here; and the whole process was possible only because I had carefully prepared those life preservers throughout. And if an impulse that had popped up only in performance came back during another performance, I recognized it and felt easier about taking a chance on it for the second, third, or fourth time. My play-throughs built upon each other.

Thus, the key to making further progress was indeed the act of performance itself, supported by the positive preparation for performance and by a continuously refreshed vision of the sublime musical image. The possibilities that occurred to me in the adrenalized state would never have popped up in my normal struggling piano practice. And without those performances, the advice that I should turn away from piano playing and resign myself to following a different life path would have been accurate. But thanks to Amelia and Eve, and the performing opportunities they created, I was taking my first steps on the path to a miracle.

Chapter Twelve

~∾

The First Miracle

From time to time Amelia would casually broach the subject of my making a trial run back onto the concert stage—preferably in a low-pressure situation. I found that idea difficult to discuss and would usually shift the conversation to my goal of a teaching career. I was hoping to apply to some of the local college and university music departments. Of course, my *curriculum vitae* would look much better if I could take the step Amelia was suggesting, even onto a small community stage.

Meanwhile, Martha and Dady had come to the United States—to White Plains, New York, where David and Eileen lived. Martha had given birth to their first child, Navroj, and she and Dady wanted me to be the baby's godmother. Their invitation was irresistible enough to tear me away from Malibu and my piano work for a while. We had a warm reunion, focused on Martha and Dady's adorable new son, with whom I fell in love at first sight.

While I was in White Plains, Webster got in touch and surprisingly suggested that I play for a well-known pianist-teacher in New York City, just to get an "objective" opinion of my playing. Although I was fearful, I didn't want to refuse the challenge.

Before the audition, I attended one of this teacher's master classes to get an idea of his musical approach. His comments to the young pianists who participated weren't especially insightful, but the attendees seemed to hang on his every word. Once the others had left, I played for him privately, and he had mostly negative comments about my playing, which reinforced my worst fears about how far I still had to go. On the other hand, I recognized those criticisms as a strategy to gain a new student: His main message was that I needed a good deal of *his* advice and help if I were ever to amount to anything. I couldn't get out of his studio fast enough.

A friend of mine in Michigan, who worked closely with a local presenter there, had set up a meeting for me with a New York artist manager, Sherman Pitluck. I didn't see how this could lead to anything, but Martha and David encouraged me to go ahead, even if it only resulted in crossing another item off my list. To my surprise, Sherman Pitluck turned out to be a quietly friendly but businesslike person who was happy to meet with me. He explained some of the realities of the concert scene and asked if I would like to play for him. An audition for an artist manager, just like that? I had figured that he was doing my friend a favor and hadn't expected that he would want to hear me play.

But could playing for a professional manager possibly be a worse experience than my recent encounter with the "master teacher"? Since I had nothing to lose, I played some of the repertoire that I had developed in my many play-throughs. To my amazement, Pitluck seemed immediately interested and suggested that I also audition for his colleague, Mark Bichurin. Bichurin, a large man with a resonant voice and a thick Russian accent, also had a friendly demeanor, liked what he heard, and seemed interested in exploring some possible tours.

The two men explained that Pitluck managed artists who toured in the United States and Bichurin handled tours for

American artists in Europe. They had both worked for Hurok Artist Management earlier in their careers, and Pitluck had also been with Columbia Artists, so they knew the ropes. They felt that the best approach was to see if Bichurin could get me some tour dates in Europe first, as those were more readily available. That made sense, as I had seen many young Americans, especially singers, turn to Europe for performance opportunities that they hadn't found at home.

Pitluck went on to explain that if the response in Europe turned out to be positive, resulting in some good reviews, he could then go after tour dates for me in the U.S. Bichurin warned that the European tour, if he were successful in setting it up, would not be lucrative; in fact, I would undoubtedly lose money by the time I had paid my travel expenses. I told him that would be OK.

This unexpected development happened so suddenly that it seemed somewhat unreal. Fortunately, neither man asked my age or much about my background. I told them a few details about my college years—studying with Webster Aitken and winning a couple of competitions—and that I had studied further in Europe. I mentioned the magic name of Nadia Boulanger as one of my teachers and referred to my study of Baroque style in Vienna. Every detail was accurate; I just never mentioned polio.

When I returned to White Plains that evening, I was still in shock over the reception I'd received from the two managers. David practically threw his hat in the air, exclaiming: "But you're *in!*" (He made it sound like "Bichurin.")

"I'm *in?* David! This is just a toe in the water!" I cautioned. But he was enjoying it so much that I let the evening be a celebratory one, while telling myself that I'd believe those European dates when I saw them. I hadn't even started to wrap my mind around how I would carry out such a tour.

Once back in Malibu, I found that Amelia and Eve were as excited as David had been. I tried not to get my hopes up, but couldn't help thinking about what program would be best to offer if the tour materialized.

I felt relatively secure playing the Bach Chromatic Fantasy and Fugue in my informal performances, so the three of us agreed that it could be a fine program opener. My beloved Beethoven Sonata Opus 111, which by then had been the focal point of many a play-through, could be a musically powerful second half of such a program. For a couple of years, I had also been preparing a group of Chopin Preludes—especially appropriate choices for me because each one was short and not too demanding on any aspect of my physical endurance. And yet each Prelude could create a unique sound picture and mood—perhaps one reason the Chopin group had become a favorite for our play-through audiences.

As I thought about the significance of such a tour, should it come to pass, I kept thinking of Mademoiselle Boulanger, and the special piece of sheet music she had given me when I left Paris. It was the Fauré 13th Nocturne, a late piano work of Gabriel Fauré, who had been her teacher. As such, this work represented her great love for his music. Mademoiselle had inscribed the piece to me, and I had worked on it intermittently, enjoying its spare, intimate beauty. If I were to put that nocturne on a tour program, perhaps it could be a talisman, carrying with it Mademoiselle's wishes for my musical recovery. Amelia and Eve both loved the idea, so I set to work making the piece secure.

To my surprise, in only a few weeks Bichurin got back to me with some specific engagements for March and April of 1964, starting with an appearance in Stockholm. It was really going to happen! I would be making my European debut at the advanced age of thirty! I just had to avoid potential questions about my "debut" age and hope that the word "polio" never came up.

I sent Bichurin the suggested program, to which I had added a couple of my favorite Schubert Impromptus. The first half had a nice variety, and the second half was devoted to Beethoven's monumental Opus 111. He liked it and said that he would pass the program along to his presenters.

Eve's immediate response was to plan a shopping trip. She wanted plenty of time to make sure that the performance gown—or gowns—would be stunning. I protested that we had months to worry about my wardrobe, but she was determined. "Stunning" was fine with me, but secondary; first and foremost, any gown we chose would have to be comfortable to play in. It was just as well that we started early. Coming up with solutions that satisfied both requirements became a major effort. But we finally found two gowns that would work.

My parents were thrilled and wanted to help set up play-throughs in Michigan. They and a few of their friends arranged a couple of appearances in the Detroit area a few weeks before the tour began. Other family friends came through with an invitation to play the program in La Jolla, California.

Meanwhile, Carolyn said that I could count on her to host any number of full program play-throughs at her house. Two new friends in Santa Monica, pianist-composer Francis Hendricks and his wife, Katie, who had a beautiful nine-foot Steinway in their home, invited me to play the program there.

As I tried to absorb the prospect of returning to the stage, Amelia and I had some in-depth conversations about mind-set. One of the principles we discussed was a simple but effective technique, useful in all sorts of situations, that she called "acting as if." When Amelia taught social workers and probation officers to work with families, one of her techniques was to "act as if" they were, for example, relaxed and calm around their clients. Amelia demonstrated how she would stretch her arm over the back of a chair or couch, or otherwise "open up" her body posture so that the client subconsciously felt more at ease. At the very beginning of a session with clients, the "acting as if" might be a conscious effort; but soon the more relaxed state becomes internalized for everyone in the room, including oneself.

If I could, to some extent, "act as if" the larger audience, the larger hall, the higher-pressure situation were similar to my play-throughs in Eve's living room, I could put myself into a state I had already experienced as a means of communicating the music despite my neuromuscular disabilities.

As in the play-throughs, the sublime musical vision needed to coexist at every moment with an artificial neuromuscular substitute. I had been learning to accept a finger stroke, or shove with the wrist, or any other "work-around," in such a way as not to disturb that exalted musical image.

In my play-throughs there was a "near place" and an "encompassing place." The "near place" was where the careful retraining of each small movement and impulse—each micro-movement and micro-impulse—happened on an ongoing basis. This was the area that suddenly seemed exposed with the time-stretch of the adrenalized state.

The "encompassing place" was the entirety of the music—beginning with the inner vision of the sublime content—flowing through me and through the instrument, becoming part of the room and the room's atmosphere. The larger the room, the larger the encompassing place.

As a teenage pianist, the encompassing place was where I had dwelled; I performed often and always thought in terms of communicating the music. I had done careful work in the near place, to refine detail and develop solid technique, but in those days it had always merged seamlessly with the encompassing-place flow.

But now, in getting used to the idea of playing for a larger audience in a more formal situation, I needed to keep all of this in focus to offer the public this music that meant so much to me. And I needed to "act as if," as Amelia put it, and see the audience as friendly if I were ever again to feel at home on the stage.

I played the concert program in performance mode twelve times in the weeks before leaving for Stockholm at the end of February. The agonizing first concert, in Detroit, took place on

November 1, which happened to be my thirtieth birthday. I had made sure Mom and Dad got the word out to their friends that I didn't want anything said about my illness to the press. The announcement that appeared was simply stated:

> *Carol Rosenberger will make her professional piano debut in a recital at the Detroit Institute of Arts November 1. The concert, which has already been sold out, will be repeated November 3. Miss Rosenberger has performed in this area since she was eight years old. She studied here with the late Edward Bredshall and in Pittsburgh under Webster Aitken, during which time she received several awards, including the Steinway Centennial Award. In Paris, she studied privately with Nadia Boulanger, and in Vienna, attended the Vienna Music Academy. Since her return to the United States, she has pursued her musical activities on the West Coast."*

The only thing I remember about those two concerts was pacing backstage beforehand, just as I had done as a teenager. I kept thinking of Bredshall, backstage there with me so many times when I had played in that hall years before. He would be smiling and encouraging me to think through the opening of the first piece I was going to play. That was the most calming thing one could do before a performance, he always said, and of course he was right. The rest is a blur, though I remember trying to focus on playing for all the friends in the audience.

Soon after I returned to California following the Detroit concerts, Amelia called from work with news so shocking that for a moment I thought it must be a horrible dream: President John F. Kennedy had been shot in Dallas. In the ensuing weeks, as Amelia, Eve, and I watched the gripping TV footage and discussed the fallout from the assassination, along with the rest of the country, everything we were working on individually felt unreal.

Just before I left for the European tour, Webster arrived in LA. We arranged to spend an afternoon together, and I was looking forward to outlining the whole tour plan with him in a leisurely fashion. But as we sipped our tea, I could tell that he was anything but relaxed. When we discussed my imminent departure for Stockholm, the first stop on the tour, I was distressed to see that the color had drained from his face. I suddenly realized that he was not just worried, but all-out frightened for me. And my own anxieties increased once it was clear that he doubted whether my reconstructed techniques would hold up in the spotlight of a strenuous concert tour.

Webster was not the only one. Even in my most positive mode, encouraged by Amelia and Eve, setting out for the tour felt more like a dangerous mission than a triumph. At my highest anxiety levels, I was just plain terrified. I tried to reassure myself that if I could just bring home a positive review or two, I might be better able to get a college teaching job.

For me, it was critical that the words "illness" or "polio" never come up. I didn't want anyone to be watching for a disability to manifest itself; and I wanted any response to my playing to be unbiased. On the other hand, I had to get help with my luggage, even the lightest of hand luggage, or I would be unable to play at all. At each stage of the journey, this was not only a constant worry but also an embarrassment.

When I arrived in Stockholm, the head presenter was out of town, and his assistant seemed bored with her job. Everything she did and said increased my fear quotient. When she only grudgingly helped with my luggage, I knew that we were getting off on the wrong foot. In the taxi from the airport, she casually mentioned that we would have a good crowd, but that some Swedish critics didn't like American musicians. If I didn't receive a warm reception, I shouldn't take it personally.

When we got out of the taxi, she asked the driver for a receipt, and once again I waited awkwardly for her help with the hand luggage. The American duo-pianists and twin brothers Richard and John Contiguglia were just coming out of the hotel, and she introduced us nonchalantly. Their performance would be the evening after mine. The brothers were friendly and relaxed, and assured me that they would be at my recital. Although I was grateful for their warm greeting, knowing that they were coming to hear me made me even more nervous. Would professional pianists of their caliber see through some of my precarious neuromuscular structure?

Both the backstage milieu and the hall itself are dim in my memory, and I was too nervous to have any idea how I'd played. The manager's assistant came backstage at intermission and tactlessly mentioned that the critics were all leaving. I knew that happened sometimes for practical reasons and tried my best not to panic.

The next morning, on our way to the airport, the assistant told me that the reviews were "all bad." I didn't even ask what they had said. By then I was just trying to hang on through ever-increasing panic. I was trying to ward off the feeling that I was a fake.

In Copenhagen, the next stop on the tour, the atmosphere was different. The concert management people were welcoming, and I knew that some of my friends from Blegdam Hospital would be coming to the concert. I also recognized that nothing could be more difficult than that first experience in Stockholm. And no matter how I played, I had come a great distance from the time I'd been in Copenhagen as a patient. Perhaps that awareness helped me relax a little, too. After I had played the Bach, the audience broke into enthusiastic applause, and I relaxed a little more. (Secret tip for all concertgoers: Applaud like mad after the first piece, as the performer will give a better performance of the rest of the program.)

Backstage after the concert, I was greeted by the Blegdam physical therapy team, Mrs. Buttrup and her relatives, and a few other acquaintances from my months as a patient. Along with hugs were wide smiles and tears of joy. At Mrs. Buttrup's side was a tall, charming young man with glasses and a big smile; it was Marcel, all grown up! After he had said something enthusiastic about the recital in fluent English, he had a question for me: "Remember when you put the bird gravel in the soup?" We had a good laugh, and I complimented him on his English. It was a kind of homecoming for me, and I could see that everyone felt the same way.

The tour took me next to Oslo, The Hague, Amsterdam, and Zurich. The Amsterdam and Hague audiences were especially warm and receptive, giving me a standing ovation at intermission. It was their custom to welcome an artist in this way, but their friendliness had a positive effect on me, and I was more relaxed for the second half. It was heartening to play the Beethoven under these reassuring circumstances, and I knew that I would always be grateful to these people no matter what the reviewers might write.

Then it was on to Vienna. Martha and Dady had returned to the Köllnerhof flat after the birth of their adorable little Nuvi (the nickname for Navroj), and it was good to be with them again. Although we were all nervous about the Vienna reception, the performance seemed to go quite well. Martha told me afterward that, in general, American pianists weren't much treasured by the Viennese reviewers, so I shouldn't be disappointed by whatever they wrote.

The after-concert party was enthusiastic and comforting. Professor Eibner was there—clearly excited that I was playing once again. We all sat around a large table, and he sat next to me, partly smiling and laughing, partly with tears in his eyes.

The last two concerts were in Salzburg and Athens. Since I had an extra day before flying back to the United States, I had a chance to visit the Acropolis and the Parthenon. I knew that Amelia would be excited to hear about these visits, as she had felt a great love for ancient Greek culture since childhood, when her father had introduced her to its language and philosophy.

Back in the States, I went first to Michigan, played the tour program at Oakland University, reunited with my parents, and then flew back to California. Once I was home in Malibu, I received two packets in the mail: one from Martha with clippings of the Vienna reviews and one from Bichurin with all the European reviews, translated by his staff. They were magnificent.

I was stunned. In review after review, the glowing comments were far beyond anything I could have hoped for. An Amsterdam review called me "a young pianist of stature." The Vienna headline read, *"Sie Kam, Spielte, Faszinierte"* ("She Came, She Played, She Fascinated.") A Zurich reviewer commented, "If we're any judge at all, a new star has appeared in the pianistic heavens." Even the Stockholm reviews, which I had been told two months before were "all bad," said simply that I was like so many other American pianists: all technique and no soul. Once I had seen the other reviews, the Stockholm comments read almost like a bitter joke.

Soon after I got back, I played a recital at the Santa Monica (Assistance League) Playhouse that had been set up before I left for Europe. A well-known Los Angeles critic wrote a laudatory review of that performance as well.

Sherman Pitluck, meanwhile, got in touch to say that he was ready to sign me up with his management and had already created a flyer with his favorite quotes from the European reviews. I could hardly believe it. Nine years after the polio attack, I was a "pro" at last!

There was one problem, however: I had never told Sherman the story of my illness and years-long struggle to recover. I felt it should be done in person, and scheduled a trip to New York, explaining that I wanted to get together and talk about the future. We had a relaxed and positive discussion over dinner and some wine, and once we were nearing the end of our meal, I leaned forward and said, "Sherman, there is something I need to tell you." My serious tone clearly alerted him. "I don't want you to tell anyone," I continued, "except perhaps Mark Bichurin, but you'd have to tell him to keep it to himself." He nodded in consent.

Then I launched into the story of my polio attack and recovery years, complete with the true state of my neuromuscular condition. I knew it would be shocking and wanted to make sure he was aware of my disability before we signed a contract. I thought he might be wary or possibly concerned about my physical limitations in terms of carrying out further tours. If this worried him, I also wanted to give him a chance to back out of our contract.

But Sherman's first response was not what I expected. "People should know about this!" he exclaimed. "There is *no* reason to keep it a secret!" I told him my fear that anyone who knew might suddenly notice some of my work-arounds and think of me as less of a pianist. Presenters might worry about my reliability.

But Sherman was on a roll of excitement. "What an inspiring story!" he kept saying. "I can't wait to tell (so-and-so) about it!" Every time he thought of someone else in the business who "should know," he would get excited all over again.

His jaw had dropped when I told him about the polio, but now mine did, as I tried to grasp his response. Every objection or "but what about . . ." that I came up with, he dismissed as totally unimportant. Finally, I gave in and told him that he had my permission to handle telling my story as he wished. I didn't have to ask Amelia for *her* opinion; I already knew what she would say. Since the very first day we met, she had thought my polio story should not be kept secret.

Both Sherman and Amelia turned out to be right. In all the years I played in public from that time on, not one negative word appeared about my disability. No one ever speculated that my such-and-such finger must be weak, or was strangely positioned in some specific musical passage, or whatever else I might have been afraid people would say. On the contrary, in countless radio interviews and other ways I was to meet the public, people wanted to discuss their own problems with a right-hand thumb or a left wrist, or all kinds of other conditions, hoping that I might have some advice. Far from being something that kept me out of the performance world, my disability enabled me to be helpful, or at least encouraging, to others.

Chapter Thirteen

Back Onstage, and
Heartbreak in LA

With reviews from my European tour in hand, Sherman embarked enthusiastically on his quest for concert dates in the United States and asked me for a list of concerto repertoire. I hadn't even thought that far. I named five of the concertos I had played pre-polio and then mapped out a plan to approach them anew with my "work-around" techniques. Considering how much thought and care needed to go into reworking all five concertos, that was a tall order.

Next, I needed to decide on repertoire for the next European solo tour Mark Bichurin was already working on. I wanted to begin the program with a Handel suite and include another of my favorite Beethoven sonatas, the "Waldstein." The all-important initial play-throughs began once more, with Eve and Carolyn hosting the gatherings.

A few invitations to play for groups in California also began to come my way—among them, a performance for a local chapter of the Music Teachers' Association. This Los Angeles performance brought me some new private students, who were enjoyable to work with and helped me stay solvent.

Between Bichurin and Pitluck, my 1965 concert schedule was dotted with performances and auditions. Besides preparing thoroughly for each one, I had to sort out attendant details: travel reservations; who was meeting me at each destination airport; prescription refills for anti-inflammatories; even careful notes about my wardrobe, so that I didn't repeat a performance gown in the same, or a neighboring, town.

Still uneasy that the polio story was out, I told myself that when people saw me walk effortlessly into a room or onto a stage, bow gracefully, and seat myself easily on the piano bench, any worries that the "polio girl" might not be able to deliver the goods would be put to rest.

If anyone asked me about problems with my arms and hands, I tried to answer in the past tense, figuring that almost everyone likes to hear a story with a happy ending. My "happy ending" was that after going through hell for a long time, I had come back to a normal life and piano playing.

Privately, however, I was grabbing every chance I could to rest and soothe, stretch and treat the most damaged and vulnerable upper-body muscles. I knew that I should take everything one step at a time, but anxiety was building. En route to Europe for my second tour, I stopped in New York for a couple of auditions and then flew to Scandinavia for concerts in Oslo and Copenhagen. By that time, I was having what felt like a sustained anxiety attack. As I wrote to Amelia:

> *Perhaps it's just the sum total of what I'm undertaking, but it seems so much larger this time! Last year in Europe I had no expectations. . . . Now, since I have hope for the first time, I'm afraid to see those hopes destroyed. There's more at stake now because I'm hoping that I can dare to give out what I feel about music. Last time was more of an experiment.*

What am I doing this for, anyway? With a new set of reflexes? When you think of it, it's absurd. As we know, the channels couldn't be as deep yet as they are for someone who hasn't had to redo it all.

If I can be this nervous after I've played the repertoire so many times, can I really trust my reflexes after all? If I tighten, I'm too tight. If I loosen, there are too many breaks in the fabric.

The tranquilizer I take late in the evening works in a strange way. I'm sleepy in between waves of anxiety. Then I hope it wears off in the course of the next afternoon. Maybe I'm building this thing up out of all proportion. Maybe last time was a fluke. I know I've gone a long way, considering where I started. But I feel as if I may have used too much to come up to this point. So there is nothing left for public performance.

Amelia responded to my letter by calling me long distance. She suggested that I first try weaning myself off the tranquilizer for a few days to see if that helped. She thought I might be having an adverse reaction to the tranquilizer itself, experiencing peaks and valleys rather than the calming effect I was hoping for.

She also understood why I felt more pressure this time around. My shoulders began to relax a little just because of her understanding. We discussed how the "acting as if" and talking myself into an attitude of communicating could begin to outweigh the fear. If I could talk myself into simulating a state of greater calm, it would gradually become internalized and integrated. Amelia was right, as usual. After the first performance, I wrote:

My God, what a relief! I don't even care what the reviewers say. After the nerves of yesterday and today I'm glad to have played decently. As it was, I think I did more than that. I almost died during the Handel. Tried

*like mad to loosen up in the Beethoven. I did, halfway
through, and simulated what I do when relaxed as well
as I could. It was basically my Beethoven, though. Musically the fabric did hold all the way through because I
gave through the tension, and kept forcing myself to play
rather than to be held back by terror.*

*After the concert I had the first meal I've enjoyed
since I left California. I have forced lots of food down;
still lost a little weight, I think. I don't mind that, but
what a way to lose it.*

During the rest of the tour I gradually became a little less
agitated, considerably helped by a few more long-distance talks
with Amelia. She would remind me of something she found
unique in my playing and that, in her opinion, this part of the
process was well worth the struggle.

Knowing about the major problems Amelia faced every
day helped me to put my own fears into perspective. She had
become the chief psychologist at Lathrop, a treatment center
for young people who had been in lockup and were potential
candidates for reuniting with their families. The Los Angeles
County Juvenile Probation Department had started this innovative treatment program, with Amelia at the helm. She held
weekly meetings with each of the youngsters in the program,
along with any family members she could pull in, and the probation officer, social worker, and nurse counselor assigned to
the case. The objective was to get the young people back home
whenever possible. During the same period, Amelia was also
driving around the county to teach probation officers how to
work with families.

My next group of performances took me to the Nether-
lands—Haarlem, The Hague, and Amsterdam. The concert
manager, Harry de Freese, was based in Amsterdam. Harry was
a lovely person, and welcomed me into both his management

"family" and his own, in heartening post-concert get-togethers. One such party, at his daughter's apartment, was memorable for the climb up very steep stairs to her sitting room. It felt like climbing a ladder, but I had lots of help in both directions, supported by smiles and laughter all around. As I had found during my first tour in Holland, the demonstrative warmth of the audiences helped me to relax and "give" more.

As I continued touring, smaller problems like saving the muscles in my hands and arms for the big job of playing were an ongoing issue. I summed up those difficulties in a letter to Amelia: "Leave out things you have to do with hands and wrists, and not much is left! I even gave up trying to cut the *entrecôte* I'd ordered from room service, and left the rest of it. Next time I'll order something soft!"

But I had an exciting bit of news to tell Amelia and Eve after my performance in Salzburg: "Imagine finding out that Wilhelm Backhaus was in the audience! He liked the 'Waldstein.' In fact, he told Gmachl [the presenter] that I was exceptional. Gmachl told me he thought I was good last year, but much better this year. He said the Beethoven was a true interpretation. One of life's pleasant surprises...."

Then it was on to Vienna to play the new program, and to London for a meeting with Wilfred van Wyck, the presenter of my UK appearances scheduled for early 1966. And finally I returned to Malibu, my two dear friends, and those much-anticipated relaxing walks on the beach.

In the meantime, Dad had retired from General Motors, and he and Mom had moved to Southern California. It was wonderful that we could see each other more often, since they were only a two-hour drive away. Typically, they had found a "fixer" in a good neighborhood, just as they had as newlyweds in Detroit and later in the Detroit suburbs in 1942. Their new home was in Rancho Santa Fe, a rustic area north of San Diego that they were enjoying, and my father was cheerfully fixing up a house yet again. I was delighted to discover that this house, like many in Southern California, had a pool, where one could swim all year around.

In early January, I began the second lap of Bichurin's European tour for that season, with performances in Brussels, Cologne, Berlin, and London. The Berlin audience was as warm as the climate was cold, but the next day something went wrong at Tempelhof airport. We were forced to sit in a cold plane for some hours, waiting for the connection to London; and as London passengers, our papers were not cleared for us to go into the terminal. When I finally arrived in London, it was too late for warm water or anything else to dispel the chill, and I woke up with a cold the next day. My main concern during that London concert was getting through it without sneezing. Fortunately, my ever-reliable performance adrenalin came to the rescue, edging out the histamine reaction until well after I had finished playing.

While I was on tour in Europe, Sherman had been busy lining up interviews and concert dates in Portland, Seattle, Indianapolis, Pittsburgh, St. Louis, Houston, and other cities. He particularly enjoyed a review by Corbin Patrick in the *Indianapolis Star:*

> *The Grieg served admirably to introduce the beauty, grace, and talent of Miss Rosenberger, a truly gifted young artist who could just as well be (and maybe she is) the heroine in a romance. She revealed style and sensitivity, not to mention the complete technical equipment we expect of young artists these days. . . . Highly expressive performance.*

Once back in Malibu, I began catching up with private students, working on a new solo program, and planning new repertoire play-throughs in Eve's living room. One day she said that in the next gathering she was going to include a young man she thought might be fun for me to meet. His name was Morrie Peltz, whom she had met a couple of times at a neighbor's house, along with his young children, Caroline and John. He was recently divorced and, in her estimation, was brilliant. He had been something of a child prodigy, accepted by the University of Chicago at age thirteen and graduating at sixteen. He had gone on to study Asian and Middle Eastern philosophy and culture, had worked abroad for a few years, and was now consulting in Santa Monica.

For the next play-through, Morrie—tall, intense, and with a winning smile—was among the guests. When I finished playing the first piece, Morrie leapt to his feet, applauding loudly and shouting, "Brava! Brava!" That didn't happen very often in Eve's living room, or in Carolyn's for that matter, so I was quite amazed and couldn't help laughing along with his lively cheers. After I had played the rest of the program, Morrie had the same enthusiastic response.

During refreshments afterward, Morrie and I fell into conversation, and I found out that he loved theater, as did I, and obviously seemed to enjoy classical music. He asked me if I'd like to have dinner with him sometime soon, and I agreed that I would indeed. We felt an instant, mutual attraction.

It wasn't long before we were seeing each other often, and soon Morrie wanted to bring his children over to meet me. They lived with their mother and saw Morrie mostly on weekends. As they were coming up the stairs, I heard a young voice say to him, "Is this the lady with the nice apartment?" Evidently the answer was yes, and both children seemed to enjoy the balcony that overlooked the Santa Monica Bay. We all went for a walk on the beach, then to dinner, and it looked as if I had passed the approval test with both Caroline and John.

Things escalated as quickly as my schedule would allow, but I was still surprised by Morrie's marriage proposal just a few months after we had met. When I told Eve, she was horrified, which somewhat confused me, as she had, after all, introduced us. "I just wanted you to have fun dating someone!" she exclaimed. "I *never* meant for you to *marry* him!"

Amelia had a far more positive reaction. She knew that, in the decade-plus since the polio attack, I had missed out on normal romantic relationships. There had been a couple of brief flings after my relationship with Sam ended, but nothing emotionally satisfying. Amelia was clearly hoping that my relationship with Morrie would be a positive experience.

When Morrie met my parents, Mom guardedly accepted him, while Dad looked as if he didn't trust him at all. On the other hand, Morrie's parents were quite friendly, and his sister, Mary, very much so. Mary was about my height, and their parents were of relatively short stature. When Morrie's tallness came up, Mary chuckled and confided the family joke that they must have brought the wrong baby home from the hospital. In general, everybody but Eve and Dad seemed pleased.

We were married in a simple wedding ceremony in September of 1966, with Amelia as my matron of honor. Morrie and I drove through some beautiful parts of California on our brief honeymoon, then settled down in my Malibu apartment. Wedded bliss was mine at last! Here was an intellectually stimulating and romantically attractive man who wanted to be in a committed relationship with me—something my post-polio experiences over the previous ten years had told me was unlikely to happen.

But soon I had concert dates, auditions, interviews and, when I was at home, my private piano students to catch up with. It wasn't long before Morrie began to mention feeling left out when I shut myself into my little studio to do the necessary piano work for these ongoing activities. Since Morrie had a job as a consultant, some of his work could be done at home, and he didn't have to go into the office every day, or at least not for long. He had anticipated fun times at home when he could hear me play pieces of music, but he found himself bored by my endless practice and teaching sessions. I had tried to explain to him what my work as a pianist and teacher entailed, but he was still unprepared for the day-to-day reality. I hoped he would get used to it as time went on.

On the other hand, Morrie and I had a great time going to out-of-the-way films and taking long walks on the beach, when he would do much of the talking about all sorts of far-flung ideas and experiences. He had an extensive knowledge of Asian culture, and he knew a lot about the Middle East as well, since he had traveled there soon after his graduate study. He'd even worked a couple of years for the Shah of Iran. Morrie was always full of surprises, and he kept me guessing and laughing.

A simple visit to the Malibu supermarket turned into a scene that lingers in my memory. Morrie—clad in bathing trunks, a loose shirt, and tennis shoes—rode the shopping cart like a slow scooter through the aisles of the market, reciting eloquent passages from Shakespeare's *Henry V* in his most resonant baritone. I expected someone to come along and ask him to keep it down, but both shoppers and employees seemed to be enjoying the show.

A few months further into our marriage, something happened that was a positive for me but probably a negative for Morrie, even though it promised to make us more financially secure. Following a *curriculum vitae* mailing I had sent to area colleges and universities, the head of the music department at Immaculate Heart College, Sister Mary Mark Zeyen, responded and asked to set up a time to talk by phone.

The ensuing conversation, a delightful meeting of the minds about many aspects of music and teaching, lasted about an hour and a half. I already knew that Sister Mary Mark and her two real-life sisters, a violinist and a cellist, had formed the Immaculate Heart Trio and built a fine reputation in Los Angeles, partly through their performances and partly through their recordings for Capitol Records. Sister Mary Mark had been teaching piano at Immaculate Heart and had recently become head of its music department. Now she was looking for her part-time replacement as piano faculty.

She was impressed by the review quotes in my résumé and not a bit dismayed when I told her about my post-polio fight back to the keyboard. But what we bonded about most was our mutual love of teaching, which for both of us had begun at an early age. By the end of that conversation, I had a job on the piano faculty, sight unseen and piano playing unheard. Mary Mark told me a few months later that when one of her other piano faculty members heard how I'd been hired, he had exclaimed, "Over the *phone?* You hired a new faculty member *over the phone?*" We laughed about that for years.

It didn't take long to recognize that the prevailing atmosphere among the Immaculate Heart College faculty was flexible and innovative. Mary Mark became a friend, as did a member of the voice faculty, Sister Theresa di Rocco; and one weekend when Morrie was off with his children and Amelia was home, I invited both sisters to come out to Malibu and meet Amelia and Eve.

Mary Mark and Theresa were part of a group of nuns who believed in the interconnectedness of education and general improvement of a community. They immediately felt a "common cause" with Amelia and her work. They were also interested to meet Eve, whose family was Catholic and whose younger cousin, Sister Joel Read, was the president of Alverno College in Milwaukee. Sister Joel was also a founding member of the then-new National Organization for Women (NOW).

I suggested to Mary Mark that at IHC we might try some joint classes with both voice and piano students working together on some of the great art song literature. She loved the idea, and we set up, together with Theresa and another member of the voice faculty, Gloria Steppe, such a workshop as an elective part of the curriculum. I also suggested an experimental class in Schenker Theory. Mary Mark welcomed that too, and as we got it going, we were all delighted at how quickly the students could grasp and make good use of Schenker's concepts.

The music department was small enough that I quickly got to know the other faculty members as well. It was the perfect job for me since it was part-time, and the piano students Mary Mark assigned to me included a diverse group of abilities, interests, and ages. Some of my students loved coming out to Malibu for their lessons, which gave me some good flexibility in my own schedule; for the most part I needed to drive into the Los Feliz area of Los Angeles—where the college was located—only a couple of days per week.

My parents were delighted that I had formal employment, as they had worried for some time about what I would do if our modest farm income dried up. Although Morrie had his consultant's job, he needed to pay expenses for his ex-wife and two children. For him, it had been a financial relief to move in with me.

One day I invited Morrie to hear some of my students play a recital at the IHC Auditorium. Since I had scheduled a rehearsal for the performers beforehand, Morrie said he would come separately. He turned up in a college football sweater, while my students, their families, their friends, and I had all dressed up for the occasion. When I thought about it, I realized that due to his accelerated intellectual development, he had been of high school age during his college years, and had probably never fit in. No wonder he might misjudge the costume for the role he was playing that evening. For all I knew, his Joe College sweater might have been to enliven the atmosphere and relieve the tension of the students' performance nerves. Morrie's thinking was unlike anyone else's, and he always had a sense of fun, along with a desire to lighten things up.

One day, Eve told Amelia and me that she wanted to take

a long-anticipated trip to Mexico and Central America. She had been experiencing some physical symptoms that had no clear diagnosis, and wanted to take the trip while she was still feeling up to it. She invited Amelia to go along and added that, as far as she could see, Amelia hadn't had a real vacation in a long time.

Eve also knew that I was discussing my marital problems with Amelia, and thought I should deal with that issue for a while without the "cushion" of being able to talk it through with my trusted friend. I encouraged Amelia to go, as I knew she loved to experience parts of the world that she had never seen. So off they went, and Morrie and I were on our own.

When I looked objectively at our relationship, it was clear that Morrie and I had met at the wrong time in my career, and probably too soon after his divorce from his first wife. Even though I was very much in love, I had already paid too high a price to let my piano work slide or to turn my back on either performance or teaching opportunities. Morrie, after being hurt by the divorce from his first wife, probably needed much more care and attention than I had anticipated.

Although I had explained to Morrie many times that I was trying to keep the piano sound contained in my home studio so that he could do whatever he wished in the rest of the apartment, that did not satisfy his expectations. He wanted more from me during the normal daytime and evening hours than I could realistically offer.

Morrie had always done a wide variety of things with such ease that he couldn't possibly have understood the enormous effort I'd had to make over the twelve-plus years since my polio attack. His brilliant brain also moved along too fast to stop and take in what I was up against, even at that stage of my recovery.

In an abstract way, Morrie knew that I was still a physically damaged person. He had heard me say that I was stretching my upper-body neuromuscular endurance as far as possible each day. It was a difficult thing to explain to most people, and I had been hoping for his gradual understanding. But Morrie could never quite grasp how far I had to push myself, and whatever I *could* give just wasn't enough to keep him content.

In a typical at-home scenario, I would emerge from a studio practice session, and Morrie would be reading. I'd say something cheerful to him; he'd look up and say, "As you can see, I'm reading," or just, "I'm reading," and then go back to his material. It was his answer to all that practicing I insisted on doing. I understood both the subliminal message and the underlying problem, but had no solution.

A revelatory moment came one evening while my close friends were on vacation. I had a performance in the Santa Monica area, the kind of event that Amelia and sometimes Eve would drive me to, if they possibly could, and then stay for the concert. They both knew that my arms and hands had a limited amount of endurance, and that it would ease that situation if someone else drove me to the venue.

I had explained all of this to Morrie many times, telling him how much it helped when someone drove me to performances. But as I got ready to leave, I could see that he hadn't dressed to go with me. I put my dress bag with gown and shoes in the hallway, where he could see it clearly. Then I went back to get my smaller bag containing various supplies, such as emergency calories, fix-it for broken skin, hair spray, handkerchiefs, etc.—whatever I might need during the evening.

When I got back to the front hallway, I explained what was in the smaller bag, too, a casual-sounding attempt to ease the conversation. He scarcely looked up from his reading when I mentioned that I had to get these things down to the car, then had to be on my way to the venue early. As he knew, I would need to try the piano before the audience got there. But Morrie didn't budge. No offer to drive me there; not even a move to carry the dress bag and other gear down to the car.

I tried one last time, mentioning that my shoulders were not in great shape—something of an understatement. Still no response. So I made my way downstairs with the dress bag and then came back for the other one. Morrie looked up just long enough to wave goodbye. When I left, mingled with my usual pre-performance nervousness was a bleak feeling. I wondered what was happening to this relationship.

When I came back to the apartment, still flushed with the adrenaline of performance, Morrie didn't even ask how the concert had gone. That was the moment when I finally became aware that something was fundamentally wrong between us, and that I hadn't truly felt the full extent of it until that evening. First, Morrie had resented my piano work in the studio. Then, he had begun to resent my going off to teach or perform. Finally, he had begun to resent *me*.

Things went downhill from there. We didn't have much to say during our last conversations while we were living together. Everything had already been said. Morrie had already commented enough on my unavailability when I went into my studio. He had expressed his unhappiness that I was always accepting tour dates, auditions, interviews, and, more recently, the teaching job. I had commented enough on my dismay that he felt that way. And I had said many times that I wished he could understand why I couldn't bypass those opportunities for which I had waited so long.

I felt tearful on the fateful day when Morrie moved his things out. After he had left, I sat in great sadness, finally moving around slowly and weeping while I aimlessly rearranged my things in bureau drawers and closets.

After a few weeks of unhappy silence on both sides, Morrie called to see if I would like to get together for dinner at The Sea Lion. I accepted, and we discovered, to our surprise, that we could still enjoy dating if we weren't living together. The chemistry was still there, once we had been freed from his resentment and my resulting distress. And when he stayed overnight, we both understood that he would be leaving the next morning, like a guest. The eventual divorce was amicable, though sad. Morrie's sister, Mary, who was devoted to him, stayed in touch and seemed to understand how I felt. Eve and Amelia gave me a lot of support, though every so often Eve would remind me that she had never thought it would work.

Chapter Fourteen

৵৯

Hope Hopkins and
the Second Miracle

I plunged into preparations for upcoming concert tours, and also began spending more time in my two-piano studio at Immaculate Heart College. My students and I were taking full advantage of the chance to rehearse concerto repertoire there, since orchestral reductions could be played on the second piano. Amelia and Eve grew concerned about how much my work schedule had escalated, and in the evenings, encouraged me to relax and enjoy the end of my day. Amelia would tell me jokingly that it was time to "stop tilling the fields," one of her references to my family's farming background.

The IHC music students were a diverse group from convent and monastic life, Catholic, or public school backgrounds. They were all attracted to the small, flexible, and active music department. Their performance levels varied from a pre-college program—which Mary Mark had initiated—to graduate proficiency. Brother Salvatore, a graduate-level student, was teaching piano at a Catholic school and wanted to increase his performance skills. Valerie, a precocious fourteen-year-old in the pre-college program, was my first-ever blind student.

Since Valerie taped our lessons on her cassette recorder, I would play in slow motion any piece she was working on, giving her something that she could replay at home to help her memorize the music more easily. I would stop the slow-motion flow to *arpeggiate* a chord—spread out, or roll, the chord, starting with the lowest note—when I thought it would help her to identify every note.

Valerie felt very secure once she had learned a piece. Since she read the Braille sheet music with her fingers, and memorized as she went along, she had committed a musical work firmly to memory by the time she could play it through. She could start cold anywhere in a piece—a skill I had learned to prize. I encouraged her to keep thinking through, in slow motion, any work she was going to perform. Valerie said she enjoyed doing that; to her, it felt like a meditation.

It was a challenge to help Valerie with her technical approach to the piano. She felt safest feeling her way around the keyboard, in motions that resembled crawling. So I tried practicing with my eyes closed, to determine how secure I could be without visual help, while still giving my hands plenty of playing space. I figured that if I could sense spaces at the keyboard with my rebuilt playing mechanism, then someone with normal hands and arms should be able to do the same. I came up with some "interval jumping" exercises that I thought might give Valerie more freedom, and she tailored them to what she could do. She said it was akin to what they were teaching her at the Braille Institute, a technique called "walking in space," in which she was learning to sense spaces rather than always feeling her way around a room.

When Valerie performed, she would turn her head toward the audience while playing and smile broadly through most of a piece. I explained that the sighted audience, used to seeing performers face straight ahead, might be distracted from her musical message and might not take her playing as seriously as she deserved. So we rehearsed a more conventional head position.

When Valerie played her first full solo recital program, she was "walking in space" to and from the piano, giving her hands space at the keyboard, and saving her happy grins for between pieces. It was a wonderful evening for Valerie and for everyone who knew her.

In one of the student group sessions, I asked Valerie to show the college students how she had to learn. I could describe my own careful preparation, of course, but thought it would be more fun for everyone, including Valerie, if she could demonstrate this technique herself.

As my relationship with the students developed, it turned into an interesting give-and-take. Just as teaching had always been integrated into the rest of my life when I was in my teens, it was developing that way at IHC.

I was always willing to give students extra time. And many of them were eager to help me in whatever ways they could. Sometimes one of my students would drive out to Malibu to pick me up for a day at the college, and then another student would drive me back home. They enjoyed coming out to Malibu for some of their lessons. On occasion, someone who needed to talk through a personal matter with a professional came out for a lesson late in the day, or even on a weekend, so that he or she could go next door to Amelia's apartment for a therapy session.

This was in many ways an ideal arrangement—incorporating music and pertinent deep conversation into everyday life, in a natural flow of people helping each other and drawing on whatever skills and insights were available. Amelia also had conferences with faculty members from time to time, once some of them became aware of that potential.

Amelia's manner was always so relaxed that the students felt partly as if they were just talking with a friend. For a short and casual session, she didn't charge them anything, and for a longer session it was still on a generous basis.

April of that year (1968) was memorable for a tragic event in American history, the assassination of Dr. Martin Luther King Jr. The day it happened, Amelia, Eve, and I sat together in a state of shock during the evening, watching the televised reports of the horrific news.

The next morning, as Amelia was preparing to leave for work as usual, Eve and I pleaded with her to stay home. She was the only white person who worked at Lathrop, which was right in the middle of the Watts ghetto. Terrible riots had broken out in Watts less than three years earlier. Now, with full awareness, she was choosing to walk into the middle of intense anger, and therefore danger.

We both begged her not to go, insisting that everyone she worked with at Lathrop would understand. But Amelia simply said, with quiet determination, "This, of *all* days, is the day I *must* be there." When she drove away, Eve and I both felt sick, fearing that we might never see her again.

Later, Amelia's staff members and colleagues reported that everyone had been astonished—some described it as horrified— when she walked into her office that morning. But they were also deeply touched that she took such a risk to be with them on that day of grieving.

When Amelia got back home to Malibu that evening, she told us that probation officers who worked with her regularly had insisted on escorting her safely out of the area at the end of the afternoon.

We also heard for a long time afterward how word had spread in Watts that Amelia had come to work that day. She was right; her act of solidarity had a lasting effect in that community, even at such a turbulent time.

Only two months later we were rocked to the core once again by the shocking news that Robert Kennedy had been assassinated at the Ambassador Hotel, in the heart of Los Angeles. At about that same time, I took what appeared to be a step backward.

Evidently the mix of teaching, classes, faculty activities, touring dates, and ongoing careful preparation for solo and concerto performances was proving to be too much for some of my weakest muscles. I had a sudden "shoulder attack" in which my right shoulder—the good shoulder, yes, but with serious weak spots—started screaming at me in pain.

My usual stretches, ice packs, and other ongoing preventive measures hadn't been effective enough. My medical team termed it a serious strain, and advised me to take time out for intensive treatment, including diathermy, electrotherapy, physical therapy, and finally, an extensive course of prednisone. Fortunately, I could have some of this treatment at the clinic just up the road in Malibu. And since I didn't have much on my performance calendar for the summer, only a few appearances had to be canceled.

The course of prednisone brought daily highs and lows, a frightening combination when mixed with natural adrenaline once I played a few concert dates in the fall. My "performance nerves" were heightened and the "post-performance letdowns" more severe. As the prednisone course tapered off, my overall energy level sagged, and I felt myself pushing through each day.

I resumed the pre-shoulder-attack schedule carefully and gradually, but even so, my right shoulder again started to cry out. Hoping to reverse this development as quickly as possible, I made an immediate trip to the Malibu clinic for some more in-office physical therapy.

The therapist that day, whom I hadn't met before, smiled and introduced herself as Hope Hopkins. She had brown bobbed hair, a direct gaze that seemed to take in everything at once, and a way of speaking that identified her as hailing from Maine. To my surprise, Hope asked detailed questions about my original polio attack and specific experiences in the thirteen years since. Toward the end of the treatment, she mentioned some exercises that might help me.

My guard immediately went up, as I had taken this journey before and felt that I couldn't face another approach at that moment, especially since the prednisone had left me with a low energy level.

"I have a lot of exercises that I do regularly," I assured her politely. Hope didn't press further, and we made an appointment for our next in-office session. But that evening, once I had rested and done some breathing with the tide, I wondered if I had made a mistake by dismissing Hope's suggestion.

"What's the matter with me?" I asked Amelia, as we discussed Hope's suggestion over dinner. "Here's someone with real interest, some detailed knowledge, and perhaps a different approach. Why didn't I at least let her explain?"

Amelia well understood why my first response was something like "Please, not again!" But she also encouraged me to explore whatever Hope's approach might be.

So during our next therapy session, I asked Hope, "About those exercises you were mentioning? I'd like to hear more."

She smiled and began to ask for more details about my post-polio experiences. Then Hope told me that she had been a physical therapist at Rancho Los Amigos National Rehabilitation Center in Downey, California, a facility that had developed a particularly effective therapeutic program to help patients deal with post-polio effects. Since the polio vaccine had been in use for some fifteen years by then, the volume of new cases had decreased sharply, but post-polio patients still came from all over the country to consult the therapists there.

My chance meeting with Hope suddenly took on a whole new dimension. After we had finished the passive treatment, she did a few muscle tests, resembling those I had undergone many times. She notated the "scores" for various muscles and muscle groups, just as the doctors and therapists in Copenhagen had done.

Then she put down her clipboard, looked me in the eye, and

said, in her down-home Maine accent, "Uh, and yuhr-ah a . . . *pianist?*" I nodded. "Uh, I'd like to see you play sometime." I had to laugh. She might as well have said *"This I gotta see!"*

"Well, I live just down the road," I replied. "I'd be happy to play for you." To my surprise she immediately accepted, and we set a time for the next day.

In the late afternoon, Hope appeared promptly, and we went right to my studio. I had put a chair in the best place for her to hear the music, but she moved it a little so that she could see every upper body movement. Then, just before I began to play, she ordered, "Take your shirt off." I started unbuttoning my blouse. "You can keep your bra on," she reassured me, then added, "OK, go ahead and play."

I felt ridiculous sitting there playing Beethoven in my bra, as Hope watched for a while, looking at my right side, then sat down on the floor peering up at me. Next, she crawled on her hands and knees under the piano, a necessary move since there wasn't enough space to walk around behind me. When she reached the other side, she peered up at me at various angles from the floor. Then she stood up and shifted to a position slightly behind me, so she could see my left side from a different angle. Finally, she crawled back under the piano to the "audience position" and said, right in the middle of a musical passage, "OK, that's enough."

Obviously, Hope was not a music lover.

"Well," she said, "I see how you're doing it."

"How I'm doing *what?*" I asked, since I was doing several complicated things.

"For one thing, your left hand," she explained. "You're throwing your wrist."

"My wrist?" I asked. "I thought you said I don't *have* much in my left wrist!"

"Well, you don't," she said, "but it's the best thing you've got."

And with that pronouncement, Hope initiated exploration of a new treatment program.

Just as I'd learned in Copenhagen ten years before, I had unknowingly been straining my damaged muscles. I had continued the preventive measures that the Copenhagen team had set up for me, but Hope said that even so, I had developed muscle contractures—the shortening of muscle fiber due to a combination of weakness and overuse.

Hope explained, much as Nybo had a decade earlier, that these contractures were part of my perceived strength. Once again, they had to be eased before she could proceed with any new exercises. Her treatments to relieve some of the contractures that had developed since Copenhagen exposed my actual weakness to a surprising degree.

Once we had finished the therapy course at the Malibu clinic, Hope came to my apartment for the one-on-one and across-the-table exercises, just as I had with Nybo in the Blegdam Hospital basement. But the exercises Hope brought, and the ones she dreamed up for me to do on the days in between sessions, were unlike anything I had ever experienced.

These new exercises, known as PNF patterns (proprioceptive neuromuscular facilitation), had been refined for use with post-polio patients at Rancho Los Amigos. Hope had been in on the ground floor with that program.

Most of the rehabilitative resistive exercises I had done before meeting Hope were in vertical or horizontal patterns. The PNF patterns were diagonal. This simple but brilliant change encouraged the patient's remaining motor neurons to participate in different ways from anything the "straight" horizontal or vertical patterns could elicit. Those remaining neurons seemed encouraged to jump into the fray as soon as they discovered more ways to help.

I felt the response in the larger muscles first—those affecting the bigger, broader movements. And then the larger muscles in turn began to pour more potential into the wrists, hands, and fingers. The hands and fingers then had to respond, with the wrists as a kind of fulcrum. Each development brought a different balance and impulse into the hands and fingers. Hope also gave my hands and fingers their own diagonal exercises that corresponded to those for the arms and shoulders.

My progress felt dramatic—as if the motor neurons were continually forming different groups and alliances to accomplish more things. I could imagine some of them getting together and saying, "Hey, let's help with this!"

As my excitement grew over the new possibilities, I told Hope that she had been aptly named. She shrugged and said, "Well, it's a family name. If the family name had been Cucamonga, I'd be Cucamonga Hopkins. Also known as Kook." Our sessions never lacked for humor.

Although each tiny change seemed huge to me, requiring a whole sequence of adjustments in my artificially built piano technique, I welcomed each one as something akin to a lifesaver. I embraced whatever enabled me to feel more natural, more integrated with the musical ideal, no matter what the cost in time and temporary disorientation.

At the piano, sometimes any movement I made seemed to overshoot its mark. Or I would set out in a new direction, even on a tiny scale, and hopelessly confuse the other motor neurons involved in the approach to a complex musical passage. But I gradually began to call on older, pre-polio motor reflexes to participate. They didn't work at first. But the larger muscles kept encouraging me to try again. Once I had admitted these impulses into the mix, they integrated relatively quickly, because they were a little closer to the natural reflexes.

These impulses presented themselves most clearly in informal, intimate play-throughs, of course. Sometimes I seemed to be kicking aside some of the careful work-around structures I had devised so painstakingly. But the goal was the same: to present this beloved music as effectively and expressively as possible. And gradually, bit by bit, I found my way into a new beginning.

Once I had gone a certain distance, I couldn't even remember where I had been a short while before. The newer combinations felt more natural and left the more restricted counterparts behind. It felt as if I were remodeling—knocking out walls, putting windows and doors in different places, enlarging rooms, and streamlining passageways that had become cumbersome.

The kind of work I had done to construct the *first* artificial post-polio piano technique now helped me to tackle a *revision* of that same work-around. I already knew *how* to rebuild a technique without losing sight of the musical goal. The tortuous accumulated experience—from Copenhagen until I met Hope—was helping me to accommodate new possibilities more readily.

Since this was an entirely new training program, I had to call a halt to all public performance for another year. But this time, there was a difference. I recognized that I would end up with something more. The sensations produced by these diagonal patterns were leading to what felt like a more integrated way of moving. I sensed that I would be able to call on some of the more natural reflexes from the distant past to a greater degree than I could ever have thought possible.

It was difficult blending this process with my teaching schedule, but Amelia and Eve explained the situation to my friends on the IHC faculty. Mary Mark, Theresa, Sister Helen Kelley, president of the college, and some of my other faculty friends gave me their wholehearted support.

Hope knew that I would be feeling stronger and more capable as we continued with the treatments. She repeatedly warned me of a factor I needed to keep in mind: As my remaining motor neurons began working harder and more efficiently, accomplishing greater things, that same polio-reduced pool of motor neurons was being used *much more* during each day and thus was *more at risk* than ever. She went on to explain that this risk would be present for the rest of my life.

Hope wanted to make sure I understood that periodic rest

throughout *each day* was essential to conserving my remaining motor neurons. She defined a rest period as simply "getting horizontal," so that the spinal, upper body, neck, shoulder, and arm muscles could relax. While I was lying flat on my back, I had to make sure that my arms rested mostly in the supine (palms upward) position, which would relax the shoulder muscles more effectively than if my arms were in a prone position.

In Hope's world, there were two groups of people: "polios" and "normals." The rules and predictions were very different for the two groups. As Hope spelled it out in elementary terms, "the polios" had to expend more overall effort to make *any* kind of movement. We had substantially *less* physical endurance, even in simple daily activities, than did "the normals."

Hope reminded me often that, as a "polio," my ambition, determination, and obsession in the realm of piano playing could pose a danger to my neuromuscular system. She warned me repeatedly of "burnout"—a lifelong risk.

After Copenhagen and the Vienna conference with Lassen and Aitken, I had been the only one who thought I might be able to play the piano again. But by the time I worked with Hope, I had been accepted in the music world as a pianist, and my only question was: How much would the therapy help in my playing—and in my everyday life?

Amelia had always noticed that it was difficult for me to do certain everyday tasks. She would open doors, pick up a purse or bag or anything else, and move it from one place to another just to save my shoulders. Eve had taken her cue from Amelia; both friends had been enabling me to feel and appear more normal.

Now, after some months of my new therapy, Amelia and Eve told me they could already see some differences. Amelia and I had a talk one evening that began with her observation that I had just offered to carry a bag of groceries from the car for the first time since she had known me. (Not a heavy bag, mind you!) This led to a discussion of the many years I had unconsciously avoided a vast number of activities. We both understood that I was always doing whatever I could, but had lost perspective on what I'd been avoiding.

In the kitchen, for example, it had long been a struggle for me to pick up pots or pans holding any kind of contents. I never removed jar lids or anything similar. My kitchen was filled with gadgets enabling me to do such things when no one else was around. As Amelia and I discussed the general picture, I jotted down some points I could pass along to Hope, who was always interested and asking for specifics.

Amelia observed that my stance had "grown younger and more vital." That was probably because I had increased strength in both the back muscles and core muscles needed to hold me up. She also commented that I seemed less withdrawn.

"I hate to say 'withdrawn,' because you've always talked with enthusiasm," Amelia explained. "Your voice was higher-pitched and had less volume than it does now. You had vitality in some ways, but especially in a group there would be a noninvolvement." We agreed that my lack of involvement was a natural attempt to save my weakest muscles from further strain. I had also modified talking, gesturing, and body stances in order to save energy by avoiding unnecessary movements.

Amelia went on, "Only in walking did you really extend yourself. Anything with your arms—you tended to break the gesture, or just let the arms lie. Neurological damage can go with supinated hands; and that was one of the first things that I picked up when I met you—that your hands were in the posture of supination. Strong people usually rest their hands pronated. All of your postures were quietly animated, but not assertively expressed."

"How did I pick up a dish, or serve you a plate of cookies, or . . . ?" I asked.

"Well, usually with the smallest gesture possible. You still rock the teapot rather than picking it up," Amelia answered.

"You would usually wait for someone else to open a car door. You didn't even notice it. When you met people, most of them thought you were very nice, and they liked you very much, but didn't see you as warm or involved. It was obviously self-protection. One of the things that I've noticed as your recovery has moved along is that everyone has suddenly started talking about what a warm person you are."

On the neuromuscular front, I still had some distance to travel, and wasn't about to turn away from treatment when I went back to performing. The ongoing therapy program—with Hope until she moved back to Maine, and then with a onetime Rancho Los Amigos colleague of hers, "MJ" Sullivan—continued to bring gradual neuromuscular improvement well through the next ten years, with occasional sessions beyond that time.

In September of 1969, I decided that the new version of my piano technique was ready to try out in live performance. I began a series of more ambitious play-throughs at Eve's, Carolyn's, my parents' home in Rancho Santa Fe, and informally at IHC to see how it might hold up under pressure. In October, Eve received the shocking news that her husband, Truman, had died suddenly. She flew immediately to Boston to be with her sons and their families, staying with them a couple of weeks after Truman's memorial service.

At about that time, our inner circle of play-through hosts suffered another sad loss: the composer Francis Hendricks. He and his wife, Katie, had been warmly encouraging and willing to host such evenings for me ever since I had begun to play again. They had both become good friends. Not long after Francis's death, Katie called to let me know that she was planning to move out of the area, and to ask if I would be interested in his piano. She said Francis had always enjoyed my interaction with his Steinway concert grand, and she knew that he would have been happy for me to have it. The ridiculously low price she quoted told me that Katie really wanted me to have the piano.

My only hesitation was not *if* but *where*. A concert grand wouldn't fit into my Malibu apartment. Fortunately, Joan Palevsky, a friend of the Immaculate Heart music faculty, had a large living room in western LA and offered to house the piano for as long as necessary. Her only condition was that I sometimes practice on it when her children were home from school so that they would hear live music played by a friend. She also offered to host as many play-throughs as I wished.

Sherman and I had stayed in touch during my self-enforced hiatus from concert tours. He had moved to Bloomington, Indiana, and his activities on behalf of the Indiana University performing artists had turned into a full-time job. He assured me that he would be happy to help get things restarted for me, but suggested that I might be better off with an artist manager based in New York City. He was interested to hear that I had already been talking with someone in Los Angeles who was willing to become an interim personal artist representative.

Chapter Fifteen

❧

A Time of Triumph
and Transition

M y new interim personal rep was Whitfield Cook, a nov-
elist, playwright, and screenwriter—most notably for
Alfred Hitchcock's films *Strangers on a Train* and *Stage Fright*. A
handsome man with silver-streaked hair and a resonant speaking voice that would easily have projected from any stage, Whit
was in his early sixties at the time we met at one of my play-
throughs, or soirées, as some of the attendees were calling them.
Whit and his wife, Elizabeth, divided their time between Los
Angeles and Connecticut, since his activities were based in both
LA and New York City. Once he had heard part of my story, he
wanted to hear more.

When we got together for a lively discussion over lunch,
Whit's enthusiasm was at a high level. He was in between projects
of his own and intrigued by a field that was new for him. Although
he had written and produced his own plays in New York, he had
not yet tackled the world of classical music performance. But that
was about to change. He was teaming up with his friend Margaret

Wharton, who booked classical concerts in Southern California, to form a partnership called Wharton-Cook.

First, Whit wanted permission to revise my official biography. Since the request was coming from a writer of his stature, I was all ears.

"Well, for one thing, *no* itsy-bitsy at the piano!" he exclaimed with a hearty laugh, referring to the usual practice of chronicling a performer's early years. "Let's get right to the drama!" His proposed revision would start in the present, with an intriguing statement, and then dip back into my earlier life to fill in details.

Next, he wanted to introduce me to some of his friends in public relations, especially Rupert Allan of the Los Angeles firm Allan & Ingersoll. Rupert's younger brother, Chris Allan, managed the firm's New York office, and Whit saw Chris as an ideal person to handle my story with sensitivity.

Joan Palevsky, who wanted to spread the word about an Immaculate Heart College faculty member performing again on the concert circuit, joined Whit and me for some lunchtime brainstorming and offered to handle any public-relations expense to get things going. The year before, Joan had gone through a divorce from Max Palevsky, an early computer developer and at that time an important figure at Xerox. The settlement gave her the funds to do anything that interested her, and she had begun to contribute to arts and educational organizations in the LA area. Joan had been a teacher at UCLA before her children came along and felt passionate about the importance of arts and education. She had no interest in spending money on material things and once confided to me, shaking her head at the expensive clothing in Beverly Hills shops, "I couldn't put *that* much money on my *back!*"

Sherman, who loved the new bio, thought Whit was on the right track and was delighted to hear about the PR potential with Chris Allan. I had been cautious about accepting any performance commitments in 1969 while my work with Hope was still bringing relatively dramatic neuromuscular changes, but I couldn't resist a couple of invitations to celebrate the Beethoven Bicentennial in early 1970. It seemed fitting that I could make yet another cautious "comeback" in the warm glow of Beethoven's last three piano sonatas—my beloved trio of 109, 110, and 111.

For the fall of 1970, another European tour was taking shape, which would include some benefit performances for the physically handicapped. Two important East Coast concerts— at Boston's Jordan Hall and New York's Alice Tully Hall—were scheduled for later that fall. The Tully Hall appearance would be my long-delayed New York City debut, by which time I would have turned thirty-seven.

I planned to devote the first half of the fall program to Bee-thoven—the Bagatelles, Opus 119, and the magnificent Opus 111—in honor of the Beethoven Year. For the second half, I decided to play the Fauré Barcarolle No. 5, along with Scriabin's Sonata No. 5.

While planning this program, I was browsing in a music store one day and saw a tall, thin volume of Karol Szymanowski's Études, Opus 33. Its text was in Polish, and its pages were still uncut. Peeking into the uncut pages, I saw some unusually inter-esting piano writing, somewhat reminiscent of Scriabin. After I had brought the volume home and carefully separated the pages, I found twelve miniature études—some only a page in length and each one linked to its successor without pause. As I began to explore them at the piano, I discovered a glowing mosaic of colors and textures, and recognized this work as the perfect addition to my fall program. The short "studies," touching briefly on a variety of piano techniques, contained considerable delicacy and subtlety. There were luscious harmonies in the more spacious pieces and sparkling passages in some of the livelier études. How Nana would have loved this, I thought, knowing that I would be calling on her Polish spirit for extra insight. The next time I talked on the phone with Mom I told her excitedly of my find. "I'll be listening!" she said, summing up her ongoing enthusiasm about my playing.

Eve was especially delighted that I would be playing in Boston, her hometown, and even thought about flying back for the concert. But her health was of increasing concern. At age sixty-three, she was experiencing some mysterious symptoms, and the health-care professionals she had consulted in Santa Monica and at UCLA had so far only pinpointed extreme hormonal imbalances. She had begun to feel that, much as she loved Malibu, she should be closer to her trusted medical people. With Amelia's help, she found an apartment in Santa Monica.

Once Eve was set up in Santa Monica, where she could feel less anxious, Amelia and I tried to figure out how we could be close by, given Eve's unpredictable up-and-down health condition. So Amelia and I launched a housing search, mostly on Sunday afternoons. We couldn't find any condos or apartments that would accommodate the nine-foot Steinway concert grand presently visiting at Joan's home. We also looked at some houses that we might share, but to get a room big enough for the piano, and to have two sets of personal quarters, made the price of a house far too high for our combined incomes. We began to view our quest as an extended one.

Meanwhile, I had to do some planning on the concert re-entry front. Whit and Rupert wanted Chris Allan to get advance PR going in New York, since Sherman was no longer able to set up interviews and meetings for me.

Chris and I first met when I went through New York in February during my "re-entry" Beethoven tour. We met at the Russian Tea Room on 57th Street, over a bowl of borscht and multiple cups of tea. Chris was wearing a blue shirt and an Italian-cut jacket, a combination that set off his dark eyes and dark hair. I was taken with him from the beginning. We talked a long time and must have lingered for at least three hours, every so often ordering more Russian-style munchies and tea.

We talked mostly about our personal devotion to music and art. I was struck from the start by Chris's attitude toward the arts, which seemed more European than American. He seemed to understand someone like me, who had been willing to risk everything to rebuild my ties to music. Chris had been an Air Force pilot in the Korean War and had survived harrowing experiences, receiving the Distinguished Flying Cross for his heroism. He had returned home to devote himself to the arts, and well understood the connection between onetime trauma and heightened dedication.

I felt a wonderful connection with Chris. When I was with him, the city itself seemed to take on a different character. Ever since the polio attack, I had felt some fear of New York—fear of how "the polio girl" would be received if I ever were to play there. Now, suddenly, New York was Chris. Because of him, the city felt friendlier, more inviting.

The Beethoven tour took me to a workshop and performance in Jacksonville, Florida. I had promised Amelia's beloved nine-year-old nephew, John Douglas Stone, who lived in nearby Gainesville, that I would play one of the sonatas at his elementary school in between the two events. Giving Dougie, as Amelia called him, the choice of which piece his schoolmates would prefer, I played through all three for him ahead of time, figuring he would choose either of the tuneful sonatas Opus 109 or Opus 110. But to my surprise, he opted for the dramatic and less immediately accessible Opus 111. As Dougie listened, spellbound, to all three, it struck me that he must have inherited the musical sophistication gene present in both his Aunt Amelia and her younger brother, his father. He wanted to introduce me himself, and prepared a speech that any PR person would have heartily approved. As he came to the close of his laudatory remarks, Dougie made a sweeping gesture toward the wings and announced, in his most resonant voice, "*Miss Carol Rosenberger!*" Fortunately, I didn't have to keep a straight face as I walked onstage and bowed to the applauding children.

Back in California, I played the Beethoven program at

IHC, to an enthusiastic reception. Webster happened to be in LA and came to hear me play those three sonatas so familiar to us both. Despite his congratulatory hug, I sensed that he was still frightened for me. He knew all too well the risk I was taking by touring and performing in public with such a damaged playing mechanism.

A few days later, I auditioned for the British conductor Neville Marriner, who had recently become music director of the Los Angeles Chamber Orchestra. Neville seemed to like what he heard and invited me to play the Mendelssohn A-Minor Concerto with LACO the following November.

While I caught up with my students and their progress, Amelia and I resumed our search for a place to live near Eve—a search that still wasn't promising. Then one Sunday morning in early July, while on our way from Malibu to some appointments with realtors, we saw an open-house sign on Adelaide Place, a little cul-de-sac on the rim of Santa Monica Canyon. Amelia wanted to stop and see it.

Since Adelaide Place was a quiet street with a beautiful view of the canyon, mountains, and ocean, I figured that the house would be beyond our financial reach. But Amelia told me how often she and Doug had driven past this street on their way into town or back to Malibu, and had agreed that if they ever had to leave Malibu, this would be a lovely place to live. For that sentimental reason alone, she wanted to take a quick look.

That Sunday turned out to be the first day the house had come on the market, and Amelia and I were the first to arrive. It sat on a narrow lot and looked small from the outside. But when we walked in, we saw a large living room that would certainly accommodate the nine-foot Steinway. And the canyon-mountain view from the living-room windows was spectacular. The house also had two separate bedroom-study "suites"—one at the front and one at the back. And even though it was indeed a modest-sized house, it amazingly had the essentials we were looking for. The asking price was $80,000, but the owners were willing to come down to $78,000. And it was a block away from Eve's apartment. Excitement was mounting steadily!

I asked to use the phone and called my parents, who had already offered to help. As Depression Era veterans, they were both great believers in owning the roof over one's head. Dad had finished their place in Rancho Santa Fe and assured us that he would be ready to help fix up anything we found. He said he would drive up to Santa Monica immediately and advised us to hang around the house for a couple of hours. Amelia quickly canceled our other appointments for the day.

Once Dad arrived, things moved swiftly, and before long Amelia and I were preparing to move, aided by my ever-helpful IHC students. Eve seemed vastly relieved that we would both be close by, as her health condition continued to be worrisome.

Just a few weeks after Amelia and I had officially moved into the Adelaide house, Eve had an acute attack—of what, no one knew—and was rushed to the UCLA hospital. Her medical team ran numerous tests, but continued to have difficulty arriving at a definitive diagnosis. Amelia took a temporary leave from her work at Lathrop to be at Eve's bedside; we were both grateful that the hospital was close by.

With her usual conversational skill, Amelia began to engage the doctors about their views on Eve's condition. The suspense seemed to drag on and on, and when they finally arrived at a diagnosis, it was the worst possible news—a rare and then incurable disease caused by a mycobacterium called Kansasii.

Only a few cases of Kansasii had been documented in the worldwide medical literature, and in Eve's case the prognosis was grim. According to her doctors, she probably had somewhere between a few weeks and a few months to live.

How could this be? Suddenly Amelia and I were moving around in a trembling state that felt like slow motion, and there was only one place in the world—Eve's hospital room. It was there that the three of us tried to process the devastating news. Eve had insisted on knowing everything at every point in her illness, so no softening or fudging of the bad news was possible. All Amelia and I wanted was to give her, somehow, our combined strength, so that together the three of us might try to turn the tide, postpone the worst, or extend her life—no matter what the doctors had said.

I told Eve, in a manner meant to be reassuring, that I was planning to cancel my upcoming fall tour, since I didn't want to leave her side. But Eve wouldn't hear of it. *"Get me out* of this hospital room!" she cried. *"You* are the only one who can get me *out* of here!"

Eve had always expected me to understand how she felt about important things, since we were both Scorpios. Now she expected her fellow Scorpio to understand that the only way she could soar during her last days on earth was for me to do my part: travel to beautiful concert halls and play sublime music on her behalf.

Eve's wish turned my focus to the preparatory pre-tour play-throughs. I was facing my second important comeback tour post-polio, after the transformative neuromuscular work with Hope, which had been going on for two years. And if I were going to do this significant tour justice, as well as symbolically getting Eve out of her hospital room, I needed to give it fierce concentration.

The play-throughs started at my parents' home, for two groups of friends, and Dad taped the program both times so I could listen back. Amelia hosted a couple of gatherings for me to "play in" the Steinway that had been moved into the Adelaide Place living room. But finding the concert grand so much at home there and sounding so beautiful, with Eve unable to join us, was a bittersweet experience.

Just before I left for Europe, I did a play-through at Carolyn Fisher's house. Amelia, who usually enjoyed going to Carolyn's for my "soirées," was with Eve in the hospital room, so I drove

myself. Once I had finished playing, I fell into an unusually serious conversation with Phil Goodwin, the psychologist friend I
had met—and been attracted to—many years before.

Phil and I had maintained a special connection during the
nearly ten years since my breakup with his friend Sam, and we
were clearly still drawn to each other. After spending time with
him over the years, I had always felt somewhat wistful. But on
this evening, our connection registered in a way that felt even
deeper and more important than ever. He walked me to the car
when I left, and we lingered in the pleasant evening air, reluctant
to see our time together come to an end. Then out of the blue,
Phil asked quietly, "Carol, would you consider marrying me?"

The moment stretched in time, as I tried to absorb what
Phil was saying and feeling. For all these years, perhaps he
too had wondered what a relationship between us might have
become. The marriage he'd been trying to save when we first met
had ended permanently while I had been involved with Morrie.
Might something have happened between Phil and me sooner if
the timing hadn't always been off? Finally, I just took his hands
and answered, with a touch of humor, "Well . . . let's at least have
dinner!" He and I had never even gone out on a date. He seemed
to understand that I meant, "I'm game to see where this might
go," and gave me a warm embrace.

I left for Amsterdam two days later. The first series of performances was booked by Harry de Freese in Amsterdam and
the second series by Wilfred van Wyck in London. The friendly
reception from the Amsterdam audience, as well as the special
welcome from Harry and his family, got me off to a good start
in the beautiful Small Hall of the Concertgebouw. From there
I went to Frankfurt, where I played a benefit concert for physically handicapped children, under the patronage of the Princess
von Hessen. My old friend Sieghart from Vienna, who was then
living in Germany, came to the concert, and we went to dinner
before I left. Then I went on to the other two stops on Harry's

mini-tour: Diligentia Hall in The Hague, where the audience welcomed me back with their characteristic enthusiasm, and an appearance in Zürich.

The London-based mini-tour included more benefit concerts—another positive outcome of sharing my polio story. In Manchester, I played a benefit for the British Polio Fellowship the evening before my appearance at the Lesser Free Trade Hall there. In London, I began by playing a benefit for the University College Hospital Music Society.

The all-important official concert at Wigmore Hall fell on a Sunday afternoon, November 1, my thirty-seventh birthday. The very next day, Eve's sixty-fourth birthday, I played a benefit for a wonderful youth club called PHAB (Physically Handicapped and Able Bodied), where both groups of young people got together for enjoyable activities and became friends in the process. At the time, I had seen no such organization in the United States—a social group where the stigma of being handicapped was transcended by friendship and group camaraderie—and was deeply moved at the party after the event, when I saw the young people enjoying each other's company with such affection and enthusiasm. I could hardly wait to report it to Eve and Amelia.

My last stop on the tour was Paris, at the Salle Gaveau, and who should come backstage afterward but Mademoiselle herself. I was glad I'd played the Beethoven Opus 111, after our history with the work. I was also glad I'd programmed the Fauré, since Mademoiselle had such a strong connection to his music. She was clearly moved to witness my comeback, and it was an emotional moment for me to have her there. There wasn't a lot that needed to be said; we both recognized that the impossible had happened after all. Our emotions, and a few tears, spoke volumes about the journey and where, at that point, it had led.

The next day I flew back to Los Angeles, where I had much to share. Eve drank in every detail I could tell her and assured me that I had indeed gotten her out of the hospital room. She loved the PHAB story as much as I thought she would, as did Amelia. Since I had been away, Eve didn't seem to have gone much farther downhill, at least outwardly, but this was a mysterious illness, and it was hard to tell.

Some phone messages had accumulated while I was away, and one was from Carolyn, asking for a return phone call. When I called her, she said she had sad news, and told me gently that Phil Goodwin had suffered a fatal heart attack. He hadn't even reached fifty. I didn't tell anyone but Amelia about my last conversation with Phil. As I grieved, I wondered if he'd had some premonition that he didn't have much time left. Whatever it was that led him to communicate his feelings for me that evening at Carolyn's, I have been forever grateful that he let me know, and forever glad that I answered him that evening in a receptive manner.

A few days later I began rehearsals for the concert with Neville Marriner and the Los Angeles Chamber Orchestra, preceded by a couple of radio interviews. Neville was wonderful to work with in many ways, not the least of which was his relaxed manner, backstage and onstage. "See you afterwards," he said that evening, with a touch of humor, as we were about to walk out onstage together. Whenever I performed with Neville in future concerts, he would make a similarly casual and amusing comment to counteract nervousness just before we walked onstage. A few days after this first concert, the well-known music critic Martin Bernheimer wrote in the *Los Angeles Times:* "Carol Rosenberger played the graceful, grateful solo with tremendous fluidity, poise, and clarity."

In a few more days I was off to Boston. Before I left, Eve had assured me the performance was especially for her. The concert went exceptionally well in the New England Conservatory's Jordan Hall—a wonderfully warm and resonant space. Afterward, the backstage door opened, and there stood a tiny dark-haired woman with dancing eyes. It was Katja Andy, who had been my teacher when I was thirteen and was my only link with Edward Bredshall and those important years.

Katja had been a favorite student of the great Edwin Fischer and had become his two-piano repertoire partner and teaching assistant. When Katja had been unable to get a work permit in the UK after fleeing Nazi Germany, Fischer refused to record the major two-piano and four-hand piano repertoire—of which his interpretations were revered—with anyone else. Katja had eventually made her way to Chicago and Detroit, and Bredshall had asked her to take over his students, including me, when he went on a sabbatical. Her insights into Bach and Mozart were unique in my experience, and I had never heard anyone who so well personified "singing fingers" at the piano. She did indeed make the instrument sing! That sound had stayed with me, in my imagination, ever after.

I had tried in vain to locate Katja when I had returned to the US in 1959 and needed help in the long fight back from polio, but hadn't known that she was teaching at the New England Conservatory. Finally, after so many years, Katja and I could reconnect as if the extended time gap between us had never existed. We had tears in our eyes as we vowed to stay in touch.

Early the next morning, I was on my way to New York. Chris met me at the airport, which was certainly not in his job description. His only concession to the cold weather was a warm wool scarf. He had a couple of interviews lined up, and I soon realized that when Chris brought me to meet a writer or a columnist, his excitement was genuine. I knew he was a fine professional, but there seemed to be a special element in his feelings for me. At one point, he mentioned something that needed to be sent to my New York address. "I don't have a New York address," I reminded Chris. "Yes, you do," he exclaimed. "My apartment!"

Chris brought a large group of his own friends to the Tully Hall concert. I found that gesture alone reassuring; it helped immeasurably to counteract my long-held fear of the milestone New York appearance. I drew on my recent experiences in Holland, London, and Boston, trying to trust my carefully reconstructed neuromuscular function as well as focusing on the sound and shaping of the musical material. As the evening progressed, I began to feel more confident about what I could achieve musically. It helped that I began the program with Beethoven, including my cherished Opus 111.

After the concert, many audience members came backstage, and I enjoyed greeting them all. During a post-concert gathering, Chris and I stayed close together, and afterward talked far into the night about life and death and the sublime arts. He was one of the few people I had met who truly understood the larger picture as I saw it.

The next day I flew back to Los Angeles, and by evening was in Eve's hospital room. Around 11:00 p.m., Eve's bedside phone rang. It was Chris, so excited that he could barely speak. It was 2:00 a.m. Eastern time, but he had stayed up so he could go out and get *The New York Times*. The headline of the review read, "Carol Rosenberger Impresses at Piano Recital in Tully Hall." Chris read the entire review first to me, then to Eve, and finally to Amelia. His voice would catch every so often, and he would stop and swallow, and then go on. He told Eve, Amelia, and me that he had never heard anyone who got the sounds out of the piano that I did. Eve said Chris made her feel as if she'd been there.

When we finally left Eve's hospital room and headed home to Santa Monica, Amelia had something to tell me. While I was in Boston, Eve had asked her a startling question: "So, Amelia, what are you going to do with the rest of it?" Amelia said that Eve's question kept resonating with her and was forcing her to take stock of her own life in a way she hadn't done in a long time.

It was as if Eve had been waiting for me to return triumphant. Her condition went downhill rapidly, and her two sons flew out from the East Coast to spend the precious last days with her. Eve's older son, Truman Jr., or "T" as she called him, was the first to come. "T" was my age; Eve had pointed out many times that he and I had been born in the same year, about ten days apart. Then her younger son, Scott, arrived.

Eve made it through the holiday season and into the first days of 1971. On January 7, she looked longingly at all of us gathered around her bedside and drew her last breath. Amelia told me later that I was trying to breathe for her until the end.

The memorial that Eve's sons, Amelia, and I hosted was a celebration of Eve's life, with her favorite music, friends, and champagne. It was exactly the kind of memorial that Eve had told us she wanted, and Amelia commented, "When I go, please, no funeral, no solemn memorial; just have such a party for me."

Chapter Sixteen

⤛⤜

Carnegie Hall and
Amelia's Brainstorm

A particularly lovely condolence note from Webster came at
just the right moment:

> *Eve's death—how really sad—and what a sense of loss it*
> *brings in its wake. . . . She was such an extraordinarily*
> *vivid person; from the moment we met . . . it was all there,*
> *suddenly, and completely . . . On many levels we seemed*
> *to speak the same language, and I think it amused both of*
> *us—at times—to strain credibility to the utmost . . . a most*
> *enchanting person. I can only try to imagine the extent to*
> *which you will miss all that she represented. . . . Wonderful,*
> *that she survived long enough to enjoy your recent scaling*
> *of the peaks; nothing I'm sure could have given her greater*
> *pleasure! I can only hope that both you and Amelia will*
> *adjust to this loss with a minimum of pain—though that*
> *is really asking for the moon. . . . My thoughts are with*
> *you—and sympathy —and concern.*

My students had been waiting patiently for me to return to normal teaching mode. I felt grateful to them for recognizing that Eve's death had been a great personal loss for me. Almost everyone had met Eve and enjoyed her company. They were sympathetic when tears suddenly overtook me during an especially beautiful musical passage.

The students who came to Santa Monica for their lessons had another reminder of Eve: She had left me her piano, which Amelia and I had placed opposite the Steinway D, at the other end of our joint living room. We moved my smaller Steinway, which had been occupying that spot, to the adjoining "TV room," which opened into the living room. So for the moment the Adelaide house had three pianos—one more than was needed for two-piano rehearsals of concerto repertoire. But as several friends and students remarked, "Well, no house can have too many pianos! Right, Carol?"

Amelia returned to her job at Lathrop, on a temporary basis, to provide continuity until someone else could take over. She retained some private patients, but Eve's all-important question to Amelia about what she was going to do with "the rest of it" had fueled a rethinking process. Amelia decided to take some time for herself and even opted to join me on an upcoming European and East Coast tour.

Meanwhile, Chris was spreading the word about my re-entry into the concert world. *McCall's Magazine* featured me in a piece called "Against the Odds." An issue of *Show Magazine* offered a section called "The Editors Bless," with a column about my comeback. Chris's activity on my behalf gave us frequent excuses for long phone calls.

Music Journal invited me to write an article about my recovery, calling it "Bridge Over Troubled Waters," a reference to the Simon & Garfunkel song that had become part of the popular culture. The editors asked me to elaborate on what they saw as the "bridge" part of my journey—some of the positives that came out of my long struggle. I wrote about my post-polio difficulties in general terms, without describing the ongoing physical therapy or mentioning any remaining impairment. I wrote glowingly about some of the people who had been helpful to me, and in the last paragraph, I summed up the positives this way:

> *Because so little was possible to me during that time, I learned to make the most of anything that came my way. Because there was so much frustration, I learned a kind of patience I had never dreamed of. In the attempt to create something out of chaos I learned a great deal about the creative process. I learned how to stretch my own abilities; I learned a deeper control of myself, a fuller access to my own powers. What seemed at the time to be fragmentary, a supplement to convalescence, became for me the truest kind of education.*

Anne J. O'Donnell & Associates, a New York artist management firm, signed me up in early 1971. Whit Cook continued to help as a devoted "personal rep" but was delighted that my tour bookings would be in the hands of a company based in New York City. Anne O'Donnell had tremendous energy and considerable expertise, having worked for Columbia Artists before going out on her own. She had grown up in London during World War II and attributed her extreme startle reflex to neighborhood bombings when she was a child. Anne was energetic and always on her toes; her speaking tempo was brisk and enthusiastic. Even though she was just beginning to explore the possibilities for me, some interesting tour dates were already on the horizon.

In the summer of 1971, I played the Grieg Concerto with the Houston Symphony and the Liszt Concerto No. 2 with the Detroit Symphony. My brother, Gary, sister-in-law, Judy, and their children came to the Detroit concert, and we had a delightful reunion. Four-year-old Karl, who loved music and the piano, wandered off backstage to see if he could reach up and play a few keys on the concert grand that I had just played. When he returned, he looked admiringly at my flame-colored chiffon gown and asked, "Aunt Carol, are you going to wear that dress when you come to *our* house?" He wanted the magic of the concert experience to last as long as possible.

While I was preparing repertoire for the upcoming fall concerts, Whit brought another Anne into our lives. The well-known actress Anne Baxter, a dear friend of Whit's, came with him to one of the home play-throughs. Anne, who loved classical music, told Amelia and me that it had also been a passion of her grandfather's, the famous architect Frank Lloyd Wright. The three of us felt an instant rapport.

At one point during the evening Anne asked if I "wore eyelashes" when I performed, since my own, almost-invisible lashes were short and thin. I showed her a set of unused false eyelashes I had bought that were too uncomfortable to wear. "Those are *caterpillars!*" she declared, in her throaty, resonant voice. While explaining that the eyelashes she wore were much more comfortable but effective, she reached up with the thumb and forefinger of each hand and carefully removed her own discreet set of non-caterpillar eyelashes. She handed them to me and said, with a broad smile, "Now these are yours! Try them!" I did, and wore them many times on photo shoots and in future performances.

For the rest of the summer I focused on the program I was scheduled to play at Carnegie Hall in November. My childhood dream was about to become a reality. Playing at Carnegie Hall was the Holy Grail of concert appearances—a lofty goal that had spawned several variations of this well-known joke: A tourist wanting to see the famed venue asks a New Yorker, "How do I get to Carnegie Hall?" The reply: "Practice, practice, practice!"

I had carefully designed the program with some rarely

heard repertoire. The first half would feature the Stravinsky Piano Sonata, which Boulanger had recommended years before, and the Boulez Piano Sonata No. 1, which I had worked on intermittently since Vienna days. In between the two, I placed my good-luck piece, the beautiful Fauré 13th Nocturne, which Mademoiselle had inscribed to me when I left Paris, and the Ravel *Ondine,* which I had first played at age fifteen.

Ondine was the piece that once prompted Bredshall to ask, "How did you do that?" when I had navigated some treacherous passages without noticing their difficulty. After my polio attack, some well-informed person might have asked, "What makes you *think* you can do that?" But I had once again figured out an approach to that piece and could only hope that my handicapped apparatus would hold up in performance. The second half of the program would be Chopin's *24 Preludes,* most of which I had already played on tour.

By the time my fall tour began, Amelia had officially retired from Lathrop and rearranged her private patient schedule to accommodate a holiday. The first concert was another appearance at Jordan Hall in Boston with the new, Carnegie-destined program. Amelia flew to Boston with me, and we both saw this concert as another personal memorial to Eve.

The performance went well in that beautiful-sounding hall, and, once again, Katja Andy was there—one of the first people to come backstage afterward. This time, I didn't have to rush off the next morning, so Katja invited Amelia and me to her Cambridge apartment.

As the three of us talked, sipped some wine, and sampled a variety of cheese with crackers and pumpernickel, Amelia spoke eloquently to Katja, telling her how much I admired her playing, teaching, and understanding. Katja and I began to reminisce about our time together in Detroit, and at one point Katja took over the conversation: "Carol had the greatest pianistic facility I have ever known," she said, speaking directly to Amelia.

I stopped in the middle of cutting a wedge of gruyere, stared at her, and opened my mouth to protest. I didn't remember it that way at all. What I remembered were the special things I had learned from Katja.

But she was nodding vehemently, turning first to Amelia and then to me. "My worst fear was that your facility would keep you from developing musically." Then, laughing her high, musical laugh, she added: "If I would challenge you about anything, you would always have an answer. You would tell me what you were trying to do, or why. And you know? It always made sense!" By then all three of us were laughing.

Amelia again quoted my comment that Katja could make Bach "sing" on the piano like no other pianist I'd ever heard. Then she asked if Katja would do us the honor of playing a little Bach. At first Katja insisted that she was out of practice and could no longer do justice to such music. But Amelia was so reverently persuasive that finally Katja sat down at the piano. It was just as I had remembered—those fingers were still singing and illuminating Bach's music as she played the D-Major Toccata. It was glorious—a moment to be cherished forever. At the end of the evening, Katja said that she might come to New York to hear me play at Carnegie Hall.

Amelia continued traveling with me and seemed to love every minute of the trip, as I went on to play the same program in Switzerland, Holland, and England. It was wonderful to have her company, which helped even more than the expensive long distance calls that calmed my anxieties in the past.

Another important concert, the last one before the Carnegie appearance, took place at London's Wigmore Hall, where I had been warmly received the year before. Amelia hadn't been in London since she was a young student and had visited the city with Ricky, her British fiancé. London had personal meaning for her, and she welcomed the opportunity to go back after so many life-changing events.

Then we went on to New York, where Mom and Dad flew in for the Carnegie concert. They say your life flashes before you just prior to death; it can also do that just before a particularly important performance. David, Chris, Eve's older son "T," and Katja were all there, along with my parents and Amelia. I still remember a few special moments during that performance. The sound floating back to me was glowing; it seemed to give the Fauré Nocturne's spare song extra warmth. There was a welcome sense of space in parts of the Boulez Sonata and an almost magical flow to the most dangerous parts of my cherished *Ondine*.

Mom dissolved in happy tears after the concert—expressing for everyone what a long climb this appearance represented. Both Mom and Amelia responded to Chris, who had brought a group of distinguished people in the arts to hear me. Dad and Chris were talking animatedly at the party afterward, and I could tell that Dad was beaming his approval.

Amelia and I lingered in New York after everyone else had left, and she had a chance to get to know Chris, who was making some exciting and forward-looking plans for me. Chris was one of the few people who knew that I was having ongoing physical therapy and that I was still climbing my personal Everest. He also knew that I had a precipitous path ahead in building a solid career; both the long delay and the lesser status of women pianists were further professional handicaps. Amelia was touched by Chris's understanding and his unwavering belief in me.

One day Amelia took a walk around Carnegie Hall and reported that, since my poster had come down, no other American artists were represented in its current displays. She felt that it was terribly wrong for Americans to be invisible in the most historically significant concert venue in New York—or in the United States, for that matter. She was in one of her reflective moods, and little did I know what would develop from that observation.

Amelia told me about her idea when we were both back in Santa Monica a few weeks later. She began by referring to the treasured record collection she and Doug had amassed over many years. I had looked at the shelves of LPs in her study and listened to many of those beautiful recordings. Amelia then pointed out that most of the artists and their record labels were from overseas, with relatively few originating in the United States. "And yet," she went on, "I've gotten to know some wonderful American artists. Why aren't they being recorded?"

I shrugged. Everyone in the performing-arts field knew that European artists were more highly regarded than most Americans. Amelia suggested that we go out to dinner at Bob Burns, her favorite low-key restaurant two blocks from the ocean, where the comfortable atmosphere resembled a Scottish tavern. She greeted everyone on the staff by name, as she usually did at any establishment we'd visited more than a couple of times. After we were comfortably settled and sipping some wine, Amelia resumed her discussion about the lack of American recording artists.

"I've been thinking of starting a classical label myself," she said. I was shocked. Before I recovered enough to ask how she would fund such an endeavor, she added, "I could start small, of course, and use some of what Eve left me." Eve had left her a modest bequest, but its purpose had been to give Amelia a little extra cushion. Eve had hoped that Amelia could then afford to leave Lathrop and figure out what shape she wanted her future life to take.

"But Eve wanted you to be more secure financially!" I protested.

"Yes, but she also asked me what I was going to do with 'the rest of it,'" Amelia gently reminded me. We both had tears in our eyes, thinking of our dear friend. Eve had recognized Amelia's enormous personal and intellectual resources, marveled at what Amelia had already achieved, and wanted her to be free to soar. Eve and I had even remarked to each other that it was no wonder Amelia loved birds so much and, throughout her life, had often dreamed she could fly.

After a pause, Amelia remarked: "And I think she would have loved the idea." I had to agree. "You know," she added, "it could help to level the playing field for some of our American artists and give them an international platform."

Finally, the strands began to come together: I saw that Amelia had a new mission.

Her new project was audacious, but it wasn't hard to see where it had come from. Amelia was always thinking of—and helping—others, in both her professional and personal life. She saw several factors coincide in this new plan. Her thinking about many subjects tended to transcend borders and limitations. She wove things seamlessly from one area or discipline into another.

Even in graduate school, Amelia had taken courses in psychoacoustics and the physics of music, along with her study of clinical psychology. She loved classical music, whether she was listening to it live or on recording, and felt that great music could and should have an important place in people's lives.

For several weeks after Amelia's startling revelation, our group of friends from the medical, psychology, and social work fields would come over to hear me play through something, and stay to discuss Amelia's idea with her. They all seemed to find it exciting and wanted to participate.

Craig and Helen Boardman, the psychologist-social work couple, said they'd be good at bookkeeping and wanted to volunteer their time. Eleanor Yudkoff, the social-worker friend whose hobby was drawing and painting, wanted to contribute a design for the new company's logo and anything else that might be required. What would the company be called? Amelia had no question about that: It should be named for Delos, the mythical birthplace of the Greek god Apollo, who set out in his chariot every morning to bring light, music, and healing to the world. Everyone loved the name. This group of friends, most of whom had the healing arts in common as well as their love of music, shared Amelia's opinion that the two were closely connected.

Jeanne Hansen, a loyal member of our play-through group, knew some aspects of the classical recording field well since she had worked in record retail for many years. She was willing to contribute her time and marketing expertise. Jeanne spoke with a French accent, and when she referred to "records," the word came out with a guttural "r" and a hint of a "w"—something like "wecawds." She always said the word with affection, so it sounded a little like a term of endearment, and was both amusing and touching.

Amelia had met and become friends with several American artists she admired, most of whom had no significant discography. A clear choice as one of the first recording artists was harpsichordist Malcolm Hamilton, whom Neville Marriner had singled out as an outstanding musician, as well as a witty colleague, and referred to affectionately as "Sir Malcolm." Malcolm had become a friend and, despite his outstanding reputation, had not yet made a solo recording. "Sir Malcolm" also introduced Amelia to someone he much admired, viola da gamba virtuosa Eva Heinitz, who would love to record with—who else?—"Sir Malcolm."

Then there was James DePreist, one of the few African American conductors active at that time. Jimmy and Amelia had developed a strong rapport from the moment they met. He was the nephew of the great contralto Marian Anderson and was just embarking on his own career. He was also "a polio," so Amelia and Jimmy had discussed in-depth how these key factors were affecting his life and career.

Around the time the Delos idea was being hatched, Amelia and I went to a party in Pasadena and happened to meet another American artist, pianist John Browning. He was well-known and had a busy career based in New York, but had spent some of his growing-up years in LA, and came back from time to time for a visit.

John was standing close to the front door, talking with our

host when Amelia and I arrived. When we were introduced, his first words to me were *"You're* the one who . . ." (I was sure he would say, as several musicians had by now, "had polio and made a comeback!") But the end of his sentence was ". . . got *my* piano!!" After much laughter, John explained that he had been a close friend of Francis and Katie Hendricks, and had long loved their Steinway D, which was now in my living room.

Sometime during our delightful conversation, Amelia, seeing that I was connecting so happily with John, gracefully drifted away into the rest of the crowd. She knew that I had long been fearful to interact with most "normal" professional concert artists, since my experience was so different from theirs. While John and I were talking about preparing repertoire, I mentioned that I had just been "cramming" a Mozart concerto I had never played. I told him that after two days of intense concentration, I could think through it from memory, so that the rest of the time could be spent building secure reflexes.

Just then another LA pianist approached us, nodded to me briefly, and then turned away from me and began talking only to John. One of my students had quoted this pianist as saying about me, "She's such a dish! Why does she bother to play the piano? Too bad. . . ."

The pianist had evidently overheard part of the conversation about Mozart, since he asked John how long it took him to learn a Mozart concerto he hadn't played before. John, who had already figured out the dynamic of the situation, looked over at me inquiringly, raised his dark eyebrows, and asked casually, "Two days?" I could hardly keep from laughing as I nodded and answered, just as casually, "Two days." The other pianist looked shocked and moved on to speak with other guests. John had a twinkle in his eyes.

That was the memorable beginning of a treasured friendship. It was especially important for me, since after polio I had kept my distance from professional concert pianists, except for

Webster and Mary Mark at Immaculate Heart. John and I were the same age, and it was healing to find that I could develop a close friendship with someone who had taken the avenues that had been closed off for me. He and his friend Van Cliburn, both top students of Rosina Lhevinne at Juilliard, had been winning international competitions at about the time when I was first trying to deal with polio paralysis.

John had made some well-known recordings earlier in his career, but none for several years, and had nothing on the horizon at that moment. Amelia thought it was time for him to plan a new project, and he agreed, saying that he had a hankering to record the Mussorgsky *Pictures at an Exhibition*. He found Amelia's mission appealing and was delighted to be part of it.

As Amelia began to make plans for these artists and others, our group of friends and former colleagues jumped in with great enthusiasm. "Sir Malcolm" had a graduate student and friend, John Wright, who also wanted to be part of the startup. Some of my students, who were already part of our informal barter system, wanted to help, too. One student, Kathline Colvin, offered not only her own help but that of her boyfriend, David Grover, a photographer, and her uncle, Bill Colvin, who was an attorney in Santa Monica and could set up the legal structure for the company.

Amazingly, it was all beginning to take shape. I saw only one problem: Amelia and her friends wanted *me* to be one of the Delos recording artists. As I attempted to process that idea, I was building up a fear of the microphone and tried to sidestep discussions of going down that path. The microphone loomed as a microscope that could spotlight my neuromuscular work-arounds in a way I would not want revealed. By then I was incorporating these work-arounds effectively in live performance and gradually building some trust in myself. I didn't even mind if one of the venues recorded a live concert, because my focus was on the performance. But a studio recording? Under the glare of the microphone-microscope?

At around the same time, I had begun to explore more of the captivating piano music of Karol Szymanowski. After the success of programming his Études, Opus 33, I had been in touch with the publisher, Universal Edition, and had acquired a copy of the *Masques,* a colorful and innovative suite that I was planning to play on my next tour program. As Amelia and her friends frequently mentioned the idea of my recording at some point, I realized that Szymanowski's *Masques* would be ideal material, once I had performed it on tour and could feel relatively sure of my ground. It was a fascinating work, and rarely heard. Maybe I wouldn't be so terrified of the microphone-microscope if I could introduce others to this as-yet-unfamiliar, but captivating music.

I had occasion to be in New York more often by then. When Anne O'Donnell learned that a close friend of hers planned to be away from her apartment on West 72nd Street for an extended period, she arranged for me to stay there. She said I could move a piano into the apartment until her friend returned in a year or possibly two. I jumped at the chance and decided to move my smaller Steinway to New York rather than rent an instrument. Chris was delighted, as was Amelia, especially since there was enough room for her to stay with me whenever she wished.

Once I was settled in, Chris wanted me to meet more people—actors, singers, dancers. Meeting them made me feel more accepted in New York. But what I enjoyed most were the quiet times with Chris, including our three-hour lunches at the Szechuan, where we would grimace about "hacked chicken" and order something else. Chris savored life and included me in his own.

Webster and Lilian were delighted that I could be in New York more frequently, as were John Browning and Anne Baxter, who was starring in a Broadway show. Anne would come by for half an hour in the afternoon, and I would do an informal run-through of something I was working on. Each time, she would tell me that the live music had given her the energy lift and morale boost she needed for her evening performance.

In November, I played a concert at Alice Tully Hall, featuring a program that had been, for the most part, long entwined with my life. I had first become acquainted with the Bach French Overture back in Vienna days, when I heard Harich-Schneider play it and was transported by its magnificence. It was another of those important pieces that had kept playing inside me, through the years, helping to keep my problems in perspective. The Schubert A-Major Sonata, D. 959, was one of the two monumental Schubert masterpieces that had also woven through my life. The third work on the program was my fascinating new discovery, the Szymanowski *Masques*.

After the concert, a long line of people greeted me backstage, including a distinguished-looking gentleman who introduced himself as Alan Barrody-Szymanowski, nephew of Karol Szymanowski. He had read about my performance of the Études, Opus 33, and was thrilled that someone, especially an American pianist, was programming his uncle's wonderful pieces. He presented me with copies of his uncle's last two works for the piano—the Mazurkas, Opus 62, which were out of print and virtually unknown. I was delighted to meet him and was touched by his gift. We arranged to get together soon.

At one point a friendly young man shook my hand, said how much he had loved the Schubert, and added, speaking particularly about the dramatic second movement, "You don't play like a woman!" He seemed to have enjoyed the concert so much that I teasingly responded, as I held onto his hand, "Thanks! Um ... Tell me ... how many women have you heard play the piano?" I ended my question with a chuckle, and he laughed, too. I also heard some delighted laughter from farther down the line of people, and glanced up quickly to see a young woman with long brown hair, who had evidently enjoyed my reply.

When it was her turn to speak with me, the young woman introduced herself as Donna Handley, an editor at *Ms.* Magazine. I was excited to meet someone from the then-new publication, headed by the well-known activist Gloria Steinem. Donna said the magazine would be interested in doing a piece about me. We exchanged contact information, and things took off from there.

What Donna and her colleagues at *Ms.* had in mind became a major feature. They decided to send a reporter to one of the appearances on my upcoming spring tour, where I would be playing a concert and then appearing as guest lecturer at a five-day piano workshop for college students and teachers. Amelia and Chris, who were also part of the post-concert crowd, were delighted.

While we were in New York, Amelia and I had lunch with Shirley Fleming, chief editor of *Musical America*, who had asked me to write an article for the magazine. Like Amelia, Shirley had also grown up in the South and shared with Amelia the sense that a meal with friends should be an unhurried experience. During our lunch, Amelia confided her plan for the new Delos enterprise. Shirley, who knew the classical music business well, listened with fascination but growing alarm.

Finally, she exclaimed: "Amelia! You'll *lose* your *shirt!*" It became an oft-quoted line, at least among our volunteer friends, as the Delos adventure continued.

I lingered a few more days in New York, meeting the *Ms.* group, including Gloria Steinem, and discussing the event they would send a reporter to cover. I was already impressed with Gloria's brilliant leadership, but what struck me most in person was her gentle and unassuming manner.

Before I left for California, Chris and I had another great get-together, and I told him what I had confided only to Amelia and my family—that in my next appearance in New York, I wanted to play the Chopin B-flat Minor "Funeral March" Sonata. It was the piece I had been playing when the polio attacked me.

Chris's understanding of my need to complete this internal cycle helped lighten the burden I carried. Although we had a wonderful working relationship, the most important aspect for me was our warm personal connection and Chris's understanding of my long—and ongoing—climb. I couldn't say to many people, "I still have a long way to go" or "Maybe the rest won't come back." Most people who cared about me or about my budding career didn't want, or couldn't stand, to hear that. But Chris could.

Chapter Seventeen

❦

Braving the Microphone—
and a Tragic Loss

My next New York appearance was a year away, so I had time to decide if I would include the Chopin "Funeral March" Sonata. Meanwhile, I focused on the music of Chopin's countryman Karol Szymanowski. When I had played Syzmanowski's *Masques* and Études, Opus 33, on tour, audiences and reviewers had responded to the music with great enthusiasm. Perhaps introducing such little-known repertoire on recording could quiet my post-polio fears of the microphone. In case I could take that leap, I started "playing in" an earlier set of Szymanowski Études—Opus 4—that could be added to my first recording program for the fledgling Delos label.

Amelia suggested inviting Katja to be with us in the recording booth, if that would help my comfort level. Katja accepted and mentioned that June would be a good month for her to come to LA.

Alan Barrody was excited that I might record his uncle's *Masques* and Études and said he'd be delighted to write the program notes. The two out-of-print Mazurkas he had brought me were enchanting, and he told me there were many more, all of which he would send along.

"Sir Malcolm" went ahead with his recording plans and became Amelia's first Delos artist—brilliant in a group of Scarlatti sonatas. The recording took place at Capitol Studios, a Hollywood landmark. Malcolm's friend John Wright turned out to be a capable producer for the album, and Amelia took on the job of executive producer. Amelia became instant friends with the chief engineer, Carson Taylor, and the second engineer, Hildegarde "Hilde" Hendel, whom she found to be highly skilled and easy to work with.

Malcolm wanted to write his own program notes for the LP, which everyone thought appropriate. Amelia and I agreed that a quote from Sir John Barbirolli would be perfect for the record jacket: "Malcolm Hamilton is doubtless Bach's twenty-first child."

The Capitol Studios team introduced Amelia to a graphic designer, Harry Pack, who had designed record jackets for other companies, mostly "the majors." Harry and Amelia immediately hit it off, and Harry recognized the significance of her Delos mission, offering Amelia very reasonable pricing for album design.

Meanwhile, some interesting performance dates came my way, including playing the Shostakovich Concerto No. 1 with Neville Marriner and the Los Angeles Chamber Orchestra in LA, followed by a Southern California mini-tour. The Houston Symphony invited me back, this time to play the Mozart Concerto No. 17 with Rafael Fruhbeck de Burgos conducting.

Several of my tour performances were linked with university-sponsored workshops. As planned, *Ms.* Magazine sent their reporter, Deena Rosenberg, to Goshen College in Indiana, where my performance was followed by a five-day workshop for piano teachers.

Shirley Fleming, who had asked me to write a piece for *Musical America* about my concert-workshop experiences, found one of my stories especially amusing, giving it the subtitle "Double Header."

> *At one university where I spent several days on campus, the student committee went with me to choose a piano for the concert. They wheeled two concert grands onto the stage, and I proceeded to play the same piece on first one piano, then the other. "I had no idea the instrument made such a difference," commented one student, "I wish the others could have this experience."*
>
> *"Would you consider doing something like this tomorrow night?" another asked.*
>
> *After introducing the idea to the audience (at the concert), I explained why I had chosen Piano A for the first piece, played a little of it on Piano B, then changed to A. In the works that followed, I continued the pattern of playing the "wrong" piano first, then moving to the "right" one. By the time I reached the last piece on the program, everyone was familiar with the pattern.*
>
> *So when I sat down at Piano A, there was a murmur in the audience. Assuming I was rejecting Piano A, students were saying to each other, "But that's the right one, she should play that one." Such was their involvement that they were upset to think I might have made the wrong choice.*
>
> *I explained how difficult this choice had been, moved to Piano B and then back to Piano A, to everyone's audible relief. A student who had missed my opening explanation approached me at the reception afterward and asked: "But what do you do when you come to a hall where there's only one piano?"*

As the university-sponsored workshops and discussion sessions began to catch on, Chris suggested that I write a general description of such events that either he or my management could send to any interested group. In the last paragraph, I wrote:

> *Such sessions help to break down barriers between performer and public. We are discussing the need we all have for something of lasting value in our lives, for something beyond the temporary or the pragmatic. We are talking about a greater awareness of our own human potential—what the arts help us to explore in ourselves, and how to go about it. And in talking about these things, and about music in this context, one usually comes away from such a session feeling that something special has happened—a kind of communication we all need in our over-mechanized, over-commercialized world.*

In June of 1973, it was time to proceed with my Szymanowski recording. The studio date was set, and Katja was arriving a couple of days early. On the drive back to Santa Monica from the airport, she was enchanted by what she saw, especially the tall, graceful palm trees. "Oh!" she exclaimed, her voice full of both wonder and laughter, "Did you put the palm trees there just for me?" It was just the right way to start our project.

I was nervous during the recording sessions, but focused on sonorities—the exotic tonal tapestry of "Scheherazade," for example, the first of the *Masques*. The adrenaline intensified everything, and I tried not to notice the microphone, but rather to concentrate on the sound of this entrancing music floating around the room. My Steinway D, brought to the studio a couple of days earlier, seemed to be perfectly comfortable there, and I willed myself to match its mood.

As the sessions progressed, John Wright proved to be a meticulous and positive producer. Katja and Amelia made warmly encouraging comments. The engineers, Carson and

Hilde, cheered me on and made helpful suggestions. Almost everything else soon became a blur, as I was exhausting myself in the process.

The moment we got back to Santa Monica after the first session, I was too tired to do anything but lie down. Amelia explained to Katja the extreme post-polio fatigue she had seen so many times and suggested that I just go to bed and stay there. She and Katja brought food and sat by my bedside, doing most of the talking while I let every muscle relax. I had no idea how the recorded takes sounded, but knew I had given my all to Szymanowski.

Once I had recovered from the sessions and was back at the piano, I began to look at the Mazurkas Alan had sent me, and decided to explore them gradually. The Mazurkas numbered twenty-two in all—fascinating pieces in the composer's late style, melding modernism with often jagged Polish folkloric elements. There was much variety from one Mazurka to the next and often variety within each short piece. Now that I had taken the first step into the recording arena, this could be a worthy follow-up project. Here again, it was little-known but enthralling music.

First, however, I needed to prepare my tour program built around the Chopin B-flat Minor Sonata—my rise-out-of-the-rubble progress marker, eighteen years after the polio attack. The program would begin with short and lively pieces by Spanish composer Antonio Soler, followed by one of the earlier Schubert sonatas. The Szymanowski Études, Opus 4, which I'd recorded but hadn't yet performed live, would be a natural to complete the program.

Meanwhile, my teaching life began to expand. After giving a couple of workshops and master classes at California State University, Northridge, I had become a member of CSUN's part-time faculty. Fortunately, my students were always happy for an excuse to come to Santa Monica, so I didn't have to drive to the San Fernando Valley campus on a regular basis. I had been offered a full-time position, and Dad loved the idea of such a secure-sounding job, but I reluctantly turned it down. I knew I couldn't handle that responsibility along with some remaining IHC students, ongoing physical therapy, and the travel for out-of-town appearances.

As it was, I continued to push myself to the limit and frequently beyond what my medical consultants advised. There was never a day when I could forget that I was really "a polio" presenting myself to the outside world as "a normal." Those in our play-through group were used to seeing me stretch out on one of my foam floor mats or air mattresses afterward, or even between sections of the program. They knew I was pushing my upper-back muscles, shoulders, and neck muscles beyond the recommended limit. They knew that I still rested in secret and avoided events where I wasn't sure there would be armrests on the chairs. Those close to me took as a matter of course the ice packs to calm down an inflamed muscle group, or heat packs to soothe a tired muscle about to go into spasm. But Chris was the only professional person in the world of the arts who knew about my double life.

In early fall, Amelia and I flew to New York for a couple of meetings and some special time with Chris, before setting out for Baltimore and Washington, D.C., where Jimmy DePreist had invited me to play the Chopin E-Minor Concerto with the National Symphony Orchestra. Before we left New York, I told Chris that I had decided to put the Chopin "Funeral March" Sonata on the program for the next spring's New York appearance. We both knew that completing what we were calling "the Chopin cycle" was a serious decision. "I can't wait to hear you play that sonata!" Chris exclaimed. "I'll play it for *you*," I promised.

Then it was on to Baltimore, where Amelia and I would be staying during the rehearsals and performances in Washington, D.C. A couple of years before, Anne O'Donnell had introduced us to Rosa Ponselle, the legendary American opera star, who lived in Baltimore. Rosa had invited us to visit at her home, Villa Pace, whenever either of us could be in the area. Amelia and I had been longtime fans of hers through her archival recordings and had much enjoyed getting to know her over several visits.

Rosa was excited about Amelia's mission of recording American artists. This led Amelia to ask questions about the early days of recording, when musicians performed in front of a flared metal horn, which gathered and funneled sound waves toward a diaphragm whose vibrations caused an attached stylus to etch the sound waves onto a wax rotating cylinder or disc. The engineers made balance adjustments by altering the performer's position relative to the horn. Rosa told us that the engineers had always made her stand "farther from the horn" than most other singers, since her voice was "too big." I was especially interested in Rosa's description of her long and careful advance preparation for recording sessions. Since editing wasn't part of the process, the takes had to be as flawless as possible.

It was relaxing to stay at Villa Pace with Rosa. She understood performance preparation and anxiety, and empathized with my strenuous climb back from polio and the musical reason behind it. She had retired from professional activity herself, but could be heard joyfully vocalizing any time she was alone in a room or on her way up or down stairs.

The concerts were intense, but another milestone for me. Jimmy, with his personal warmth and sensitivity, was a very supportive conductor. I had played the Chopin E-Minor Concerto effortlessly in my teens, but wasn't yet sure how it would hold up with my rebuilt playing mechanism. Both Jimmy and Amelia had encouraged me to take the step, and so I did, with Rosa cheering from the sidelines.

Back in Santa Monica, I began my play-throughs of the program for the "Chopin tour" that was set to start in November of 1973 and climax at Alice Tully Hall in New York in

April of 1974. On Sunday, November 4, just after my fortieth birthday and a few days before I was to leave on tour, I had an excited call from Chris. He described a project he was working on for me and a party that was taking place at his apartment that evening. We discussed the *Ms.* article to be released that month and some plans he had for future PR projects. Then he mentioned needing to do some window cleaning, apartment tidying, and other preparations, and promised to call after the party or the next day.

The next morning, I got a call from Chris's brother, Rupert, whose voice sounded strange. He could hardly get the words out. "Carol, I have terrible news," he managed to say. "Chris fell out of his apartment window . . . yesterday . . . onto the sidewalk . . . eleven stories."

I was frozen in shock. Everything went out of focus, and I couldn't take in what Rupert was saying. When he could speak again, he went on: "Some are suggesting that it . . . might have been . . . suicide."

At the word "suicide" my voice suddenly returned. "No, Rupert!" I cried. "I talked with him . . . yesterday! He was excited . . . about the party!"

When I could continue, I told him that the last thing Chris had mentioned was the need for some window cleaning and tidying up before his guests arrived. Rupert hung gratefully onto everything I said, and there were more silences while we both tried to speak again. I explained that Chris had told me about some of the people who were coming that evening and repeated that he had been excited about the event. I insisted that suicide was out of the question and that it must have been the most tragic of accidents.

As soon as I told Amelia, and added that some were suggesting suicide, she shook her head. "Chris would *never* endanger the lives of others," she assured me. "If he had been suicidal, he would have found another way."

I called Rupert back immediately and repeated what Amelia had said. Evidently no one else had thought of that important factor. Amelia's insight was clearly reassuring to him.

This devastating event cast the imminent tour in a completely different light. Chris and I had been discussing the significance of the Chopin B-flat Minor Sonata, and its place in my internal cycle. Now, with terrible irony—if I could bring myself to do it—I would be playing the sonata built around the famous Funeral March, with its transcendent middle section, in Chris's memory.

I couldn't get past the horrifying image—Chris setting out to clean his living room windows, leaning out to get a swipe at something on the other side of a window, his foot slipping on the hardwood floor, the terrifying recognition that he couldn't save himself, the unthinkable moments of plunging to the sidewalk below. It haunts me to this day.

But soon I had to set out on the first part of my fall tour. I hoped I could find a way to keep it together despite my profound grief at the loss of such a beloved and irreplaceable friend. One of the first performances was back in Baltimore, at the College of Notre Dame, where I also did a workshop with students. Rosa came to the concert, and her presence and understanding were reassuring. The young students seemed excited about what we worked on, and their excitement carried me through the workshops. The tour also took me to Jacksonville, Florida, where I had done previous concert-workshop appearances. The warm reception from people I'd come to know there helped, too.

Throughout the next five months of touring, especially before each solo program, I questioned how I could make it through the Chopin "Funeral March" Sonata. And I worried even more how I could get through that piece in New York. In my mind, the city was intertwined with Chris, and he had been planning a celebration there after the event on April 22. Amelia promised to fly in for the concert, and thought the music would be especially meaningful to Chris's friends, many of whom would undoubtedly be there. That was a powerful argument.

A couple of days before the concert in Alice Tully Hall, a memorable note arrived from the entire *Ms.* Magazine group, in anticipation of my upcoming performance. "Give 'em hell!" it read, signed first by Gloria and then, in two columns, by everyone else on the staff. When I walked onto the stage, I saw Gloria, Donna, and a substantial number of my other "sisters" in the front rows, smiling broadly. They had been extraordinarily kind to send me their vote of confidence. But it was quite another level to come to the actual event and seat themselves up front so I would see them and feel their support. That act of "sisterhood" has stayed with me ever since.

Many of Chris's friends were there, tearful but grateful that I was going through with the performance. It was unspeakably difficult when I got to the Funeral March. I wasn't sure I could make my way through it without breaking down. But the collective support from all of Chris's and my friends helped give me strength to focus on what I was there to do: playing for Chris, in memory of him, and completing an important step in the back-from-polio cycle, which he had been anticipating with such confidence.

The *Ms.* group's strong support that evening went farther than coming en masse to the concert. Gloria was watching for a review, as she had noticed a *New York Times* critic in attendance. After a few days went by with no sign of a review, Gloria called the *Times* and asked to speak with the Arts Editor. She gave specifics about the concert, mentioned that she had seen the reviewer there, and asked when the review would be published. No specific date was given, but a couple of days later a glowing review appeared, bearing the headline: "Carol Rosenberger in Elegant Pianism." As a career journalist, Gloria knew that, in general, other topics tended to edge out arts news; and in her friendly but fearless way, she had made a difference.

Amelia and I had been planning to invite all of our "sisters" to the little apartment on West 72nd Street for a party, and once we agreed on a time, nearly everyone came. At one point, I was standing right behind Gloria and Amelia, who were engaged in animated conversation, when Donna sat down at my piano and silently pressed a couple of keys.

Gloria leaned toward Amelia and said to her, sotto voce, "The hem of the garment!"

That casual comment really hit me. Did I perhaps have a little magic back, after all this time?

Chapter Eighteen

∾

A Concert and Recording Diary

I rarely made diary-style notes during my tours or after other concert performances. In the early days, I wrote a few letters. But during most of my tours, I chose to call people rather than write them—in order to save my shoulders, arms, and upper back for the scheduled activities. Still, I made a few exceptions to this pattern, two of which I've included in this chapter. I wrote some of these notes in the present tense, as the events were so fresh that I could easily relive them afterward.

The first two entries describe a two-concert, one-workshop appearance at UCLA in late February and early March of 1976. The third and fourth entries describe a Delos recording session about three weeks later.

February 28, 1976
I am sitting on the stage of Schoenberg Hall, UCLA, in Los Angeles, at a nine-foot, ebony, concert grand piano. Behind me is a dark acoustic shell. The house lights are dim, so I can't see out into the hall very well, but it is empty except for the ushers getting the programs ready for the evening's performance.

The piano is silent for the moment, as I have just finished my pre-concert warmup—an hour and a half of playing slowly through the three Beethoven sonatas that make up the program. I've been thinking through the music, listening to it in the hall, getting acquainted with the sound and feel of the piano. The piano is dull on top and too bright in the middle register, which means that I cannot shape some things—especially in the first two sonatas—as I had planned. I have decided what compensations I can make: how I can best work with the unevenly voiced instrument.

I think back over the three sonatas, wondering if there is anything I should go over again. I decide that I have done what I can, that I'm at about the right point—warmed up but not yet fatigued.

If I were to look back through my life, I would find that much of it has arranged itself around concerts—the high spots of a life I will probably remember through events of this kind.

Barbara, the stage manager, opens the door of the green room and looks in. She has close-cropped blond hair and an open smile. She is dressed casually in shirt and slacks. She knows her job and does it calmly; her routine is well established.

I glance at my watch, which is lying on the table. 8:35. So they wait only five minutes for latecomers here.

"Ms. Rosenberger? It'll be about five minutes."

Barbara has everything under control. However, she can't do anything about the women who are bustling around the kitchen attached to the Green Room. They are going to sell cookies and coffee at intermission, so of course they are preparing the refreshments just as I am trying to calm myself before the concert.

Barbara opens the door again and smiles. Rare to find a woman stage manager. It's nice to work with Barbara; she's gentle at a time when my nerves are taut. She doesn't have to say anything; her wordless smile means it's time to start.

My stomach gives the familiar lurch, my heart starts pumping blood at a faster rate. I force myself to move slowly, to breathe deeply. I have my handkerchief in one hand and my thermos cup of warm herbal tea in the other. My parasympathetic nervous system has it all wrong. It's not the internal organs that need the blood now; it's my hands. But they always get cold before a performance, and the tea is a good antidote. I smile back at Barbara and demonstrate—more to myself than to her—that I am in control.

"Guess it's that time then," I say, nonchalantly, brightly, as if I think it doesn't matter that much. There are concerts in this hall all the time, I tell myself. I have played many concerts that were harder to do, and were crucial to my career. But my gut knows it's important. It's always important.

I've got a lot of friends out there, I tell myself. But I know that's one thing that makes my heart pump at its present rate. A lot of friends who say, every time I come back from a concert tour, "When are you going to play here in Los Angeles?"

So here I am at UCLA, about to play two programs. They haven't heard me here publicly for a couple of years. A lot has happened since then, and I want the performance to be the best I can do.

Barbara and I walk back behind the stage, between two sets of black curtains, to the other side. There are two bouquets on the table, one of yellow roses and one of red carnations. Barbara had asked if I wanted them in the Green Room, but I told her about my hay fever, and suggested that she keep them at a distance until after the performance. There they were—the promise of the other side of the performance, that there would be an Afterwards.

"Your dress is lovely," Barbara says. Flame, my best color. A strong color that won't wash out under the stage lights, that looks good with blond hair, and that gives a warm tone to an otherwise severe setting—an imposing-looking black piano in front of a dark brown shell, and, for the audience, a pianist in profile.

"It's marvelously comfortable," I answer. "The fabric is stretchy and moves with me." Almost as comfortable as the jerseys I always practice in. I swing my arms to help circulation and relax the muscles, and to illustrate my point.

I put my cup of tea on the little ledge, where Barbara has also placed a pitcher with cold water and a glass. I'll need that later, when I come off between sonatas, hot from the stage lights. She takes her position at the light board. She looks over at me and raises her eyebrows.

"Any time," she says. "Whenever you're ready." I breathe deeply again and let my arms hang loose. The muscles want to tighten, but I try not to let them. Fight or flight is not appropriate here.

I remind myself what I am here to do; that for right now the last three Beethoven sonatas belong to me, or I belong to them, and the fusion belongs to the audience. That fusion has already taken place. I can't undo it by nervousness or a mediocre piano, by cold hands or sweaty palms or strange shadows on the keys. It will be there always, slightly different, but there at the core. Nothing will shake it now. Like the mountains I look at every day across the canyon from my house, they will appear in different lights, but they will always be there.

Three magnificent works about life and death and transcendence. They have woven their way into the drama of my life over the past twenty years. They have seen me lose everything and gain much of it back. I had only to look around, and they were there. A soundtrack of my last twenty years would have them as a leitmotif.

Appropriate that I should play all three of them here in Los Angeles, at this point in the journey, when I am feeling very strongly that I am coming full circle. An ever-widening circle in some ways, and yet one that seems to be coming ever closer to the center.

Mom and Dad have driven up to be here tonight; they have seen the whole cycle from the beginning. Amelia is here; she came into that cycle at its lowest point. I think of all three, and imagine their thinking in perspective, which helps me to do so.

I nod to Barbara. I'm ready. The house lights go down slowly, and the volume of audience conversation follows like an echo, as if Barbara were gradually lowering the level of voices with one of her levers. I take one more deep breath and step out onto the stage.

How familiar it all is: the lights that seem too bright after the dimness of backstage, the slight ringing in my ears, the knees that feel a little shaky as I bow. I bow low and slowly, thanking the people in the audience for their presence here. Maybe they had to worry about babysitters or fight freeway traffic. Maybe they spent time dressing for the concert, finding a parking place, standing in line at the box office for tickets. They have made the effort, in this age of televised and recorded entertainment, to get to the concert hall to hear Beethoven and me, this evening. I am grateful for their confidence, for their interest. My warm feelings for them expand and edge out the nervousness. I smile my greeting to them and sit down.

The concert bench seems too high now that I am full of adrenaline. From experience, I know to leave the bench the way it is; I know that it will seem right again shortly. I make my gestures slow and smooth as I put my handkerchief on the piano, into the metal hollow where the serial number is stamped. I have carefully dusted out that hollow beforehand.

I turn toward the audience from my seat on the bench. "There are a couple of mistakes in the printed program," I say, noticing that my voice sounds natural, though lower than usual. "The second Sonata on the program, the Opus 110, is not the Sonata customarily known as the *Hammerklavier.*" I am interrupted by delighted laughter—scattered chuckles telling me that many in the audience know very well that the gentle Opus 110 is quite different from the massive Opus 106. It is like listing velvet as a "rough and ready" fabric.

I think my way into the gentle color of the opening of the Opus 109. I want to start it as if it has been going on for a while under the surface, and I have joined it at the point where the audience can hear it. Once I begin to play, I give myself fully to the fusion. If I keep it coming from the core, it will be all I am capable of at this moment. I am trying to give this performance everything I am and know, up to this point in my life.

Gradually the adrenalized state smooths out, and there is fusion between the musical intent and the audience—flowing through me, through the instrument, out into the hall to the people there, and circling back to the starting point—all one continuous circle. The beautiful Opus 110 enchants, exhilarates, and takes both performer and listeners on an inspiring journey to luminous glory.

During intermission, I think toward Opus 111 and reflect on Opus 109 and Opus 110. Barbara locks the door. I have a little applesauce and the rest of my tea. I get a dry handkerchief out of my backstage bag. How can hands be cold and perspiring at the same time? Now I'm warm.

What does one remember from a performance? Each performance gives the work more substance, more dimension. Webster said of the Schubert sonatas that they hang inside him like chandeliers. Performance also gives the work more sheen, luster, more illumination. Webster's description is good, except that the Beethoven sonatas are more substantial for me than chandeliers, and they seem an integrated part of the whole of me rather than identifiable parts of my inner dwelling.

Now it is after the concert, and my dear friend Whit, in a buoyant mood, is driving me home. While he parks his car, I walk toward the front door. It's ajar, and I hear excited voices inside. The after-concert party is well underway, as I knew it would be by the time I had greeted people backstage—hugs from acquaintances and friends, smiles from shy students, autograph requests—all most welcome.

My dress is damp and I feel a slight chill from the outside air. I step inside the house. I should probably change to something dry, but I would rather join the party, so I wrap my stole around my shoulders. There is my mother—slim and dark-haired and beautiful in her dark wool dress that she likes so much. Her eyes are moist with emotion, and her head held proudly but tilted shyly at the same time. My father is smiling the broad Rosenberger smile, his cheeks pink, his face always looking polished when he's excited. How can they have changed so little in twenty years? I hope I age as beautifully and as vitally as they have.

Amelia is moving back and forth, making punch, caring about everyone, seeing that they're comfortable, that they meet each other. I am drained; I have nothing more to give. But I know it's OK.

My friends gather around me—two, three, four at a time, giving me their energy and enthusiasm, giving me back something I've spent in the performance. Gene Ling, the screenwriter who lives down the street, brings me some punch. He and his wife, Betty, have become good friends. They keep their pool water warm all year long so that any time I'm home I can do early morning water exercises, so important for "polios."

Anne Baxter is there, and says, "Well, I love the dress . . . and the eyelashes. . . ." Then she stops speaking and just gazes at me, shaking her head slightly, eyes misting. Meaning that there are no words to describe the Beethoven.

Michael Kermoyan, Broadway actor-singer and longtime friend, brings me some hummus in a pocket of bread, a treat that he has spent the day making. I'm not hungry yet, but he is standing there waiting to see if I like it, so I make an attempt.

"You hate it," he pronounces in his deep bass voice, trained to project from the stage.

"No," I protest, "it's really delicious," and I mean

it. Even if I weren't convincing, it wouldn't really matter, because I've *played*. I could do absolutely anything for the remainder of this evening, and it would be all right. Giving a concert performance absolves me from any further responsibility.

My friends not only understand, but they want to take over. I relax into their warmth. Those few hours after a performance—or two or three days after a long concert tour—are the only times I feel totally free, as if I could allow myself anything. After that "the drive," as Amelia calls it, sets in and I have to work—whether for immediate or long term, it must be for a purpose. Without that, the story of these last twenty years would be quite different.

Tomorrow morning I'll have to let "the drive" take over. The Chopin/Szymanowski program is only six days away. It will take place in the same hall, with many of the same people in the audience, perhaps; but with strenuous and totally different repertoire. That means five days of slow practice, thinking through the music away from the piano, playing it through for a few friends a couple of evenings; every kind of careful preparation. Amelia suggests that I have my own piano brought to UCLA for the performance. I am more nervous about the next concert, in some ways, than I was about tonight's program.

March 19, 1976
The Chopin/Szymanowski program is now a memory; a memory of slow warm-up in a hot pink gown, the surprising beauty of my own piano in the hall, the responsive feel of the instrument in its home territory—it was meant for a concert hall, of course, and I felt during that evening that I was, too.

The most delightful memory is of two handsome little Polish boys coming on stage in native costume at intermission to present me with some red roses. Flowers from the "Disciples of Szymanowski," as they signed themselves, with their marvelous unpronounceable Polish names. The children made the presentation midway so that they could get home in time for their regular bedtime. I sent them each an autographed program and a Szymanowski record.

This morning I'm filing newspaper clippings in case anybody should want them: pre-concert interviews, reviews of the past week's programs, and an announcement of my one-day "residency" at UCLA. They've been called workshops, discussion sessions, rap sessions, master classes—and now a residency.

The UCLA event was an afternoon of talking with an eager group of music students. I opened it up to questions right away, and it went on for over three hours. There was some red punch in a big glass bowl and a huge plate of cookies. The discussion was so absorbing that I completely forgot about taking a break; and none of the students mentioned it. Evidently it was up to me to suggest the break. I felt embarrassed later when I realized that it was dinnertime, and that the whole point of the punch and cookies had been to give us all a break in late afternoon.

I'll be recording the Szymanowski Mazurkas in ten days. A year spent learning them and a year to let them settle. Two years of work and I have to record the sum of it all in two evenings. Jane Turner gave me a recipe for bran cake the other day—a basic recipe with suggestions about ways to vary it according to one's mood and what one has in the house. Her little note said, "It's like a Mazurka!"

A longtime member of our play-through group, she had listened to a few of the Mazurkas and remarked on their spontaneous quality. I was showing her some of the different possibilities with one of the pieces that sound somewhat improvised. I told her that I kept playing it differently, and she found that fascinating.

What would be a recipe for a Mazurka? You take a dotted rhythm like this, put the accent either on the second beat or the third, or both; elide it to the next measure or hold it back. Start it slow and dreamy and improvised, or moderate and free, or moderate and strict, or fast and free, or fast and strict. It may be a *Mazur*, or it may not; it may be an *Oberek*, or a *Kujawiak*. It may be like the dance or it may be an impression of several dances. It may be a mood, with mere suggestions of dance rhythms here and there to remind one of the piece's inspiration. Or it may be, in turn, all those things. You may feel that you could dance for a few measures, and then you are left swaying dreamily while the musicians improvise.

And then you hope that your Polish blood will aid you. Is there some understanding of the mazurka in my genes somewhere? Nana, when you taught me to say "I love music" in Polish, did you ever dream that I'd be squeezing those genes for some Polish insight?

There are twenty-two Mazurkas in all—elusive, complex, rich in folk material, and yet the ultra-refinement of the Polish aristocrat. Can I play them so all those qualities are there?

March 26, 1976
Today my piano was carted off by the piano movers. Mr. Gregory, with his tam and slight Scottish brogue, turned the heavy nine-foot piano on its side, and onto

the dolly, as if it were a delicate invalid. He wrapped it tenderly in the quilted blankets and wheeled it out of the house as if he were taking it for a stroll, a little fresh ocean air, and California sunshine. By now it will have arrived at the recording studio, two days early so that it can accustom itself to the temperature and humidity.

Later today I will be going over to the studio to practice on it there. I think of the practice as being for my benefit, but I am told that the piano needs it, too. If I practice on it for two days, it will respond by going out of tune, i.e., relaxing all it wants to do, so that by the recording session on Monday, it will hold its pre-session tune more reliably. It's odd to think that the instrument needs me.

March 30, 1976

This was to be the second day of my recording project. A project I looked forward to, and worried about, for the past two years. All the while the Szymanowski Mazurkas have been taking shape, I have been wondering how I could possibly let only one version stand. I've also been wondering how my right hand could hold up under the pressure of continued stress under the microphone-scope. Why did Szymanowski write so many chords with just the wrong stretches for me—placed just so that a strain is put upon my weakest spot? MJ said that those very passages would build me up—to keep practicing them. But under the microphone-scope I knew I would feel the pressure, and that my arm would tense. Then the very muscles I needed the most would be stiff the next day.

As it turned out, there was no next day. After two years of work, off and on, and at least as long of worry, I recorded all twenty-two of the Mazurkas in one five-hour session. Recording time, playback time combined. Some of them went in one take.

The recording took place at Capitol Studios, where I had recorded the *Masques* three years before. There is an old scratched-up piano in one corner—hardly a fitting companion for my Steinway. Behind a screen is an enormous pile of machines of all description—tape recorders, monitors, microphones, and other recording paraphernalia, stacks of amplifiers, equalizers. . . . There is a gray couch toward the back of the studio, a lifesaver for me. I can lie down there while the others go out to dinner. I have learned by now to bring my lunch so that I can eat in solitude and quiet and use the dinner hour to rest my back "in the horizontal."

The recording booth is double-glazed. I can see lips moving, but can't hear voices until someone presses the intercom button on the Big Board. Carson, the chief sound engineer, sits at this mixing board, with its multicolored buttons, knobs, levers—red, green, yellow, and white buttons, dials, and needles that swing with every sound. Hilde, the second engineer, stands at the back of the booth in front of two freestanding giant tape machines. She makes notes on the takes so that they can be located precisely on each huge reel. She controls both machines—the "A" and the "B" or backup reel.

We started at three o'clock, adjusting microphones, moving them around. "Carol, play the biggest, loudest section of . . . Something with more bass. Better come in and listen."

And so I would unseal the recording studio by opening the inner door, then the outer one, and go next door to the booth, listening to what I had just done. I liked the sound—warmer, more reverberant than my last recording. Was it as easy as that? No, Carson wanted to get another equalizer. I could continue to warm up while he sent for it.

I played slowly and lightly through some of the more treacherous Mazurkas. "Warm up, get the hands and brain ready, but don't tire the hands. Don't take the edge off the day's energy or endurance by overworking now," I kept telling myself.

Carson came back with the equalizer. Now I was to do the same passages again. "Come and listen now. We think it's better." John Wright, our producer, has a cool, rather expressionless manner. He smiles at me, comes over, and touches my shoulder. Even though I know he's working on being warmer, more supportive, it helps—I respond. The muscles can't help relaxing if everybody thinks the session will go well.

I open both doors and go back to the booth. The sound is beautiful. Hilde is beaming. "It is really a concert hall sound, now!" she says in her high-German accent. Hilde and I have become friends since the first session we did together three years ago. She has since heard me play in public and insisted that I try to play in the recording session more the way I do on the stage.

"Maybe we should turn off all the lights and have a spot on you," she suggested. "Then you would think it's a performance, and you wouldn't be so stiff." We go back into the studio and try turning off the overhead lights. The spotlights are colored and strange. They make shadows on the keys, and I shake my head. "I think I'll just have to use my imagination and the overhead lights," I decide.

Finally, everything is set, and we are ready to go. I pour myself some decaf tea to make sure circulation is good. I am nervous during the first Mazurka, but the sound is good. The first take goes well, but I do another just for good measure. The second Mazurka goes quickly, also; two problem spots go by without showing themselves. Carson is smiling. I begin to relax.

I play the third Mazurka in one take. "That's beautiful, Carol," the monitor in the studio says. It's John's voice, and I can see him. He's pleased, and thinks I should leave it at that and go on.

We started recording at about 4:00 p.m., and by 7:00 p.m. I had completed twelve Mazurkas. I had been worried about Nos. 8 and 12—so strenuous that I didn't think I could do certain sections enough times to get a clinker-free take. The tricky section in No. 8 had gone well on the second take; in No. 12, I got it the first time.

We started again at 8:30, and by 10:30 I had finished six more Mazurkas. John suggested that I come in and listen. I hesitated.

Amelia understood. "I think Carol just wants to go on through," she said. I nodded, and plunged into the final group. I was tired by then, but still in control. When I had finished the last Mazurka, I heard excitement in John's voice as he said over the monitor, "I think we have it!"

Chapter Nineteen

✥

New Frontiers

During the next couple of seasons, my tours brought some memorable experiences. An invitation to play in Pittsburgh turned into a kind of homecoming, where I reconnected with former classmates from Carnegie. When I appeared on Eastman School of Music's Great Performers Series, the *Rochester Times-Union* reviewer mentioned my spoken comments to the audience: "The statuesque blonde appeared in a tangerine-colored gown and verbally delivered program notes on the more unusual items, Schubert's *Seventeen German Dances* and four Mazurkas from Karol Szymanowski's Opus 50, Book IV. . . . She scored a genuine triumph with Beethoven's Sonata in C Minor, Opus 111."

He was the first to write about something I was doing more frequently—finding opportunities to establish rapport with an audience by saying a few words about the music. Amelia was delighted that I was beginning to feel comfortable talking to the audience, and joked, "Any excuse will do."

There was a new recording frontier, too. Jimmy DePreist proposed a Hindemith program, to be recorded at Abbey Road Studios in London with the Royal Philharmonic. I traded two shipboard performances on the QE2 for tickets to London for

Amelia and myself, and Jimmy flew in. We were all excited to be in London and felt an instant rapport with the Royal Philharmonic musicians and with the British producers.

My role in the project was as the soloist in *The Four Temperaments*, a superb work for strings and piano that had been neglected in the concert world. Since the piece's theme and four variations portray an ancient psychological theory of personality traits (melancholic, sanguine, phlegmatic, and choleric), everyone told Amelia that she should write the album notes from her psychologist's point of view. She described "Choleric" this way:

> *The* Choleric *personality, with his overflow of yellow bile, is hot-tempered and irritable. The movement opens with a quick, emphatic pronouncement from the strings. The piano immediately reacts with a slow burn, a gritting of the teeth that erupts into an outburst. The strings insist on their earlier statement, followed by more outbursts from the piano. Suddenly, our fiery friend is contrite in two charming recitatives from the piano. But he must win his point, and soon he's back to insisting violently that he's right.*

To those of us who knew Amelia well, reading her notes on the music was like hearing some of her frequent insights and observations about people. Writing later about the album, she recalled:

> *This recording did considerable Delos consciousness-raising worldwide. The Balanchine revival of* The Four Temperaments *ballet in New York around the same time came as a surprise to us—a welcome one, for ours was the new recording, and available everywhere.*

Between sessions, Jimmy and I began comparing polio treatment experiences, and he described what I considered to be basic—but far from extensive—physical therapy. When I started telling him about the benefits of further, and more targeted, therapy, he said reflectively, "Well, if I had been in your situation, I would've continued, but since I was still able to conduct . . ." He stopped and shrugged. His upper body was in very good shape. And because he could conduct from a wheelchair and get onstage with a cane, he had lost only a year or two in his career trajectory. He had found considerable acceptance as a conductor abroad and, prior to his "gig" at the National Symphony in Washington, had been an assistant conductor to Leonard Bernstein at the New York Philharmonic.

One thing Jimmy and I shared as "polios" was a lack of overall physical endurance. We both tired quickly. Jimmy described the photo shoot at the end of *The Four Temperaments* sessions as "a few happy people and one worn-out conductor who couldn't keep his eyes open."

Back home in Santa Monica, I found out that James Goodfriend, Music Editor of *Stereo Review*, had included me in a survey he called "All the Young Pianists." There were twenty-three of us—twenty men and three women in *Stereo Review's* international survey—and to my astonishment, I was the only American woman to be included.

Around that time, my teaching took another step up when I was invited to join the University of Southern California music faculty, whose roster had long included some of the great names in music. As part of my USC faculty activity, I offered to create a Preparation for Performance course—or semester-long workshop—for music students. The course would be open to singers, organists, string players, harpists, woodwind and brass players, percussionists, and, of course, pianists. The proposed subtitle was "Psycho-Physical Elements in Performance," as I would be sharing with normal student performers techniques and insights acquired in my long journey back from polio to professional piano playing.

More than thirty students enrolled in the first class. The classroom was a sizable one, allowing plenty of room for everyone to stretch out on the floor for muscle-relaxing exercises. The first time we did this, I demonstrated a stretch and suggested that the students stay in that position as long as it felt helpful. One of the students, a harpist, called out, "How about all day?"

My favorite memory is the time the students were all stretched out on the floor, thinking through in slow motion a piece of music they would be performing. I had asked each student to choose one piece for some experimental kinds of performance preparation. As they were thinking through their self-assignments, they closed their eyes, and the room fell into absolute silence. At one point, a door leading to the hallway opened, and there stood a group of people, led by the head of the USC School of Music. He was saying "and this is our Preparation for Performance . . ." then suddenly broke off, as he and his visitors saw the array of motionless bodies, all with their eyes closed. It was too soon after the Jonestown Massacre media coverage for the visitors to feel anything but visceral alarm at such a sight. I hurried to the door and explained.

As the class continued, we discussed subjects I had long brought up with my private students and in concert-connected workshops. A topic that everyone seemed to like was the musician's focus in performance—the other side of the painstaking preparation that involved the performer's slow-motion internalizing of musical detail. We discussed the all-too-common thinking that accompanied playing for "juries" and competitions: "How well am I doing? . . . Can I measure up? . . . What will they think of me? . . . Can I do this?"

Here, however, we emphasized a performance focus that projects to the audience one's own understanding of, and feelings about, the musical material. Just as it helps while practicing to respond silently and continuously to an entire piece, a section, or even a single phrase with whatever emotions the music elicits, so it helps to focus on those emotions in performance. "You are so beautiful! . . . How you sparkle! . . . You are magnificent! . . . Ah, now you're preparing me for something startling!"—and on and on, with infinite variations and intertwinings—are all expressions of feelings that direct the shaping and character of one's playing.

The class turned out to be so popular that the head of the USC School of Music soon asked me to repeat it the following semester.

Meanwhile, Amelia had become excited about the then-very-new digital recording process. She had met and conferred at length with a fascinating pioneer in digital recording, scientist-inventor Thomas Stockham, who had invented the prototype Soundstream Digital Recorder. As she was pondering what might be a suitable project for Delos's first venture into the digital realm, Amelia and I were invited to a concert featuring trumpet virtuoso-conductor Gerard Schwarz in Los Angeles. He was succeeding Neville Marriner as music director of the Los Angeles Chamber Orchestra, and neither of us had yet heard him in live performance. We were both bowled over by his joyful virtuosity and captivating musicianship, and when Amelia came up with a brilliant idea, I agreed wholeheartedly: Why not try to work out a digital recording with him?

By the time we went backstage, Gerard ("Jerry") Schwarz was about to leave the auditorium to catch a plane back to New York. But in the few minutes we had together, he expressed great enthusiasm for Amelia's project and said he wanted to get the New York Chamber Symphony and the New York Trumpet Ensemble involved.

Amelia and Jerry pursued the project with continued excitement, and in early 1979 two landmark digital recordings, the *Haydn/Hummel Trumpet Concertos* and *The Sound of Trumpets*, were made in New York, at the 92nd Street Y. These recordings would mark Jerry's last appearances as a trumpet virtuoso and his first as a conductor.

Amelia had invited her friend, American composer Ellen Taaffe Zwilich, to help on the production side in New York. She had gotten to know Ellen a few years earlier, during the Delos recording sessions for the Boston Musica Viva's American Composers Series. California engineer Stan Ricker traveled with Amelia to New York, and Tom Stockham brought his Soundstream equipment and his own engineers. The series of sessions attracted a great deal of music-industry attention.

During the first session, there was a glitch in the Soundstream recorder, which erased part of Jerry's cadenza in one of the concertos. Tom and his engineers were distressed, but when Amelia broke the news to Jerry, he was unfazed. "His lip was swollen out to here," she demonstrated, "but he just said cheerfully, 'No problem. I'll do it again,' and went back out on stage and did a brilliant cadenza."

Jerry marveled at Amelia's ability to create an atmosphere of calm and focus for everyone. "We must have had thirty music writers at that session," he said afterward. "I was oblivious to them all. That's how it felt with Amelia—nothing else mattered except the music."

I went with Amelia to Salt Lake City for the editing sessions, which took place in Tom's basement. The hard drives went into machines of a size and shape that very much resembled electric washers; in fact, Amelia and I called them "the washtubs." Each huge hard drive held approximately seven minutes of music. The editing process was basic and cumbersome by today's standards, but a brave new world to us at the time.

The transfer from the recorder to the editing equipment was especially sensitive, as we had to go from one "washtub" to another during a take, and preferably not near an edit point. "Stand by, Amelia!" Tom would call in a clarion voice. "Stand by, Jim!" "Stand by, Jules!" And on through the list of those controlling the various posts through which another seven minutes of source takes would be transferred. We labored far into the night at the editing console, and Amelia and I took turns working with Tom's engineers. Whoever was on break was free to take a catnap on the floor.

I was enjoying my new role as an audio editor—partly because of the chemistry between Tom and me, partly because Amelia and I were having a great time with his young engineers, and partly because I was finding a new use for my lifelong musical training. I didn't have to spend much of my shoulder-and-arm capital during the process. I just had to indicate where the edit should be made, if the edit point should shift to the left or right, or what we might try that could smooth the edit. Those decisions required a nuanced grasp of the musical shaping and pacing and a sense of what would enhance the presentation.

As Amelia, Tom, Stan, and I worked on further recordings, my new role became a more active one. Amelia planned a recording with the Sequoia Quartet, a beautiful group that played frequently in the Los Angeles area. Susann MacDonald, an internationally renowned harpist who was living in Los Angeles, was also interested in making a recording. We thought the Sequoia Quartet and Susann's harp would record beautifully in the intimate, warm-sounding Immaculate Heart Auditorium, so I arranged some evening sessions. My friend and onetime colleague Theresa Di Rocco was thrilled at the idea and came on board as assistant producer for both recordings.

Amelia, Stan, and Tom started trying to persuade me to record some Impressionistic music, mostly Ravel and Debussy, which I had been playing on tour. They all thought this special "sound world" could become a particularly exciting venture in the new digital medium.

It occurred to me that my repertoire already included a group of Impressionistic pieces that were all about water. I had been drawn to them as music, of course, but there were other factors, too. Water had helped restore some of my life perspective in the years I had been living near the ocean. Water continued to be my salvation for rehabilitative exercises. And who knows what subliminal forces drew me even closer to the Impressionists' "water music"? But I sensed that such a project would not only be meaningful for me but probably of interest for the new medium, too.

While discussing the "water music" recording project, Tom mentioned having heard a Boesendorfer Imperial Concert Grand the year before and being stunned by its range and beauty. I had admired Boesendorfers during my years in Vienna and marveled at their singing sound. As we began looking around, it was exciting to discover that one of the few Boesendorfer Imperials in the United States could be found in Southern California.

Amelia and I soon made a trip to the Colton Piano Company in Orange County for a live encounter with the exotic Imperial. After an hour or so of playing a variety of repertoire on the splendid instrument, I had fallen hopelessly in love. Amelia, who hadn't encountered a Boesendorfer up close, was ecstatic. We inquired about rental availability for possible sessions in June.

"Yes, it's available, if it hasn't been sold by then," the manager answered. Sold? This glorious instrument was for sale? And someone else might buy it?

I did a quick but intense soul-search, made my peace with a long-term financial obligation, and became the lifelong guardian of "Boesie," as we came to call the magnificent Imperial. Boesie must have been comfortable with the arrangement, as it has been singing happily ever since.

Amelia and Stan decided that Bridges Auditorium in Claremont, California, would be the right place to make the *Water Music of the Impressionists* recording, preferably when Boesie could spend a couple of days before the session, getting acclimated to the hall. As Amelia later wrote, the hall was "a large, warm room with height . . . irregular surfaces and lots of wood . . . we tried to create the sensation that you (the listener) are seated in choice seats—about ten to twelve rows back in the hall . . ."

Boesie revisited Bridges Auditorium the following year, when Jerry invited me to record the Shostakovich Piano Concerto No. 1 with the Los Angeles Chamber Orchestra, of which he was by then music director. Jerry's Los Angeles audiences, along with the players and his Delos fans, were excited by his brilliant, joyous, and lyrical performances as a conductor. His first recordings for Delos, with both his New York and Los Angeles orchestras, had those same qualities and were being celebrated worldwide—receiving such honors as a Grammy nomination and a Record of the Year award from *Stereo Review*.

Chapter Twenty

❦

My Walk with Beethoven

I'm not sure who first brought it up, but soon Amelia, Stan, Tom, and the Delos volunteer group began talking about another solo recording for Boesie and me: Beethoven's magnificent Opus 111.

My friends knew that the Opus 111 had decades of special meaning for me. They had heard my stories of "living with" that piece while I was a polio invalid. They knew that I had performed it many times on tour over a period of some fifteen years. So, they asked, what could be better for the next project? The prospect of recording what was, to me, an almost-sacred masterpiece was both exciting and frightening. But excitement won out.

The next step was to decide on a companion piece for the album. Tom jumped in enthusiastically with a vote for Beethoven's Sonata, Opus 57, the "Appassionata." He couldn't wait to hear it played on Boesie. Tom's excitement about the piece, the light in his eyes and special resonance in his voice as he spoke its name, were contagious.

I had a special history with the "Appassionata" as well. It was the masterpiece whose architectural wonders Franz Eibner was exploring when I chanced upon his Schenker-theory seminar in my

Vienna days. The "Appassionata" had drawn me into those Schenker explorations and, in that sense, had also helped me through the polio years.

The recording was set for March of 1981, and once again Boesie traveled to Claremont. If a single event symbolized reaching the summit of my personal Everest, it would be the day Boesie and I recorded the Opus 111 together. There had been other progress markers in my twenty-five-year climb out of the polio rubble, but recording Beethoven's final testament for the piano represented the peak of that climb—and always will.

I took some notes immediately after the recording experience, and here they are, as I wrote them.

March 21, 1981
I walk through the neighborhood in Claremont. Flat-roofed ranch houses across the street from the Griswold Motel—what everyone thinks of as California. Beethoven loved to walk, too, but he would have been walking in Doebling, outside of Vienna. The *Beethoven Gang* (Beethoven Walk) and its little signs that point you in a certain direction so you can retrace Beethoven's path exactly . . . People there speaking as if they had known him personally: "Beethoven used to stand right here. Then he would walk that way." You have the feeling that you, too, are seeing that eccentric genius.

Claremont is so different from the "Beethoven Walk," and yet here I am, walking with Beethoven's music playing in my head. He wouldn't think it too daring of me to record his Opus 111, would he?

Trees still grow and people still go shopping—and worry about other things besides the Opus 111. I must do some more relaxation exercises. But don't plan in such an anxious fashion. I need to take everything in sequence, in an unhurried way.

As I let the *Arietta* and the gently rolling first variation play through in my mind, it seems as if I must have walked here many times. But I know that feeling is overlaid with other familiar things. The short red raincoat I've taken on tour with me for years, the scarf of many colors that I've worn so many times, the mounting adrenaline and half-conscious relaxing of neck and arms that I do automatically when working up to a performance.

I wonder if I should think through every note, as I do before a performance, going back if I have let my mind wander, lingering on every chord or passage that might be in the least fuzzy.

But today I decide that isn't necessary. After all these years of performing Opus 111, I don't need to practice it mentally at present. And yet it keeps playing in my mind. It might well be the sum of all the times I've played, and thought through, and heard the piece. I want it to be all of that, when I record it a couple of hours from now.

By then I'll be fighting anxiety, and now I am remembering many of my peak times with the sonata . . . and some of my lowest moments, when the music seemed in greatest contrast with my life. The seemingly endless failures as Webster tried steadfastly to help me, day after day, some twenty years ago. Mom and Dad never losing hope on my behalf. Dad grinning affectionately, with tears in his eyes. . . . Mom always saying, lovingly, whether in person or on the phone, "I'll be listening!"

All the way back to a very sick version of myself, semi-reclining on cushions in Boulanger's studio some twenty-five years ago. Mademoiselle wanting to know what music would mean the most to me just then. I knew that she was asking, "What would help you to feel that you haven't lost everything?"

The answer was the musical-philosophical world of late Beethoven and musical essences . . . life essences . . . the beauty of Opus 111's *Arietta* . . . the warm glow of Opus 109.

I had needed magnificent creations to dwarf that devastating blow, to make the polio losses seem temporary. As with so many good things, my relationship with the Opus 111 began in pain.

As I return to the motel, Amelia is about to get some refreshments for the recording team at the local supermarket. I go with her, as I am most comfortable when in her company. I'm sitting on the sidelines in the supermarket, waiting while she selects the groceries. I'm doing finger stretches. First, with thumb hooked under chin, I stretch the fascia between each finger. Then I pull each finger gently, in line with arm and wrist. I'm also doing shoulder rolls and neck stretches.

Amelia says laughingly after this routine that she was getting looks of sympathy from other shoppers who had seen us come in together, as if to say that it can't be easy having such a strange adult daughter. People look at me disapprovingly as we leave and she opens doors, handles all the bags, and puts everything in the trunk, while I stand idly by, shrugging my shoulders and doing head rolls to relax neck muscles. When looked at from that perspective, she has a lot to put up with.

Once we get to the hall, Amelia tells the rest of the team the supermarket story with that rich, relaxed laugh of hers, enjoying the phenomenon of what is about to take place. She and I already know that each recording session where I manage to hold up and hit performance level for the entire span feels miraculous to us both.

My contact lenses are getting cloudy for some reason. I think I'm probably exuding anxiety from my eyes. Am I only pretending to be a pianist? (The same old question that keeps popping up in important moments.)

And yet just recently I received word that *Water Music of the Impressionists* was named Critics Choice in *Gramophone* magazine. It's that "if they only knew" feeling. But they *do* know by now, at least part of it. My polio story has been out for some fifteen years.

And there is one thing I know for sure: Opus 111 is one of "my" pieces.

The "Downward Leap into Space," or "Leap into the Abyss," in the opening movement . . . like my own leap into space—in how many performances of this piece, and in how many life situations surrounding it?

The "Deep Song" of the *Arietta* . . . letting it flow out into the hall, joining every experience I've ever had with this music.

Overcoming the feeling that the microphones are closing in . . . moving past them and taking the space as my own . . . filling the empty hall with the sound . . . letting the sound float back to me.

In between sonic adjustments I smile and remember Martha's little three-year-old niece, who thought that the music was there in the piano and I was the person who knew how to turn it on—how to make it work. What I have to do now is release the music into the room. It helps to feel that it's all there, waiting to be let out, waiting to be tapped into.

I come downstairs to listen to a playback of a complete take. I hear the sound and the flow, and a few isolated errors. But I can't focus on it. The active involvement is too great. I am too excited, too adrenalized, too grim, too anxious.

Stan hands me the headphones. "Listen through these." I hear more hall resonance. It sounds bigger than it does to me upstairs.

Amelia and Stan turn to me with raised eyebrows and smiles. Amelia says, "Good take, don't you think?" George Baker, our brilliant organist friend, and today the assistant producer, enthusiastically nods his assent. I tell them honestly that I don't know.

There are various layers of uncertainty, of having to accept something my hands could do, rather than what I sought. These layers could accrue—they're there if I look for them—but the Opus 111 has been purified many times in that white heat of performance, where the focus is so intense that the hesitations have to drop away. All that is left is the idea—the sound. One's limitations are simply not part of that focus. This is true particularly of the masterpieces that have seen me through the recovery from polio, the slow climbing out of the rubble.

I try to call upon that continuous thread that stretches from the days with Boulanger in Paris through Vienna, Copenhagen, Santa Fe, Detroit, Los Angeles, Stockholm, London, and New York. Now that thread needs to be ongoing through Claremont for another day or two.

The magnificent *Arietta*—Opus 111's final movement, with its inspired variations—brings us a great, strong spirit in a gentle and transcendent mood. Beethoven has said it all; and those final, accepting chords of the *Arietta* tell us that we have reached the end of the road.

Chapter Twenty-one

❦

To Everything There Is a Season

Just before the release of the Beethoven recording, Lilian Aitken called me with shocking news: Webster had died suddenly at their home in Santa Fe. During our long phone conversation, Lilian filled in the details of his last days and mercifully short illness. She also reminded me how pleased Webster had been that the dreaded "one dried-up flower" had become, after all, part of a long-lasting bouquet. Lilian and I reminisced about those long Santa Fe summers more than twenty years before, when Webster had tried with all his might to help me rise from the ashes. We agreed that the Opus 111/"Appassionata" recording symbolized that intensive effort. With Lilian's tearful appreciation, I dedicated the Beethoven recording to Webster: *In memoriam, Webster Aitken (1908-1981)*.

My focus soon began to change from strenuous solo tours to more recording projects, with a few tour dates sprinkled throughout. As my physical endurance was defining its limits, and I was becoming more comfortable with the microphone, the shift in emphasis seemed the natural way to go. And after daring to record the Opus 111, the pinnacle of piano sonatas, further studio projects seemed less daunting.

The Beethoven recording received splendid reviews, as did *Water Music of the Impressionists*. Amelia remarked that a review in *Audio* magazine was especially interesting because the reviewer was the celebrated audio engineer John Eargle. John had written a series of books considered the "bibles" on modern sound recording and was revered by the international community of recording engineers. He was based in Los Angeles, though he traveled frequently to give classes and workshops in universities with outstanding graduate sound-engineering programs.

Soon afterward, Amelia met with John, and that pivotal encounter led to a close friendship. John had been a pianist and organist before turning to audio engineering, and he was also an advisor to JBL in loudspeaker design. As our friendship grew, John took on the role of Delos Director of Engineering, attracting a steady stream of young engineering graduates, who were eager to train at Delos under his guidance.

Tall and slender, John was focused, often amused, and so passionate about music and audio that at times his eagerness resulted in a slight stammer. He spoke clearly and precisely. He would smile and joke with the Delos team, and then say something serious like, "I think we should consider the following. . . ." And in a very few minutes, everyone would have a clear vision of how we were going to approach a project.

Since John loved the pipe organ and relished opportunities to record celebrated instruments, a distinguished Delos organ series took shape. When the organist and recording team took a break during sessions, John would often say, with a broad smile and a twinkle in his eyes, "I'll catch up with you in a bit." We all knew that he looked forward to playing the organ himself when no one else was around, and often the rest of the team would return to find John still blissfully playing.

John's living room became a second Delos studio-listening room. It was furnished with the finest listening equipment, thanks to John's ongoing work with JBL and other audio equipment developers. Adjoining the living-listening room was a dining room, which, instead of a table, housed a lovely Steinway B grand. I knew that John practiced almost every day on his Steinway, but whenever I was there he encouraged me to play something so that he could just listen to it.

Meanwhile, Tom Stockham and one of his top engineers had set up an editing facility in the Los Angeles area, which opened the door for me to participate even more. Soon Delos had its own editing setup as well, supervised by Amelia and John. I continued to enjoy editing, since I could listen to takes and map out edits in a posture with minimal neuromuscular strain.

Working "on the other side of the microphone" involved me more closely with Delos's musical growth, which in turn limited the amount of teaching I could take on. Soon I retired from an active role on the USC faculty and kept just a few private students whose schedules could be flexible.

One of my first ventures into the session-producer role was for my dear friend John Browning, in a Liszt solo piano album. John Eargle was the engineer, and it was fun to be part of the sessions while those two brilliant minds were interacting. A couple of years later, John Browning was easily persuaded to follow his Liszt album with an all-Rachmaninoff program.

A new friend from Santa Monica, Phyllis Bernard, wanted to sponsor a jazz series for Delos, coordinated by jazz producer Ralph Jungheim and engineered by John Eargle. Amelia was knowledgeable about jazz, and the series brought back happy memories of her husband, Doug, and being with him when he sat in at the keyboard with high-level combos. One of the first projects was an album featuring the great jazz singer Joe Williams. His *Nothin' But the Blues* turned out to be an irresistible, one-of-a-kind album, and brought Joe his first Grammy at the end of a long career.

From the very beginning of her startup mission, Amelia had referred informally to Delos as "the Baby" when something was needed for its health or welfare. Usually, Baby Delos's need would supersede anything personal on her part.

"Where does she get her money?" I had overheard someone say about Amelia, shortly after she started the label. I felt like responding, "What money? She has a mission and close friends who want to help make this work." As a psychologist, Amelia was fully aware that people often project onto others their own feelings or motivations or perspectives. Yet even with this awareness, Amelia still anticipated that others would treat her with the same goodwill that she felt toward them. I saw her disappointed many times, but she would approach the next situation with the same openness and lack of fear, and always with positive expectations.

Amelia was not a businessperson. She made decisions based on musical worth and personal enthusiasm, not financial gain. After the Delos team had put a great deal of work into a song album with the superb American soprano Arleen Auger, Arleen had mixed feelings about the result. Although the renowned singer gave the go-ahead to release the final edit of her album, she apologized for not having been in the best voice. "I'm afraid I spent too much time out in the California sunshine before the sessions," Arleen confessed to Amelia.

Amelia responded with a question: Would Arleen prefer to rerecord the program? Arleen jumped at the chance. The resulting happy ending was that Arleen's *Love Songs* album was nominated for a Grammy and singled out by *Billboard* as an All-Time Great Recording.

Amelia put a lot of effort into enterprises that included trips to Washington, D.C., to request NEA funding for recording American composers—in particular, a series featuring the Seattle Symphony with Jerry Schwarz at the helm. The orchestra's administrators assumed that Delos must be making a lot of money from these projects—otherwise, why would Amelia continue? It didn't occur to most people that Amelia simply believed that the recordings should be made. As Jerry knew—

and had expressed at the time of his first Delos recording—for Amelia, it was always about the music.

Jerry kept coming up with recording plans that sounded exciting, and some of them included me. He and I recorded eight piano concertos together during the 1980s and early 1990s. Among them were Falla's *Nights in the Gardens of Spain,* the Strauss *Burleske,* and two little-known concertos by American composer Howard Hanson. The concertos were all part of programs Jerry had planned with his own orchestras—the Los Angeles Chamber Orchestra, New York Chamber Symphony, and Seattle Symphony—as well as the London Symphony and Scottish Chamber Orchestra.

In London, Jerry decided to do a Beethoven program, which gave me a chance to record my all-time favorite piano concerto, the wondrous Fourth, in G Major. In Edinburgh, Jerry recorded a four-disc Haydn series. The great Janos Starker joined us to record two Haydn cello concertos, and I played a pair of Haydn's piano concertos. We all loved spending time with Janos, and during some post-session happy hours, planned further recordings with him. Amelia had a soft spot for anything Scottish and considered that unforgettable sojourn a high point. We all called the experience a "Haydn high."

During the 1980s, I began to have increasingly severe post-polio episodes that limited to an even greater extent what I could accomplish, and threatened to shut down my playing yet again. This time, the ongoing medical team suggested a consultation with Dr. Jacquelin Perry, head of the Rancho Los Amigos Post-Polio Rehab Center in Downey, California (where Hope Hopkins had once worked). Dr. Perry was chief of their pathokinesiology service and a professor of orthopedics at USC. Dr. Perry and her associates diagnosed my condition as "acute post-polio syndrome representing accumulative strain from chronic overuse of muscles with less than the normal number of motor units." She suggested some assistive devices—frames with moving parts—to support my arms and upper body when I was at the piano and at my desk. I found them cumbersome from the beginning, and never felt that they could be harmonious with my work. Nevertheless, Dr. Perry and her associates had succeeded in reminding me that only a finite amount of life was left in the areas that had been hardest hit by polio.

Dr. Perry and her staff presented me with a plan that would increase my rest periods and decrease strain on my upper back, shoulders, and neck muscles. She also had an interesting handout for post-polio patients. It explained more precisely why and how muscle function could appear to be lost suddenly, after a period when the patient has been overusing damaged muscles, which was a technical explanation of the "burnout" Hope Hopkins had often warned me about. It also explained why such a loss of function could seem almost random.

I kept recording anyway. After Jerry and the great clarinet virtuoso David Shifrin had completed a landmark Delos recording of the Mozart Clarinet Concerto, David and I came up with the idea of recording the Brahms Clarinet Sonatas together. We made it a re-creation of a famous "soirée" at Clara Schumann's home in 1894, which had included the Robert Schumann *Fantasiestücke.* That project led to another delightful experience— playing and recording the Mozart and Beethoven piano-wind quintets with David and three other wonderful wind players who led their various sections in the Los Angeles Chamber Orchestra. David and some of the leading string players from LACO also joined me for a recording with Martha and Dady's younger son, Bejun, who was a remarkably gifted boy soprano.

In 1988, I made a solo recording called *Night Moods,* a dreamy, lyrical program suggesting evening and romance. Not long after its release, Amelia and I decided to go a step further and create a lullaby album. We both felt strongly that one of the best gifts anyone could give a young child, even from babyhood, is the experience of great music—and the younger, the better. So

I began putting together a program of simple, comforting works by great composers that could be suitable for a nursery, for the elderly, and for everyone in between. I invited Amelia to listen to some of the material I was considering. Every so often she would say something like, "That's lovely, but it's not pre-pubertal enough." So I would go back and choose something else that had that kind of perfect innocence.

Amelia wrote children's notes for the album. She always knew how to talk with kids in a very direct, and as she used to put it, eye-level manner. My favorite phrase in her notes was that Robert and Clara Schumann "lived in Germany in a big house." We decided to call the album *Perchance to Dream: A Lullaby Album for Children and Adults.*

A whole world of listeners welcomed the "Perchance" program, which spoke to every human condition, beginning with the prenatal, and brought comfort and beauty to all ages. In her introduction to the CD, Amelia wrote,

> *Good music, like good books, can provide a haven throughout life—a shelter against the heavy weather that comes to us all. At Delos it is not unusual for artists to receive grateful letters from individuals who have found refuge in the artist's recorded music when experiencing overwhelming events. We are grateful for these letters. And we are very happy that the writers of these letters had learned to listen to good music at an early age.*

The worldwide response to *Perchance to Dream* inspired us to create an entire Young People's Series on Delos: albums for babies, and albums that included both music and children's stories. This series was one of the most satisfying projects we undertook in those years. It managed to combine the lifelong love of music Amelia and I shared, my love of teaching, and her deeply felt wish to heal.

Amelia's understanding of the benefits of classical music for the young led her to write a statement that was widely received across many fields:

> *Developmental enrichment programs for the very young are important not only to parents but to all who care about our collective future. The healing and developmental properties of music have long been recognized. The ancient Greeks believed that music, healing, and enlightenment all come from the same source.*
>
> *One of music's properties, rhythm, is as elemental as the mother's heartbeat. Another of its properties, melody, is first experienced in the loving sounds the infant first hears from its mother.*
>
> *Great music is the form of beauty and symmetry that can be experienced before the eyes can focus. Great music is the form of logic and order that can be experienced before the brain can differentiate words, designs, or numbers.*
>
> *Music is often called the "universal language," because its truths precede words and transcend words. Music speaks to the entire being, and as such engages the senses, the emotions, and the spirit. Great music thus becomes a magic potion in a child's early brain development, an ever-renewable source of enrichment.*

Some of the most fascinating projects for the Young People's Series involved narrations. We had a wonderful time with the great ballerina Natalia Makarova, who narrated two Russian fairy tales for us, with piano music of Prokofiev and Tchaikovsky, and a Stravinsky "Firebird" story interwoven with the ballet music. Two memorable projects for the American Composers series also included narrations. For those recordings, we had the privilege of working with James Earl Jones on the voice-over narration for Copland's *A Lincoln Portrait,* and with Michael York for *The Rubaiyat* in its setting by American composer Alan Hovhaness.

Around the time that *Perchance to Dream* was released, my mother began to have memory problems. The cause wasn't entirely clear, as she had taken a fall while on a walk. But in our daily phone conversations, if I gave her items to be discussed, her thinking, judgment, and perspective were unimpaired. We continued to have our good talks until the day she took another fall, and this time the effects were indeed serious. She was hospitalized, and I dropped everything to rush to her bedside at the hospital in Tucson. (Mom and Dad had moved to Tucson from Southern California a few years earlier.)

Dad and I couldn't do much but just be there, and it wasn't even clear that Mom knew who I was. "Mama?" she asked at one point when I was stroking her hair. At least she knew that I was someone who loved her very much. One day the phone by her bedside rang. Dad had gone down the hall, so I answered the phone. It was Amelia, and as we exchanged a few words, I noticed that Mom looked interested. On an impulse, I handed her the phone. To my amazement she said, "Oh hello, Amelia!" She listened for a moment, and then answered, "Oh yes, it's wonderful!" There were a few more snippets of conversation, and then she handed the phone back to me. When I asked Amelia what elicited the "wonderful" comment, she replied gently, "I said, 'Isn't it wonderful to have your daughter there?'"

Later, in the hospice, we were able to play the *Perchance to Dream* CD in Mom's room. Little had I known when I was recording the program that, before long, it would be playing soothingly for my beloved mother in her last days.

A few months earlier, I had recorded a program of serene piano music that was about to be released under the title *Reverie.* The last piece on the recording was the Liszt *Consolation* in D-flat. Dad particularly loved that piece and had once commented that he would like to have it played at his own memorial. Now, he and

I agreed that I would play it at the informal memorial we were having for Mom at their home. My dedication on the *Reverie* recording reads:

> *Dedicated to the memory of my mother*
> *Whilamet Gibson Rosenberger (1904–1992)*
> *whose beauty of spirit will be with me always*

I was worried about Dad being alone after Mom's death. They had been together for sixty-seven years. He wanted to stay in their house, and it was reassuring to see that his friends were gathering around. Especially heartwarming was the support from his neighborhood friends Bob and Mary Ann Calmes. They included Dad in their plans, called unfailingly to wish him good morning and good night, and in many ways brought him into their family. Their beautiful white Samoyed, Thundress, was a daily companion as well. She adored Dad, recognized the sound of his car as he approached the Calmes' house, and would rush to the door, wagging her tail joyously.

Bob and Mary Ann spent the hot Tucson summers up in the Colorado mountains, in Steamboat Springs, and invited Dad to go with them. In the summer of 1995, shortly before I was to fly to Colorado for a visit, a call came from Mary Ann. Dad had taken Thundress for a walk in the late afternoon and then had gone upstairs to rest for a bit. When he didn't appear after his usual half hour or so, Mary Ann had gone up to check and found him unconscious. He had had a fatal heart attack. Dad had always said, even in shock after receiving word that a friend had dropped dead suddenly, "But *that's* the way to do it!" And that's the way he did it.

Ironically, I had just finished recording another Impressionistic water-themed program, which would be called *Singing on the Water*. It was an album of barcarolles, including the Liszt transcription of Schubert's *Auf dem Wasser zu Singen* (To Be Sung on the Water). My dedication on that recording reads:

Dedicated to the memory of my father
Maurice Seiberling Rosenberger (1903–1995)
whose fearless and generous spirit
will always be my North Star

That same year Amelia, at age seventy-five, was diagnosed with cancer. Her first request was that we not tell anyone but her closest friends, fearing that any news of her condition would damage Baby Delos. She knew that hers was still the name most closely associated with the label.

From that time on, Amelia had periods of intensive cancer treatment, followed by periods of remission. When I went with her to chemo appointments, I was touched, but not surprised, by the way she could change the atmosphere in a room where several patients were undergoing the same kind of IV treatment. Whether in the waiting room or in the treatment room itself, people would be sitting mostly in silence, looking weary and sometimes depressed. Amelia would look around the room and catch someone's eye, smile, and make some comment about a scarf or a shirt or something that happened on the way up to the office or any other random topic that might start a conversation. And once an exchange started, most people would brighten up and join in.

Amelia's strategy worked partly as a distraction from that omnipresent IV in the treatment room and partly as a bit of community to offset the loneliness patients can feel at such times. It was the sort of thing Amelia could always do when working with families—as she had brought them together with social workers, probation officers, and nurse counselors at Lathrop or any other psychological-medical facility. Or it could be anywhere, in any meeting, with any group of people. But it was deeply touching to see her do this when she herself was undergoing treatment, and yet making the day just a little better for the others in the room. Amelia's battle with cancer would go on for more than a decade.

Although she needed time for rest and recovery, Amelia was always optimistic, and she was determined to continue Delos projects with as much enthusiasm as ever. We even put together a follow-up album to *Perchance to Dream,* this one also drawing on Shakespeare for its title: . . . *Such Stuff as Dreams . . . A Lullaby Album for Children and Adults.*

In the summer of 1998, Amelia and I went to a Chinese restaurant in Los Angeles for a get-acquainted lunch with the brilliant American pianist-conductor Constantine Orbelian. He and Amelia had talked by phone, but this was our first in-person meeting. It may have been the longest-lasting lunch any of us ever had experienced.

Constantine, a dynamic, outgoing young man with a resonant voice and a contagious laugh, was a San Francisco native, and had grown up speaking both English and Russian at home. His Ukrainian mother, Vera, and Armenian father, Harry, had survived unspeakable tragedies during World War II and the Stalin era. They had come to the United States as refugees and had, over time, made substantial contributions to their community in San Francisco. Constantine grew up playing the piano and had continued his studies at Juilliard in New York.

In 1991, a few years into his successful career as a concert pianist, Constantine became the first and only non-Russian ever to be offered the music directorship of a top Russian orchestra. Since that time, he had been touring worldwide with the Moscow Chamber Orchestra, bringing American artists to Russia and Russian artists to America—applauded in both diplomatic and music circles as a cultural ambassador. Now he was eager to go to the next level and begin a recording series with his remarkable orchestra—a state-supported group of virtuoso players who loved what they were doing.

By the time we came to the first pause in our conversation, all three of us knew that this meeting was life-changing. Just at the point where "Baby" had been experiencing a slight lull, we were sketching out an ambitious and exciting new recording plan.

During the Moscow Chamber Orchestra's 1998 fall tour, Amelia, John, and I began the new recording series in what had become our favorite Los Angeles venue, the First Congregational Church. The resulting CDs were *Russian Soul,* which Constantine dedicated to his mother, Vera, and *Mozart Adagios,* with oboe virtuoso Allan Vogel and other American artists (including me) taking solo turns with the MCO. One of the sessions fell on Thanksgiving Day, so Amelia treated the orchestra members to their first-ever Thanksgiving dinner.

The following spring, Amelia and I, along with two John Eargle protégés, Jeff Mee and Ramiro Belgardt, flew to Moscow to continue the recording series. This was a dramatic development for both Amelia and me. In her teens, Amelia had been fascinated by socialist ideals of equality, wherever they could be found. She had taken Russian language classes along with her International Law studies in college, but even while working as editor of a State Department publication in Washington, D.C., had never thought she would have an opportunity to visit Russia. In my teenage years, I had read Russian composers' and musicians' biographies and had imagined their Mother Russia, as it was often called. But as an American in Vienna during the Cold War, I hadn't even been allowed to go as far east as Budapest or Prague. Now, suddenly, we were bound for Moscow.

The four of us flew from Los Angeles to London's Heathrow, where we changed planes. We had dozed for a while when suddenly I woke up, looked at my watch, and realized that we must have reached Russian airspace. That's when I found myself saying excitedly, "Amelia, we're flying over Mother Russia!"

We were to have a number of memorable recording trips to Moscow in the years that followed. Amelia and I were always welcome to stay at Constantine's flat, which was a short walk from the Great Hall of the Moscow Conservatory, where we made most of our recordings. Constantine also found inexpensive lodging for other members of the Delos team. The sessions began around 11:00 p.m., as the hall was usually booked for concerts in the evenings and rehearsals during the day. No one seemed to mind the late hour, and there was a feeling of excitement and joviality among these outstanding musicians, who would often line up to greet Amelia and me when the session was over.

We also had opportunities to record Constantine and his orchestra during their subsequent American tours. John, Amelia, and I had a wonderful time at Skywalker Sound in California's Marin County, working with Leslie Ann Jones, Director of Music Recording and Scoring. Leslie, John, and Amelia had long respected each other's accomplishments, and we all enjoyed getting better acquainted during our memorable lunches between sessions. In one program we recorded at Skywalker, a Shostakovich/Schnittke album, Constantine was both the piano soloist and the conductor. In another, the music of British composer Frank Bridge, I was the soloist in a lovely work Constantine had arranged for piano and orchestra. The great Polish contralto Ewa Podles recorded an album of Handel arias with such virtuosity, and such blazing tempi in the fast sections, that the *Opera News* reviewer Judith Malafronte referred to Constantine as "driving the getaway car." It was indeed quite a ride!

The *Opera News* review also singled out Constantine as "the singer's dream collaborator," a gift that Amelia and I noticed in him from the outset. He always seemed to intuit exactly what a vocal soloist was about to do so that his orchestra could be the ideal complement. The Moscow sessions brought us together with some wonderful opera stars who came to record with Constantine and his orchestras (both the MCO and its expanded version, the Philharmonia of Russia), including Siberian baritone Dmitri Hvorostovsky and American soprano Sondra Radvanovsky. Our first recording with Dmitri, in 2001, was followed by many more, and Sondra, in addition to a solo album, also joined Dmitri for a memorable duet album.

Throughout the many recordings we did with Dmitri, Amelia and I reveled in his incomparable artistry. He was always highly prepared for the sessions, and his breath control was mind-boggling. Each take was beautifully thought out and executed, and sometimes in the booth, between takes, he'd be doing one-armed push-ups to keep his energy level high. When he sang in one breath a phrase that any other opera singer would have split into two, my hands would immediately start sweating in a sort of visceral panic. It felt as if no one could possibly have enough breath left to finish the phrase. And yet, of course, Dmitri always did, and beautifully. Amelia and I agreed that comments about his "singing like a god" were right on target.

I hadn't been touring during the seven years since Mom's death. But in the summer of 1999, Constantine got me started again with an invitation to play a concerto with the Moscow Chamber Orchestra on his Palaces of St. Petersburg Festival series. Constantine said that after the festival Amelia and I could go on to Moscow with him and the orchestra for two more recording projects. My performance anxiety started creeping in again, but the chance to spend time in fabled St. Petersburg, the Venice of the North, was stronger.

The festival took place every summer during the city's "White Nights" season in some of its most glorious palaces, such as Peterhof, the Winter Palace, and Catherine the Great's Palace. Amelia and I drank it all in while I worked myself back to performance pitch. Shortly before walking onstage, I found out that Russian television was filming the entire concert, and my anxiety level rose a few more notches. But Constantine's relaxed manner helped me focus, and I cleared that hurdle.

Toward the end of the festival, Amelia and I attended a lavish banquet in one of the splendid palaces. Constantine had placed his Russian cousin, Vladimir, who spoke good English, next to Amelia, and I was sitting across from them at the long banquet table. When the vodka was served in what looked like jumbo shot glasses, Vladimir explained to Amelia that Russian custom was to make a toast and then drink the entire contents of the glass before putting it down. Amelia was nodding as he explained this custom and proposed a toast. After they clinked glasses, Amelia downed hers, Vladimir took a couple of sips, and they both put their glasses onto the table. When Vladimir looked over at Amelia's empty glass, his jaw dropped and he burst out laughing. Amelia had learned the chug-a-lug technique in her college years, at fraternity beer parties, so downing an oversized shot glass of vodka was no big deal.

From St. Petersburg we went on to Moscow, where Constantine and his orchestra recorded an album of Shostakovich waltzes. The sessions ended on July 14th, and we were to begin the next recording, an all-Tchaikovsky program, on the 16th. July 15th was set aside as a rest day and, not coincidentally, to celebrate Amelia's eightieth birthday. Constantine invited the Delos team to what he called "a relaxed birthday dinner" at a restaurant that had already become our favorite in the capital: The Boat, on the Moscow River. The host seated the five of us at one end of a long table more fit for a banquet, but Constantine shrugged and said it was early for Muscovites to go to dinner. As we settled down to have a celebratory vodka, Amelia and I marveled that she was spending her birthday in Moscow. But soon we learned the secret reason for the large table: Some of our favorite orchestra members began to arrive, bearing gifts and flowers. A little later a large, decorated birthday cake and champagne arrived at the table. Constantine and I will never forget the look on Amelia's face when she realized that the orchestra was in on the surprise.

That St. Petersburg/Moscow trip broke through a personal barrier. Since I had thought that my hard-won concertizing years had ceased in the early 1990s, I had accepted the miracle and felt blessed that I had already enjoyed some twenty-five years of successful touring. But after the St. Petersburg concert,

Constantine continued to invite me to perform with his orchestra on tour. From Juneau, Alaska, to Marathon Keys in Florida; from Town Hall in New York to Philharmonic Hall in Moscow; from Italy to Finland and Sweden, and many venues in between, the next few years were sprinkled with performances. I happily rode in tour buses with Constantine and the orchestra members, many of whom became my friends. Amelia usually joined us, depending on her health and Delos's needs. The orchestra loved her and always cheered when she could come along.

We did programs for all sorts of audiences, in a wide range of venues with a variety of pianos. I would play one or another of my favorite Mozart concertos on every program. The spectacular Italian saxophonist Federico Mondelci, who had been the star of our very first Moscow recording, joined us for some of the tours. Presenters always requested some of his wonderful arrangements of Piazzolla tangos, the repertoire on his first Delos recording.

Whenever possible, Constantine would offer an open rehearsal for schoolchildren, parents, teachers, and anyone who couldn't come to the concert itself. He made it informal, usually introducing some of the orchestra members. Once when he had introduced the concertmaster, Dmitry Khakamov, someone asked how old Dmitry had been when he started playing the violin. Dmitry answered that he had begun lessons at age five. "I'm five!" came an excited, high-pitched exclamation from one of the front rows. That little boy's horizon had just been expanded.

Through all of this, Amelia was valiant in the face of spreading cancer and the need for debilitating courses of treatment. But she was determined to care, or plan care, for her "Baby," even while her own health was impaired. Up to that time, only a few close friends knew about Amelia's illness, and she had asked them to continue keeping the information to themselves. Constantine knew, and always showed his concern for Amelia's welfare, helping when needed while we were recording or traveling together.

In late August of 2006, Amelia and I were in the Bay Area for a celebration of Constantine's birthday and that of his mother, Vera, who had also become a good friend of Amelia's and mine. Immediately after both celebrations, a meeting took place with a bicoastal group that was proposing a series of joint projects with Delos. Although Amelia was not feeling well, she held up during the birthday festivities, and then conducted an "Amelia-style" meeting in the conference room of the West Coast group's quarters. Constantine and I were marveling at the way she could still open communication channels among people who had never met or worked with each other—even though she was suffering from intermittent nausea, weakness, and "chemo brain." It was a brilliant meeting, and everyone left the room in high spirits.

I tried always to be on the alert, making sure that Amelia was holding on to someone when we were walking even a short distance, as her frequent dizziness could come on at any time. But she was in high gear at the end of the meeting, and set out on her own, talking excitedly with one of the New York people. Constantine and I were trying to make our way toward her, to insist that she hold onto one of us, when we saw her grab at a doorknob for support. Evidently the door had not been firmly closed, and it swung open just as Amelia took hold of it. She fell backwards, hit her head on a hardwood floor, and immediately started bleeding.

The emergency team arrived quickly and rushed Amelia to Marin General Hospital. Over the next few days, she seemed to recover sufficiently for the medical staff to approve a flight back to Santa Monica. She was told to take it easy over the next few weeks.

But then one day in early October, something seemed to go haywire. Amelia couldn't control the movements of her legs or arms and wasn't making sense when she spoke. Once again, she was rushed to the hospital, this time to St. John's in Santa

Monica, where a brain scan revealed that a severe hemorrhage had occurred. She sank into a comatose state, and only gradually and episodically began to emerge.

Throughout the years I had known her, Amelia had often said, "We'll find a way!" when a problem came up, whether at Delos or in any other part of life. But how could we "find a way" now? Her oncologist told me gently that the brain injury would preclude any further cancer treatment. In other words, even if Amelia continued a gradual recovery from the brain hemorrhage, she was doomed.

John Eargle wanted to be by my side. Other friends, too, came to the hospital. But there was no one who could help me fix any of this or help me "find a way." The extraordinary person who had encouraged me to take the precipitous climb out of the rubble, and who had given me the great gift of believing once again in myself, was now herself beyond help. All I could do was be there every waking hour with my lifetime closest friend and keep watching for some way to make that day a little better for her.

There were tests and attempts at some therapeutic passive movement, but they all seemed to result in one heartbreaking failure after another. Amelia would mumble something about "getting out of here," as if I could perhaps help her to escape from this purgatory and get back home. She even tried to figure out how to do it, gesturing toward the window and the street below as the place I should bring the car. It was agonizing to watch, and it must have been agonizing to experience. She couldn't tell me much, but her desire to "escape" was strong.

Thanksgiving, Christmas, New Year's Eve, New Year's Day—2006 into 2007—all came and left sickening trauma that I can scarcely bear to remember. One of the hardest things was having to avoid speaking the truth for the first time in Amelia's and my many years of deep friendship. I would tell her anything that I thought would give her hope and any kind of positive feeling. Yet I knew there was no hope. That same sick feeling—literal heartache—has echoed every year since, especially during the holiday time.

This agonizing situation went on for three long months, during which I would tear myself away from Amelia's bedside only to go home and try to get a few hours of sleep. Finally, Amelia's doctors decided that she could go home as long as there would be round-the-clock hospice care.

I thought that once Amelia was at home, it would feel as if she were making, or had made, some form of progress, and I wanted her to feel that way as long as possible. I decided to have her hospital bed put into the TV room that had once been an extra piano room, then a partial editing room, but was also a lovely spot that allowed her to lie in bed and look out at the canyon and mountains in the distance.

When friends came, it could seem more like a social time than a visit to her bedside, since we were in a room associated with beautiful scenery, music, and being together. John was there frequently, and one remarkable time the three of us listened to the final edit of *Heroes and Villains*, an album Constantine and Dmitri had recorded in Moscow. Afterward, our conversation was animated, and Amelia even recalled some earlier recording sessions. John was thrilled, and as he was leaving, exclaimed to me, "She's back!" He was jubilant, but at the same time we both realized that it was temporary. The unthinkable had permeated everything, and all I could do was treasure any time when my dear friend could, by some miraculous means, find her way "back" for a few precious minutes.

Two months after we had brought Amelia home, her doctors began to say we should let go and stop the life-support measures. Amelia was increasingly in pain and would need a proportionately increasing dose of morphine. To this day, I can hardly bear to think of that heartsick time when the decision had to be made. Once I had given in to the inevitable, the hospice caregivers stopped the intravenous feeding. As the *Perchance to Dream* CD played continuously for an irreplaceably beloved person, Amelia was slowly drifting away. She died on March 19, 2007, at age eighty-seven.

My best friend was gone. John stayed close, extending his hand to me, sometimes beginning to talk about practical matters that I couldn't even take in, but mostly just saying, "Lean on me, Carol. Lean on me."

Constantine, who was on an American tour with the MCO, stayed in touch almost daily. He wanted to make sure he could be there for the memorial party, just as Amelia had requested. The best day turned out to be April 1, a Sunday, and doubly appropriate since it had been her husband, Doug's, birthday.

Tributes poured in from far and wide—newspapers, artists, music journalists, publication editors, radio commentators, and, of course, friends. I welcomed them all, and wished Amelia could have read these heartfelt messages with me. One from our dear Santa Monica friend Phyllis, who after her collaboration with "Baby Delos" on the jazz series had stayed to work on many a classical project, summed up many people's sentiments:

> *Amelia thought of the large picture and lived by her convictions—she had no ambivalence on a matter of conscience. She lived by her courage . . . was ageless in outlook and focus. She was one singular, admirable, complete and outstanding woman who lifted all those around her.*

Jimmy DePreist spoke for many Delos artists when he wrote:

> *Amelia was there from the start . . . it was her dedication to American artists without an entrée into the world of commercial recordings, her feistiness and her humor . . . Amelia was the plow that broke the status quo plains of American recordings, but beyond that she was a passionate advocate for her artists and a friend now truly, truly missed.*

KUSC Radio host Jim Svejda, hailed as The High Priest of Classical Music by the *Los Angeles Times*, dedicated a special radio program to Amelia's memory, reminding his listeners that she was one of his inspirations and commenting between selections from the Delos catalog:

> *Yesterday I got the sad news that one of my genuine heroes passed away. Amelia Haygood, the Founder and President of Delos Records, died after an heroic—I should say typically heroic—twelve-year struggle against cancer. Over the years, I knew that if Amelia was bringing something out it was going to be a recording of the highest possible quality, not only in terms of the performance but the recorded sound. And it was going to be immensely interesting and worth hearing, for the simple reason that Amelia Haygood and Delos never brought out anything that wasn't. . . . One of my White Knights passed away this Monday at the age of eighty-seven.*

Dmitri Hvorostovsky wrote a touching dedication on his *Heroes and Villains* album:

> *I remember my first talks with Amelia, strolling in the little forest just outside of Moscow, where she listened to my life stories and talked and talked in return, with charm and wisdom. . . . Ever since, whenever we've been together, something important was happening in my life. . . . And through it all, Amelia's wholehearted interest and enthusiasm, her great knowledge and experience, her ongoing advice, have protected me from many mistakes and have encouraged me to be brave and honest with myself and with other people. . . .*
>
>   *I loved Amelia and love her still. I am sad that I won't see her coming toward me, with her outgoing,*

warmhearted smile, holding her usual glass of vodka in her hand. . . . I am honored to dedicate this album to Amelia.

When we made a special Thirty-fifth Anniversary Delos Opera Gala album, Constantine wrote this dedication:

> *In my opinion, Amelia DaCosta Stone Haygood was one of the truly great artists of the twentieth century. Not that she danced or sang (publicly at least), but in the thirty-four years she created and developed Delos, she was an inspiration and guiding light to everyone who had the very good fortune to meet her and work with her.*
>
> *During recording sessions at the Great Hall of the Moscow Conservatory, which typically would begin at 11:00 p.m. and go through to 3:00 a.m., Amelia was there. Music in hand, she would turn to us as soon as we walked into the control room, greeting us with a big smile and words of encouragement. She would give us the impression that this sounded great, that that sounded wonderful, that we were creating something very special, that it would be a glorious recording of the aria, that no one has ever sung it better. . . . Nerves and throats relaxed and invigorated, we would all go back to the stage, reassemble the orchestra, and do another take, probably the one you are listening to now. . . .*
>
> *A superb clinical psychologist before she founded Delos, Amelia was highly educated, idealistic but worldly, and downright smart. She had the optimum of what many call women's intuition, was keenly interested in her fellow human beings, and was a joy to be around. And Amelia's greatest joy was to be around her beloved artists and the music they made. So Amelia, this is for you! Missing you always.*

Not long after our memorial party, John began to talk with me about living situations, now that I was alone. He knew that, over many years, Amelia and I had put a lot of debt on the Santa Monica house to keep things going for numerous recording projects and other "Baby" matters. He also knew that I had turned my back on everything but Amelia's condition for six months. He had found a retirement community not far from Claremont that appeared to be appropriate for both of us and suggested that we might want to move there together. He was seventy-six at the time, and I was seventy-three. I couldn't focus so soon on any thought of moving, but agreed to go with him to look at the place. Through the fog of grief, I was also thinking that if John wanted to make a change in living situations, maybe he could move into my house instead.

But before we had even decided on a date to check out the retirement community, I had a call from one of John's friends at JBL. He said that he had some things to discuss with me and suggested that I sit down somewhere while we talked. Assuming John's friend wanted me to take some notes about a potential project, I picked up pencil and paper and sat down at the round glass table in the little dining-conference room that now seemed so forlorn. He mentioned something about an audio engineering meeting the evening before, and I replied that I knew John was going to speak at that meeting.

Then he told me that John had not shown up, whereupon he and another friend and colleague had tried to call John, with no response. My anxiety level was rising rapidly. He went on to say that he and the other friend had driven to John's house, had managed to get in through the side door, and had found him lifeless on the couch. John had apparently died in the early evening—on May 9, a scant six weeks after Amelia's memorial.

How could this be? I had scarcely begun to take in the enormousness of Amelia's death. And now my dear friend John, who was encouraging me so lovingly to "lean on" him, was also gone? I tried to look back and recall any sign whatsoever of health concerns on his part, but I could come up with nothing. What had taken him must have been completely unexpected. As Dad, who had loved getting to know John, would have said, "But *that's* the way to do it!"

John's audio engineering and JBL colleagues set out to arrange a memorial for him, a more formal one than the memorial party I had hosted for Amelia. The event in John's honor, too, seemed unreal. I couldn't bring myself to read all the touching tributes others left in the memorial book. Leslie Ann Jones from Skywalker Sound, who had become a good friend of Amelia's, John's, and mine since our recordings at Skywalker, flew down to Los Angeles for John's memorial. She had made that same trip just six weeks earlier to participate in the memorial for Amelia in Santa Monica. At John's memorial, Leslie sat reassuringly by my side, and at one point went up to the podium and gave the most eloquent tribute of the day.

An incident during the weeks that followed illustrates my own state of mind after two such devastating blows. I was picking up some mail at a business mailbox service we had been using for Delos in Santa Monica and was on the way back to where I'd parked my car. As I began to cross a side street that led to Wilshire Boulevard, a car sped up to the crossing, slammed on the brakes, and came within an inch or two of running me over. I was aware that the vehicle was headed straight for me, and had quickened my pace to avoid it, but there was no rush of adrenaline, no instant reaction to danger, no feeling at all. As I reached the curb, a woman who had stopped in her tracks when she witnessed the near-accident, asked me anxiously, "Are you OK?" It was obvious why she, as a witness, would be startled, but I couldn't feel anything. I was numb even in the face of acute danger.

In the months that followed, I kept trying to care for Delos as well as I could. One by one, our group of volunteer friends had died, or moved away, or were no longer able to help. "Baby" was ailing. I tried to learn some of the business side, but it was slow going, and I made mistakes. Ana Poveda, a lovely person at one of the sub-distributor accounts, patiently explained some essential business practices to me. I knew that she had a demanding job as Alliance Entertainment's music media buyer, and I was touched that she took the time to help me. I'll never forget her kindness. But it was looking as if I couldn't keep Delos alive by myself.

Then one day, out of the blue, a call came in on my cell phone. The caller identified himself as Jim Selby, CEO of Naxos of America. Evidently Ana had told him that I was floundering and had given him my private number. Jim asked if I might welcome an offer from Naxos to take over the distribution—worldwide, if I wished—of Delos. At one point during our conversation, as I was explaining some things very openly to Jim, he exclaimed, "If *Delos* were to go under, that would be a *tragedy!*" I was surprised and touched by the emotion in his voice.

When I explained that I wouldn't even have the funds to get the inventory to him, he assured me that would be no problem. His company was willing to fund and carry out the entire transition. Costs could be taken care of over a period of our first year or so together. When could I make a trip to Nashville to meet him and his staff? As I took a moment before replying, he quickly added, "We'll send you a plane ticket!" The entire conversation felt like a hand extended to me from heaven. And so it was that Baby Delos was rescued and able to live on to celebrate the legacies of its founder, Amelia, and its chief engineer, John.

Another chapter in the Delos rescue was coming to terms with selling my cherished Santa Monica house, which was overloaded with debt. I went through that painful process about a year and a half after Amelia's death. At Constantine's suggestion, I relocated to Sonoma, California—with the help of my nephew, Karl; Amelia's nephew, Doug; one of my USC students, Carl Dominic; and my dear friends Dena and Brad Horton. Constantine and Vera welcomed me into their family-and-friends circle, and Vera became an even closer friend and confidante, as if she and I were "family." We lost her in May of 2015, when she had a stroke at age ninety-six.

Since Sonoma is the place Constantine always returns to when he is in California, he and I are able to spend quality time together and work on new projects for "Baby." Recently created treasures, under Constantine's direction, have been American tenor Lawrence Brownlee's Grammy-nominated Rossini album, Dmitri Hvorostovsky's *Wait for Me*, and the complete opera *Simon Boccanegra*, starring (who else?) Dmitri as the title character. In the works, as of this writing, are a second album with Larry Brownlee, a new aria and duets album with Dmitri, and other projects with international opera stars.

As I continue as caretaker of Delos, there are always exciting developments on the horizon—some carefully planned and others completely unexpected. And I always wish I could share them with Amelia and John. One such delightful surprise project was American composer Mark Abel's *The Dream Gallery*.

I had settled down one afternoon to listen to a stack of demo CDs, which usually means listening to about ten minutes of each demo and then putting it into one of two piles: "To Be Explored" or "Not Right for Delos." When I got to *The Dream Gallery*, however, time stopped. The song cycle for seven different vocal soloists and orchestra drew me into its drama for its full seventy minutes. All I could do was marvel at the musical and dramatic ingenuity that made me eager to know more about each of the seven California characters I was meeting during the cycle. I laughed in some places and wept at the end, when the last character sings of picturing "the setting sun over the Pacific's horizon . . . it will inspire eternally." I kept thinking how much Amelia and John would have loved it. And now we are working on another of Mark Abel's unique creations: a poignant new opera *Home Is a Harbor*, about a California family and a veteran of the war in Afghanistan. Amelia and John would have loved this one, too.

Amelia used to say that immortality is the extent to which those left behind can incorporate the qualities they most admired in the departed person. I hope that I have incorporated even a fraction of what I admired in my parents, Nana, Bredshall, Webster, Eve, Chris, John, and, of course, Amelia herself.

I am still working around post-polio problems, and some have worsened as I inevitably experience the long-term effects of post-polio syndrome. But my beautiful Boesie is still singing joyously. Lately I've been playing through Beethoven's glorious Sonata, Opus 110, almost daily. This timeless masterpiece weaves beauty, joy, sorrow, acceptance, and finally redemptive triumph through its twenty-minute journey, and never fails to thrill and inspire.

Carol Rosenberger, November 2015

Acknowledgments

Special thanks to the wonderful composer/writer Mark Abel, who consistently encouraged me to finish this book, helped greatly with the shaping and editing, and has become a dear friend in the years since I first discovered his unique compositions. Thanks also to Anne Maley, our Delos copy editor par excellence, who cheerfully surveyed every sentence for clarity and readability. And thanks to cellist/music scholar David Brin, who offered his personal and musical perspective in reassuring me about this book's value and in making many helpful suggestions along the way. Thanks also to my friends, relatives, and colleagues who cheered me on and kept expressing their interest in this evolving project: Henry Bargert, Phyllis Bernard, Sharon Burt, Kathline Colvin, Thu-Nga Dan, Suzanne Denison, Elena Fadeeva, Katie Hackett Ferguson, Caroline Greenleaf, David Hedden, Sean Hickey, Dena and Brad Horton, Ali Khan, Lindsay Koob, Lonnie Kunkel, Lea Maitlen, Constantine Orbelian, Augusta Petroff, Gary Rosenberger, Karl Rosenberger, Gerard Schwarz, David Shifrin, Keiko Shimizu, Matthew Snyder, John Douglas Stone, David Weuste, Kira Bielfield Williams, Brian Zeger, and Jane Zimmerman.

Please visit www.carolrosenberger.com for in-depth information about a variety of topics.

Quotes from
Recording Reviews

Water Music of the Impressionists
Critic's Choice, *Gramophone*
All-Time Great Recording, *Billboard*
Best Classical Compact Disc, *Stereo Review*
"Defines the state of the art in piano recordings." *CD Review*
(Delos DE 3006)

Beethoven: Sonatas Opus 57, Appassionata, and Opus 111
"A splendid, large-scale recording. Carol Rosenberger is a formidable talent, and her performance of these Beethoven piano sonatas is powerful and intense." *Audio*
(Delos DE 3009)

Night Moods
"Performance: 10. Sound: 10. Rosenberger is absolutely marvelous."
CD Review
(Delos DE 3030)

Mozart and Beethoven: Piano and Wind Quintets
"Rosenberger's playing sparkles with wit and intelligence, as does that of her colleagues." *Los Angeles Times*
(Delos DE 3024)

Beethoven: Piano Concerto No. 4 in G Major
"Rosenberger's playing is poetic as it is brilliant . . . remarkably impressive." *Gramophone*
(Delos DE 3027)

Reverie
"Serene renditions of contemplative piano pieces . . . perfect for late-night listening. . . . Dreamy in every sense of the word." *Stereo Review*
(Delos DE 3113)

A Concerto Collection
"Hanson's concerto is one of his most attractive pieces. Rosenberger has fun with the piece and plays it for all it is worth. Schwarz shares her enthusiasm . . . a brilliant, exciting performance." *American Record Guide* (DE 3306)

A Concerto Collection
"Rosenberger brings to these three nocturnal movements *(Nights in the Gardens of Spain)* improvisatory, introspective subjectivity." *High Fidelity* (DE 3306)

Please refer to the Delos website (www.delosmusic.com) for more information about these and other recordings.

A special playlist, *"To Play Again—the playlist,"* can be found on www.carolrosenberger.com

Carol Rosenberger Discography

Concerto Solo with Orchestra

A Concerto Collection • Falla: *Nights in the Gardens of Spain* • Hanson: *Variations on a Theme of Youth*; Piano Concerto, Op. 36 • Haydn: Piano Concerto No. 2; Piano Concerto No. 5 • Strauss: *Burleske* • Gerard Schwarz, conductor; Seattle Symphony/New York Chamber Symphony/Scottish Chamber Orchestra/ London Symphony Orchestra • *Delos DE 3306* • This two-disc set features concerto recordings originally issued on six separate Delos CD releases.

Beethoven: Piano Concerto No. 4 in G Major • Gerard Schwarz, conductor; London Symphony Orchestra • *Delos DE 3027*

Bridge: Chamber Concerto, arr. Orbelian • Constantine Orbelian, conductor; Moscow Chamber Orchestra • *Delos DE 3263*

Hindemith: Four Temperaments • James DePreist, conductor; Royal Philharmonic Orchestra • *Delos DE 1006*

Mozart Adagios (from Piano Concertos K. 595, K. 488, K. 491) • Constantine Orbelian, conductor; Moscow Chamber Orchestra • *Delos DE 3243*

A French Romance (Ravel: Piano Concerto in G Major, Adagio)
• James DePreist, conductor; Orchestre Philharmonique de
Monte-Carlo • *Delos DE 3202*

Shostakovich: *Piano Concerto No. 1* • Gerard Schwarz, conductor;
Los Angeles Chamber Orchestra • *Delos DE 3021*

Piano Solo

Water Music of the Impressionists (Debussy, Ravel, Liszt, Griffes)
• *Delos DE 3006*

Beethoven: *Piano Sonatas: "Appassionata," Op. 57; Op. 111* • *Delos
DE 3009*

Schubert: *Sonata in B-flat; Impromptus, Op. 90* • *Delos DE 3018*

Szymanowski: *Masques, Études, Mazurkas* • *Delos DE 1635 (a
2-CD set, with complete Mazurkas, Op. 50 & Op. 62)*

Night Moods (Chopin, Debussy, Fauré, Griffes, Granados) • *Delos
DE 3030*

Reverie (Bach, Chopin, Debussy, Fauré, Griffes, Liszt, Ravel)
• *Delos DE 3113*

Singing on the Water: Piano Barcarolles (Bennett, Chopin, Debussy,
Diamond, Fauré, Griffes, Liszt, Rachmaninoff, Ravel) • *Delos
DE 3172*

The Boesendorfer Sound: (Debussy, Ravel, Chopin, Bennett, Griffes,
Liszt) • *Delos DE 3460*

Theme & Variations (Beethoven: Sonata Op. 109; Mozart: Sonata K. 331; Schubert Impromptu Op. 142#3) • *Delos DE 3452*

Piano by the Sea: Classical "Water" Masterpieces Surrounded by Surf and Stream—recreates the experience of listening to beautiful piano music near the seaside, lakeshore, or a flowing stream. • *Delos DE 3242*

Chamber Music

Mozart, Beethoven: *Quintets for Piano and Winds* • with David Shifrin, clarinet; Allan Vogel, oboe; others • *Delos DE 3024*

A Brahms / Schumann Soirée: Sonatas and Fantasiestücke for Clarinet and Piano • with David Shifrin, clarinet • *Delos DE 3025*

Presenting Jian Wang • Chopin: *Polonaise Brillante; Sonata Op 65;* Barber: *Sonata Op. 6,* Songs; Schumann: *Adagio and Allegro Op. 70* with Jian Wang, cello • *Delos DE 3097*

Bejun: Songs and Arias of Handel, Schubert, Brahms, and Britten • with Bejun Mehta, boy soprano; David Shifrin, clarinet; Principals of Los Angeles Chamber Orchestra • *Delos DE 3019*

Time and Distance • Songs by Mark Abel • *Those Who Loved Medusa,* with Hila Plitmann, soprano; *Invocation,* with Janelle DeStefano, mezzo-soprano • *Delos DE 3550*

Recordings for Young People

Perchance to Dream: A Lullaby Album for Children and Adults (Kabalevsky, Tchaikovsky, Mozart, Schumann, Beethoven, Chopin, Bach, Haydn, Brahms) • *Delos DE 3079*

. . . Such Stuff as Dreams . . . A Lullaby Album for Children and Adults
(Mozart, Beethoven, Schubert, Kabalevsky, Schumann, Beethoven, Grieg, Ravel, Debussy, Satie, Mendelssohn) • *Delos DE 3230*

Baby Needs Lullabys (Schumann, Schubert, Mendelssohn, Liszt, Debussy, Tchaikovsky, Haydn, Bach, Brahms) • *Delos DE 1619*

Prince Ivan and the Frog Princess: A Fairy Tale Music of Prokofiev, with Natalia Makarova, narrator • *Delos DE 6003*

The Snow Queen: A Fairy Tale Music of Tchaikovsky, with Natalia Makarova, narrator • *Delos DE 6004*

My Keyboard Friends: Piano Music of Bennett and Walton with Richard Rodney Bennett, narrator and piano • *Delos DE 6002*

Heigh-Ho! Mozart: Favorite Disney Tunes in Classical Style • Fraser: "Beauty and the Beast" in the style of Rachmaninoff; "With a Smile and a Song" in the style of Chopin • Donald Fraser, arranger and conductor; English Chamber Orchestra • *Delos DE 3186*

Bibbidi Bobbidi Bach: Favorite Disney Tunes in Classical Style • Fraser: "A Whole New World" in the style of Chopin; "So This is Love" in the style of Debussy • Donald Fraser, arranger and conductor; English Chamber Orchestra • *Delos DE 3195*

The Best of Peter Pan • Fraser: "I'm Flying," "Nocturne," "Distant Melody" • Los Angeles Opera Orchestra; Grant Gershon, conductor; arrangements by Donald Fraser • *Delos DE 3201*

About the Author

author photo © Millard Tipp

"Ravishing, elegant pianism" wrote *The New York Times* of American pianist Carol Rosenberger, whose four-decade concert career is represented by over thirty recordings on the Delos label. Many are enduring favorites worldwide, and have brought her a Grammy Award nomination, *Gramophone*'s Critic's Choice Award, *Stereo Review*'s Best Classical Compact Disc, and *Billboard*'s All-Time Great Recording. When Carol was twenty-one, her career was interrupted by an attack of paralytic polio, which destroyed her piano-playing apparatus. The dramatic story of how she overcame her "musical death sentence" has been an inspiration to many, as she has passed along her hard-won techniques to young musicians in performance workshops nationwide and at the University of Southern California, where she was a faculty member. With Delos founder Amelia Haygood, Carol coproduced many recordings by world-class artists, and after Haygood's death in 2007, became Delos's director.

Selected Titles from She Writes Press

She Writes Press is an independent publishing company founded to serve women writers everywhere. Visit us at www.shewritespress.com.

Rethinking Possible: A Memoir of Resilience by Rebecca Faye Smith Galli. $16.95, 978-1-63152-220-8. After her brother's devastatingly young death tears her world apart, Becky Galli embarks upon a quest to recreate the sense of family she's lost—and learns about healing and the transformational power of love over loss along the way.

A Leg to Stand On: An Amputee's Walk into Motherhood by Colleen Haggerty. $16.95, 978-1-63152-923-8. Haggerty's candid story of how she overcame the pain of losing a leg at seventeen—and of terminating two pregnancies as a young woman—and went on to become a mother, despite her fears.

Body 2.0: Finding My Edge Through Loss and Mastectomy by Krista Hammerbacher Haapala. An authentic, inspiring guide to reframing adversity that provides a new perspective on preventative mastectomy, told through the lens of the author's personal experience.

Beautiful Affliction: A Memoir by Lene Fogelberg. $16.95, 978-1-63152-985-6. The true story of a young woman's struggle to raise a family while her body slowly deteriorates as the result of an undetected fatal heart disease.

Learning to Eat Along the Way by Margaret Bendet. $16.95, 978-1-63152-997-9. After interviewing an Indian holy man, newspaper reporter Margaret Bendet follows him in pursuit of enlightenment and ends up facing demons that were inside her all along.

There Was a Fire Here: A Memoir by Risa Nye. $16.95, 978-1-63152-045-7. After a devastating firestorm destroys Risa Nye's Oakland, California home and neighborhood, she has to dig deep to discover her inner strength and resilience.

31901062651528